John Davenporte

Engraved for The Colonial Society of Massachusetts from the original in the possession of Yale University

THE NEW HAVEN COLONY

BY

ISABEL MacBEATH CALDER

ARCHON BOOKS
1970

SBN: 208 00863 5
Library of Congress Catalog Card Number: 71-95022
Printed in the United States of America

PREFACE

IN writing the *History of the Colony of New Haven, before and after the Union with Connecticut* (New Haven, 1838), Edward R. Lambert examined the manuscript records of the colony and of some of its towns, and broke the ground for later writers, but left much to be done. In preparing *The Republic of New Haven* (Baltimore, 1886), Charles H. Levermore used the *Records of the Colony and Plantation of New Haven, from 1638 to 1649*, and *Records of the Colony or Jurisdiction of New Haven, from May, 1653, to the Union*, edited by Charles J. Hoadly and published at Hartford in 1857 and 1858, but made scant use of manuscripts, and labored under the influence of a theory that has long since been discarded. Carrying their narratives beyond the union of the New Haven Colony and Connecticut in 1665, both Lambert and Levermore devoted but little space to the history of the New Haven Colony and confused the history of the colony with that of the town after 1665. In the *History of the Colony of New Haven to Its Absorption into Connecticut* (New Haven, 1881), Edward E. Atwater used the published records of the colony and town of New Haven and manuscript records of the town, and limited himself to the history of the New Haven Colony, but he failed to exhaust other manuscript sources of information in either America or England. This defect a second edition in 1902 failed to remedy. Misled by the ambiguous and obscure language of the early records, all three writers have misinterpreted the constitutional and legislative efforts of the founders of the colony.

For these reasons, almost three hundred years after

the founding of the smallest and strictest of the Puritan commonwealths, a fourth history seems in order. Settled by ultra-conservative Puritans, unrestricted by royal charter, far removed from the ecclesiastical organization of England, the colony on Long Island Sound served as a laboratory in which Puritan theories of ecclesiastical and civil organization might be tested. More than any other colony in New England it represents the goal toward which the most orthodox wing of the Puritan party was striving. With the rise of the Puritans to power in England, the colony on Long Island Sound increased in prestige, but at the same time it became less necessary. With the restoration of the Stuarts to the throne it disappeared, and today it is almost forgotten.

From the undergraduate courses of Professor Albert Beebe White of the University of Minnesota the writer carried a love of historical research and the vision of a problem to be solved. Under the guidance of Professor Charles McLean Andrews a doctoral dissertation presented at Yale University has gradually evolved into the present study. Professor Leonard W. Labaree of Yale University has made valuable suggestions regarding both text and notes. Miss Anne S. Pratt of the Yale University Library has freely given her assistance. Other librarians and archivists in the United States, England, and the United Netherlands have furthered the work. The Bulkley Fellowship in American History and the Bulkley-Currier Fellowship in the Graduate School of Yale University and a fellowship of the American Council of Learned Societies have made possible the leisure necessary to complete the study. For the interest, guidance, and assistance of all, the writer will always be indebted.

I. M. C.

Wells College, June 4, 1934.

CONTENTS

ILLUSTRATIONS

THE NEW HAVEN COLONY

CHAPTER I

ST. STEPHEN'S, COLEMAN STREET

THE parish of St. Stephen, Coleman Street, London, extends from about a hundred feet west of Coleman Street to Drapers' Gardens, and from Lothbury to beyond the Wall. The church stands on the west side of Coleman Street, in the southwest corner of the parish. In the seventeenth century Coleman Street was "a faire and large street, on both sides builded with diuerse faire houses," and the principal artery between Moorgate and Lothbury. To the east and west of this main thoroughfare was a network of alleys: Chimney Alley, Nunnes Court or Alley, Swanne, Whites, Bell, and George Alleys on the east, and Gleane and Byrdes Alleys on the west, "with small tenements in great number."[1] With the parish of St. Olave in the Old Jewry on the south, and part of the parish of St. Margaret, Lothbury, on the east, the parish of St. Stephen, Coleman Street, constitutes Coleman Street ward.

The right to present a vicar to the church of this parish originally belonged to the prior of Butley in Suffolk, but with the dissolution of the monasteries in the reign of Henry VIII, it passed to the crown, and in the year 1590, rectory, advowson, and fee farm were granted to the parishioners by letters patent of Queen Elizabeth. A vicar was always chosen subject to the approval of the Bishop of London, but through their control of the purse, the

1 John Stow, *A Survey of London* (2 vols., 1908, Charles L. Kingsford, ed.), I, 284; St. Stephen's, Coleman Street, Churchwardens' Accounts, 1586-1640.

parishioners guarded against undue interference from without. To their vicar they granted an annual salary of £11, and the Bishop of London could force the installation of a candidate only at this nominal remuneration, but to the vicar of their choice, they granted both salary and a gratuity of £39.[2]

In the early seventeenth century ecclesiastical and civil affairs of the parish were conducted in general vestries and in vestries of committees. The former were meetings of between thirty and eighty householders of the parish who paid scot and bore lot and were probably free of the city. The committees were a self-perpetuating group of the more important householders who, in the intervals between general vestries, managed the affairs of the parish. At a general vestry which assembled in Easter week, the householders chose churchwardens and sidesmen,[3] in accord with the canons of 1603, collectors for the poor, and auditors of the accounts of churchwardens and collectors. At a general vestry which met as a precinct of the ward in December of each year, they chose two common-councilmen, two constables, seven members of the wardmote inquest, and two scavengers. They had difficulty in filling these offices in parish and ward, and often fined several individuals for refusal to serve before they elected a man willing to undertake the duties of constable or scavenger. The wealthier householders of the parish bought immunity from all offices by paying a fine of £10. At special meetings of the general vestry, the householders chose a new vicar or filled a lesser office that had become vacant, audited the churchwardens' accounts, and levied tithes. At the vestries of committees, the select

[2] Edwin Freshfield, ''Some Remarks upon the Book of Records and History of the Parish of St. Stephen, Coleman Street, in the City of London,'' *Archaeologia,* L, 17-57.

[3] At St. Stephen's, Coleman Street, elected in March, 1624, and April, 1625, but not thereafter.

group in charge of parish affairs nominated vicars, and after their election made settlements with them regarding salary, benevolences, gratuities, gifts, and tithes. They designated groups of themselves as feoffees in whom the title to the real property of the parish rested, decided all questions regarding the property of the parish, directed law suits in which the parish was involved, and assessed tithes on new houses. They granted allowances for the archdeacon's visitation and for the dinner which followed the annual perambulation of the parish by its officers and young urchins. They voted to make a collection for the purchase of communion silver. They settled questions regarding the poor within their bounds, ordered the churchwardens to take out letters of administration of the estates of orphans, directed the overseers of the poor to apprentice poor children, took charge of the poor chest and its keys, made regulations regarding coal for the poor, granted pensions, and regulated the pensioners. In characteristic seventeenth-century fashion, no distinction was made between parish and precinct business. The deputy alderman of the ward often attended general vestries in Easter week for the choice of parish officers, and sometimes served as a committee of the parish, and a vestry of committees occasionally filled an office vacant in the precinct.[4]

In the concluding year of the reign of James I, at a time when the church established by Henry VIII contained within itself some who accepted high-church Anglicanism and others who wished to replace the hierarchy with Presbyterianism or Congregationalism,[5] a group of seventy-four householders of the parish met as a general

[4] St. Stephen's, Coleman Street, Vestry Minute Book, 1622-1726, *passim;* Sidney and Beatrice Webb, *English Local Government, The Manor and the Borough,* II, 586-593.

[5] Perry Miller, *Orthodoxy in Massachusetts, 1630-1650* (1933).

vestry, October 5, 1624, to elect a vicar.[6] At this time there were two candidates in nomination for the office, one Wilson and John Davenport.

Of Wilson, only the fact that he had the support of George Abbot, Archbishop of Canterbury, is known.

John Davenport was the son of Henry and Winifred (Barneby) Davenport. He had been baptized by Richard Eaton, vicar of Holy Trinity Church, Coventry, April 9, 1597.[7] After preparation at the Free Grammar School, Coventry, he enrolled as batteler at Merton College, Oxford. Dismissed by Sir Henry Savile, warden of the college, because he refused to become a commoner, he migrated to Magdalen Hall, but soon left Oxford without a degree, "not from any want of tyme, or of willingnes, or of sufficiency (as was well knowne in Oxford)," he explained, "but from want of meanes (my freinds being unwilling) to keepe me longer at the University."[8] Probably at the invitation of Lady Mary Hilton, the eighteen year old youth found employment as preacher in the chapel dedicated to St. Katherine attached to Hilton Castle in the parish of Monk Wearmouth, palatinate of Durham.[9] Sometime within the next four years he married Elizabeth Wooley.[10] Elected lecturer and curate of the church of St. Lawrence, Old Jewry, London, June 4, 1619,[11] he held that office for more than five years. In 1624 he was living in Milk Street, near Cheapside. Al-

6 Public Record Office, State Papers, Domestic, James I, CLXXIII, no. 64 i.

7 Franklin B. Dexter, "Sketch of the Life and Writings of John Davenport," New Haven Colony Historical Society *Papers*, II, 205-238.

8 State Papers, Domestic, James I, CLXXIII, no. 44.

9 Yale University Library, Sermons of the Reverend John Davenport A.D. 1615.

10 "The Visitation of the County of Warwick in the Year 1619," Harleian Society *Publications*, XII, 373.

11 Guildhall Library, S[t] Laurence Iewry London Vestry Book 1556 to 1669, p. 234.

most unanimously the young curate was elected vicar of St. Stephen's, Coleman Street.

Just as John Davenport was about to enter upon his first real charge, perhaps because of his popularity, perhaps because he had aroused the enmity of the king's page, he was charged with Puritanism. "It hath bene the will of God," he wrote, "(against my naturall desire of privacy, and retirednes) to make my ministry, for the space of this sixe yeares, in London, publick, and eminent, wch hath Caused some to looke upon me wth a squint eye, and hearken to my sermons wth the leaft eare, and, by all meanes, to endeavor my discouragment, and disgrace; insomuch that I am traduced (as I heare, and feare) to his Ma. for a puritan, or one that is puritannically affected."[12] Again he wrote, "I heare that Mr Sidnam, the Kings page, hath incensed his Matie against me, because above a yeare since, I reproved him for swearing, at my Lady Veres, wch I marvayle at, since, at that tyme he pretended not onely a favorable acceptance, but also thanckfulnes, wth a free promise of future reformac̄on."[13] James I ordered George Montaigne, Bishop of London, "to call Mr Damport in Question for some pointes of doctrine wch he had preached," and because "he was reported to be factious and Popular and to draw after him great congregations and assemblies of Common and meane People," and the bishop refused to admit as vicar of St. Stephen's one who did not "stand so right as he should do in his ma^{ties} favour," until the king's pleasure might be known.[14]

The vicar-elect of St. Stephen's was not without friends at court. The protégé of Lady Mary Vere, wife of Sir Horace Vere and sister-in-law of Sir Edward Conway, one of the secretaries of state, he turned to both

[12] State Papers, Domestic, James I, CLXXIII, no. 42.

[13] *Ibid.*, no. 51.

[14] *Ibid.*, nos. 42, 43.

Lady Vere and Sir Edward Conway, and besought the secretary of state to intercede with James I and Bishop Montaigne in his behalf. His later conduct indicates that he was not whole-heartedly in sympathy with the Church of England, but at this time he was one of those who hoped to bring about change from within, and meanwhile were willing to conform to the discipline and ceremonies of the church. Fearful that the charge of Puritanism would not only prevent his induction as vicar of St. Stephen's, but endanger his curacy at St. Lawrence's, he emphatically denied the accusation. "If by a puritan is meant one opposite to the present government," he wrote, "I profes . . . the Contrary. . . . I have baptized many, but never any wthout the signe of the Cross I have monethly administred the Sacrament of the Lords Supper, but at no tyme without the Surplice, nor to any but those that kneeled. . . . If by puritanically affected, be meant one, that secretly encourageth men in opposition to the present Government. I profes an hearty detestac̄on of such hypocrisy. my publick sermons, and private discourses have ever aimed at this, to persuade men to give unto Caesar the things that are Caesars, and unto God the things that are Gods."[15]

Sir Edward Conway took up Davenport's cause. Interceding in behalf of the vicar-elect of St. Stephen's with the Bishop of London and the Archbishop of Canterbury,[16] he met with such success that, after an examination, the Bishop of London certified Davenport's conformity to the king.

After dispatching a letter of deep gratitude to Conway, on Wednesday, November 3, 1624, Davenport was

15 State Papers, Domestic, James I, CLXXIII, no. 42. Although undated, the letter was written on or before October 11, for on that date Conway wrote to the Bishop of London in Davenport's behalf. See the letter of the Bishop of London to Conway, October 14, 1624, *ibid.*, no. 43.

16 *Ibid.*, nos. 47, 58.

inducted into the office of vicar of St. Stephen's, Coleman Street.[17] On the following Sabbath, in a surplice, he read and assented to the thirty-nine articles and administered communion at the church.[18] At a vestry of committees on December 7 he agreed to preach twice every Sabbath in person or to furnish a godly substitute, and to perform all ministerial functions and offices belonging to the vicarage and ministry. In return the committees agreed to bestow upon him an annual salary of £11, a gratuity of £39, a house in Coleman Street worth £14 a year, and all profits from christenings, weddings, and burials from the preceding Michaelmas day—the great bell, ground in the church and choirs, and the Easter book excepted.[19]

In the year of Davenport's induction, tithes were levied on three hundred and eighty-five houses in the parish, and some years later the vicar of St. Stephen's reported to the Bishop of London that he had fourteen hundred communicants. Men interested in the livery companies of London and the great trading companies of the day occupied the "faire houses" which lined Coleman Street and stood in Swanne Alley; and shopkeepers and craftsmen and the poor in great number lived in the less pretentious dwellings in the parish. The neighborhood offered habitations to the wealthy and to the poor, but was "not a place convenient for shop-keepers to dwell in," and members of the middle class who lived in the parish changed their residences so frequently that Davenport seldom learned to know them.[20]

In the affairs of the parish, Davenport was deeply interested. He attended general vestries and vestries of committees. He served as a committee, feoffee, and audi-

17 *Ibid.*, CLXXIV, no. 14.

18 American Antiquarian Society *Transactions and Collections,* III, cxxxv-cxxxvi.

19 St. Stephen's, Coleman Street, Vestry Minute Book, 1622-1726, p. 18.

20 State Papers, Domestic, Charles I, CLXXXII, no. 60.

tor of the parish. He was a member of groups appointed to negotiate with the Company of Mercers regarding their poor in Byrdes Alley, and to present a petition of the parish to the lord keeper. With others he viewed the pensioners of the parish, carried on negotiations for the purchase of an almshouse, and viewed the writings in the great chest. He kept one of the keys to the poor chest and distributed alms to the poor. In these multifarious duties he was sometimes assisted by a curate toward whose maintenance the parish contributed. At the time of his induction one Barricke was reader. On April 18, 1626, Francis Bright, bachelor of arts, and on September 22, 1627, John Williamson, master of arts, were licensed as curates of St. Stephen's, Coleman Street. Some years later Timothy Hood was Davenport's assistant.[21]

Although a young man at the time of his ministry in Coleman Street, Davenport was considered "a great Preacher in London."[22] Numerous gifts and bequests indicate his popularity with his parishioners. He attracted individuals from beyond the limits of the parish, among them Robert Keayne, merchant taylor, and William Kiffin, at the time a young apprentice in London.[23] He was in demand for sermons on special occasions, and on June 23, 1629, preached to a general meeting of the Artillery Company at St. Andrew's, Undershaft.

The vicar of St. Stephen's, Coleman Street, also found time for many extra-parochial activities. Before his induction he had assured Sir Edward Conway that as soon

21 St. Stephen's, Coleman Street, Vestry Minute Book, 1622-1726, p. 18; George Hennessy, *Novum Repertorium Ecclesiasticum Parochiale Londinense*, p. 384; State Papers, Domestic, Charles I, CLXXXII, no. 60.

22 *Ibid.*, XXVII, no. 46.

23 Massachusetts Historical Society *Proceedings*, L, 204-207; Walter Wilson, *The History and Antiquities of Dissenting Churches . . . in London, Westminster, and Southwark*, I, 403; William Orme, *Remarkable Passages in the Life of W. Kiffin*, pp. 4-5; Joseph Ivemey, *The Life of . . . William Kiffin*, p. 5.

as he was "settled in a certayne competencye of meanes," he intended to take the university degrees which some thought that he had lost through delay.[24] On Wednesday, May 18, 1625, he attended disputations in the Divinity School at Oxford, and with John Prideaux, rector of Exeter College in the chair, and a great host of juniors and seniors assiduously taking notes, debated with George Palmer of Lincoln College the theses: "*An 1. Reconciliatio per mortem Christi sit singulis hominibus impetrata. 2. Vere renati possint gratia finaliter aut totaliter excidere.*" The performance won him the approval of Prideaux and on June 28, 1625, the degree of bachelor of divinity.[25]

In 1627 he wrote an introduction to Henry Scudder's *The Christian's Daily Walk in Holy Security and Peace*, and in 1629 published the sermon which he had preached to the Artillery Company as *A Royall Edict for Military Exercises*. As literary legatees of John Preston, friend and disciple of John Cotton, rector of St. Botolph's at Boston in Lincolnshire, Davenport and Richard Sibbes edited the sermons which Preston had preached at Lincoln's Inn, and published them in four volumes which passed through many editions.[26]

He was one of a group of four clergymen, four lawyers, and four citizens of London, who, in an effort to mould the Church of England more to their liking, erected themselves into a self-perpetuating society and undertook to raise funds for the purchase of impropriations or ec-

[24] State Papers, Domestic, James I, CLXXIII, no. 44.

[25] Yale University Library, John Davenport, Note-Book; State Papers, Domestic, Charles I, XXVII, no. 46; Anthony à Wood, *The History and Antiquities of the University of Oxford*, II, Part I, 354; Joseph Foster, *Alumni Oxonienses*, 1500-1714, I, 376.

[26] *The New Covenant or the Saints Portion* (1629); *The Saints Daily Exercise* (1629); *The Breast-Plate of Faith and Love* (1630); *The Saints Qualification* (1633).

clesiastical revenues in lay hands, the income to be bestowed upon able, preaching, conformable ministers appointed by the group. From February 15, 1626, to March 15, 1632, the feoffees for the purchase of impropriations or collectors of St. Antholin's, as the group was sometimes called, met in one another's houses and chambers two or three times a term, penalized absentees, and admitted only such outsiders as they chose. They appointed a president, treasurer, secretary, and two auditors, and engaged a servant who wore their livery. They drafted twenty orders in the form of a constitution for the society, providing among other things that eight of their number should be residents of London at the time of their election to the society, and passed three hundred and ninety-eight ordinances or by-laws. They kept a great parchment ledger for the entrance of all purchases, a parchment book relating to St. Antholin's, a book of orders, and the necessary accounts. They elected a thirteenth member to the society and filled vacancies which occurred in their number. In 1628 they considered procuring an act of parliament erecting the society into a corporation, but took no steps to do so. They raised £6361 6*s.* 1*d.*, including £1554 13*s.* 4*d.* contributed to a special fund for the maintenance of lectureships established in the time of Queen Elizabeth by the parish of St. Antholin and the city of London in the church at the intersection of Sythe Lane and Budge Row. To this latter enterprise several inhabitants of the parish of St. Stephen contributed. Disbursing £8073 9*s.* 1*d.*, the group acquired title to ecclesiastical properties and revenues scattered throughout England and Wales. Toward a deficit of £1712 3*s.*, the feoffees contributed £516 5*s.* from their own purses, and went in debt to the amount of £1195 18*s.* They took bonds from their appointees to the effect that they would forfeit £1000 if they accepted a second cure or lectureship without the consent of the feoffees, and manipulated stipends to encourage ministers who had their favor and to get rid of others of whom they disapproved. Had the enterprise gone unmolested, a self-perpetuating group of twelve or thirteen individuals would eventually have controlled the lay fees of England![27]

[27] Through ceaseless activity, the feoffees for the purchase of impropriations acquired the rectory and impropriations of St. Peter's and St. Paul's, Dunstable, a market town in Bedfordshire, at a cost of £350; the rectory and impropriations of Cirencester, Gloucestershire, at a cost of £350; a lease for lives of the prebend and rectory of Aylesbury, a market town and borough in Buckinghamshire, at a cost of £2830, and the promise to erect and maintain a school and master; the advowson of High Wycombe in Buckinghamshire, Sir Richard Burrell of London giving £80 to purchase the vicarage; the rectory and impropriations of Presteigne in Herefordshire and Radnorshire, bought from Sir Robert Harley at a cost of about £1400; the nomination of a preacher at Bridgnorth, a market town, borough, and peculiar with ecclesiastical jurisdiction, and a curate at Claverley, Shropshire, with £500 the gift of Sir William Whitmore on condition that the feoffees increase the annual stipends of preacher and curate from £5 and £8 to £50 apiece; a perpetuity of the rectory of Mainstone in Shropshire at a cost of £500; the vicarage and impropriations of All Saints' in Hertford, the gift of Gabriel Barber, who bought them from Sir William Soame; the advowson of St. Peter's and St. John's at Dunwich in Suffolk at a cost of £10 given for the purpose by one Coppyn, a London merchant; the lease of certain glebe lands and tithes of the prebend of Prees in the cathedral church at Lichfield, at a cost of £180; the advowson of St. Alkmund's at Shrewsbury in Shropshire, the leases of barn and tithes at Cotton nearby, the gift of Rowland Heylyn, the tithes to be paid to Heylyn during his life, and to the feoffees for the maintenance of a preacher at St. Alkmund's after his death; a lease of the rectory of Tipton in Staffordshire; the nomination of a curate and a schoolmaster and the lease of certain tithes and offerings of the rectory impropriate of Kinvere in Staffordshire, given by the town on condition that the feoffees maintain a preacher and schoolmaster at that place; the chapel and a little house called the Hermitage at Harringworth in Northamptonshire, the gift of Sir Edward Southe; the next advowson of the church at Birmingham in Warwickshire at a cost of £100; the advowson of the vicarage of Neen Savage, Shropshire, at a cost of £80; the rectory and lands and tenements in the parish of St. Thomas, Haverfordwest, Pembrokeshire, South Wales, at a cost of £360; perpetual nomination of a curate, a house, and tithes at Lingfield in Surrey, the gift of one Newton; the advowson of All Saints' in Worcester, at a cost of £100; messuages and lands in Southwark to be used to build a church on the bank of the Thames,

Also without letters patent from the crown, on March 2, 1627, John Davenport and three other ministers were the authors of a circular letter advocating a collection for the exiled Protestants of the Palatinate.[28] For this unauthorized interference with affairs of state, the authors of the letter were summoned before the Court of High Commission, but the question of conformity was not involved, and the misdirected efforts of the four ministers were without serious consequences to them. At a later time William Laud probably referred to this incident when he said that Davenport had meddled with civil affairs "to no small hindrance to Westminster-Hall."[29]

Both Davenport and his parishioners were interested in the great trading companies of the day. As a young curate at St. Lawrence's, Davenport preached before the Virginia Company of London, and on May 22, 1622, was admitted a member of the company.[30]

One of his parishioners at St. Lawrence's was Roger Conant, who in 1623 migrated to New Plymouth. Finding himself out of sympathy with the Separatism of the Pil-

by the will of John Marshall; the advowson of Mayfield in Staffordshire; the lease of certain tithes at Lyme Regis and Halstock in Dorsetshire; and the promise of an estate in one of the Bardfields, Essex. These properties were conveyed to one, two, or three of the feoffees, their heirs, and assigns, for the uses specified. They attempted to secure the nomination of the preacher at Lewes in Sussex in return for repairing the church; considered purchasing the rectory at Plumstead in Kent; negotiated with Francis Russell, fourth Earl of Bedford, regarding St. Paul's in process of erection in Covent Garden, offering £1000 for the vicarage worth £100 a year; but refused the nomination of a commissary. Public Record Office, Bills, Answers, etc., Charles I, London and Middlesex, no. 533; British Museum, Harleian MSS., no. 832. For these references I am indebted to Mrs. Frances Rose-Troup, Ottery St. Mary, Devonshire. See also Public Record Office, Exchequer Decrees, IV, 88-91.

28 State Papers, Domestic, Charles I, LVI, nos. 15, 16; CCII, no. 3.

29 William Laud, *Works*, VI, 214.

30 Edward D. Neill, *History of the Virginia Company of London*, p. 260; Susan M. Kingsbury, ed., *The Records of the Virginia Company of London*, II, 20, 26; Public Record Office, C. O. 1: 2, no. 33.

grims, he first removed to Nantasket and later undertook the management of the plantation of the Dorchester company at Cape Ann and was responsible for the removal of the settlement to Nahum-Keike or Salem.[31] A few years later John Davenport, Sir Richard Saltonstall, Samuel Aldersey, Theophilus Eaton, Mathew Cradock, and George Foxcroft were members of the group who took over the rights of the Dorchester company, perhaps with the idea of providing a refuge across the seas for non-separating Congregationalists. Sir Richard Saltonstall and Samuel Aldersey both lived in Swanne Alley in the parish of St. Stephen, Coleman Street. About 1630 Theophilus Eaton took over the house vacated by Sir Richard Saltonstall in Swanne Alley. He was the son of Richard Eaton, who had baptised Davenport at Holy Trinity Church, Coventry. Although he was Davenport's senior by at least seven years, Theophilus Eaton may have been the playmate of the future vicar of St. Stephen's until 1604, when his father removed from Coventry to Great Budworth, Cheshire. He was a member of the Eastland Company and had served as deputy governor of the company, probably at Elbing. Mathew Cradock had married Damaris Wine or Wynne at St. Stephen's, December 10, 1622. He was also a member of the Eastland Company. George Foxcroft lived in Coleman Street at a slightly later date. As "the New Engl: Company for a Plantac̄on in Mattachusetts Bay," on March 19, 1628, the group received a grant of territory from the Council for New England, and as "the Governor and Company of the Massachusetts Bay in New England," on March 4, 1629, a charter from the crown. Toward the cost of procuring this latter document Davenport contributed £50 and Eaton £100, but to spare the vicar of St. Stephen's

31 Frances Rose-Troup, *Roger Conant; The Massachusetts Bay Company and Its Predecessors; John White, the Patriarch of Dorchester.*

the enmity of William Laud, who on July 25, 1628, succeeded George Montaigne as Bishop of London, and opposed the enterprise, Davenport's name was omitted from the royal grant. The charter authorized a governor, deputy governor, eighteen assistants, a commonality of freemen, four great and general courts to be held each year, monthly courts of governor, deputy governor, and assistants, the annual election of officers at a general court to be held on the last Wednesday in Easter term, the admission of freemen by the general court, and legislation in harmony with the laws of England by the general court for the good and welfare of the company and the government of its lands and plantations. Only in the omission of a place at which meetings of the company must be held did the document differ from the usual trading company charter. Mathew Cradock was appointed the first governor of the company. Sir Richard Saltonstall, Samuel Aldersey, Theophilus Eaton, and George Foxcroft represented St. Stephen's, Coleman Street, in the first court of assistants, and John Davenport, Robert Crane, Owen Rowe, William Spurstowe, Edmund White, all living in Coleman Street, and possibly Francis Bright of Swanne Alley represented the parish among the commonality. For a brief two months in 1629 John Washborne of Byrdes Alley served the company as secretary.[32]

As long as the Massachusetts Bay Company remained

[32] St. Stephen's, Coleman Street, Churchwardens' Accounts, 1586-1640; *Massachusetts Colony Records*, I, *passim;* Frances Rose-Troup, *The Massachusetts Bay Company and Its Predecessors;* State Papers, Domestic, Charles I, CXLIV, no. 181; CCLXVIII, no. 62; CCCVII, no. 80; DXXXIII, no. 47; State Papers, Poland, IV, 213; VIII, 9-10, 13, 38, 174, 182-183, 186, 187-188, 191-192, 206-207, 210-214, 216-219; John Davenport to John Leverett, June 24, 1665, printed in Thomas Hutchinson, *A Collection of Original Papers* (1769), pp. 392-396; John Davenport, *A Sermon Preach'd at The Election of the Governour, At Boston in New-England, May 19th 1669* (1670), p. 15, reprinted in Colonial Society of Massachusetts *Publications*, X, 6.

in England, Davenport was in frequent attendance at meetings of the group. He was probably responsible for the unfortunate choice of Francis Bright, his former curate, as minister for New England. He recommended Richard Ewstead, a resident of Bell Alley, "a very able man, though not wthout his imperfeccons," as wheelwright to the company. He served on a committee appointed to reduce the orders of the company to a method, and was named one of a group of arbitrators to settle a dispute between Governor Endecott and others in New England and John and Samuel Brown. On August 28 and 29, 1629, he was present at meetings to consider the advisability of transferring the charter of the company to America, and after the decision to transfer the charter and the government of persons to New England but to leave the government of trade and commerce in London, he was appointed a member of a committee to draft articles of agreement between members of the company who intended to migrate to the New World and the adventurers in England. On October 19 and 20 he attended meetings "to resolue of the alterac̄on of the gouernmt," and to elect officers, for not all at that time in office intended to migrate, and he was named one of three umpires to settle differences which might arise between planters and adventurers. In the spring of 1630 he may have been present when John Cotton preached his memorable sermon on the text, "Moreover I will appoint a place for my people Israel, and I will plant them, that they may dwell in a place of their owne, and move no more,"[33] to the great company about to sail from Southampton for New England; for at this time Sir Richard

[33] John Cotton, *Gods Promise to His Plantation* (1630). The text occurs at II Samuel 7.10. See also Edwin D. Mead, "John Cotton's Farewell Sermon to Winthrop's Company at Southampton," Massachusetts Historical Society *Proceedings*, 3d series, I, 101-115.

Saltonstall of Swanne Alley, and Robert Seely, who had married Mary Mason at St. Stephen's, December 15, 1626, and since then lived in the Mason home in Coleman Street, and probably others of the parish were among the emigrants to Massachusetts Bay, and during ensuing years other inhabitants of the parish followed.

As Davenport preached before pews vacated by the great exodus to Massachusetts Bay, he probably meditated on the changes in episcopal policy which made migration to an unknown wilderness seem preferable to longer residence in London, and perhaps on his own change of heart. In 1624 he had emphatically proclaimed his conformity. Soon after his induction, the vicar of St. Stephen's, Coleman Street, had maintained in argument with Alexander Leighton, the Scotch physician and divine at the time residing in London, that kneeling at the sacrament of the Lord's Supper was not only in harmony with the scriptures but an ordinance of God.[34] But as William Laud added to the discipline and ceremonies of the Church of England, and labored to enforce conformity in the minutest detail, Davenport's zeal waned. About January, 1631, a bitter quarrel between the vicar of St. Stephen's and his curate over the wearing of the surplice, the reading of the litany, the significance of the cross in baptism, the admission of strangers to communion, and the curate's refusal to live in the plague-infested parish was brought to the attention of Laud. At this time Davenport was not ready to refuse to conform, and excused his actions on grounds other than doctrinal, but was far milder in his denial of non-conformity to the canons of the Church of England than he had been in 1624.[35] To the charge that he administered communion to those who did not kneel, he replied that St. Stephen's

[34] Yale University Library, John Davenport, Note-Book.

[35] State Papers, Domestic, Charles I, CLXXXII, no. 60.

was too crowded for all to kneel, an excuse identical with that which John Cotton of Boston had given to the Bishop of Lincoln on January 31, 1625.[36] Although at this time Laud had Davenport "at advantage enough to have put extremity upon him," he forebore to act, for which Lord Vere came and thanked him.[37] But the activities of the company of feoffees for the purchase of impropriations were destined to result in an open breach between the vicar of St. Stephen's and his diocesan.

Laud desired the return of impropriations to the Church of England, and the attempt of a group of unauthorized individuals to acquire this revenue, and bestow or withhold it at will, seemed a cunning scheme to gain control of the ecclesiastical hierarchy. Perhaps at his instigation, Peter Heylyn, grandnephew of the treasurer of the company of feoffees but also the "great minion" of Laud, denounced the undertaking in a sermon preached at Oxford, July 11, 1630. "The Corporation of *Feoffees* for buying in of Impropriations to the Church; Doth it not seem in the appearance to be an excellent piece of *Wheat?* A noble and gracious point of piety? Is not this *Templum Domini, Templum Domini?* But blessed God, that men should thus draw near unto thee with their mouths, and yet be far from thee in their hearts! For what are those intrusted in the managing of this great business? Are they not the most of them the most active and the best affected men in the whole cause, and *Magna Partium momenta,* Chief Patrons of the Faction? And what are those whom they prefer? Are they not most of them such as must be serviceable to their dangerous innovations? And will they not in time have more preferments to bestow, and therefore more dependencies than all the Prelates in the Kingdom, *etc.* Yet all this while we

36 British Museum, Additional MSS., 6394, fols. 35-36.

37 William Laud, *Works,* IV, 260; V, 318-319.

sleep and slumber, and fold our hands in sloth, and see perhaps, but dare not note it.'"[38] Laying the matter before Charles I, Laud was referred to William Noy, recently appointed attorney general of the kingdom.[39] Noy was quick to see that the feoffees for the purchase of impropriations were without authorization from either crown or parliament, and, charging that in erecting themselves into a society as though incorporated, the group had infringed the royal prerogative, in Easter term, 1632, he filed an information against them in the Court of Exchequer.[40]

On January 31, February 7, and February 11, 1633, the case of the crown against the feoffees for the purchase of impropriations was heard by the barons of the Exchequer. On the last day of the trial the attorney general announced that he had been instructed by Charles I not to proceed against the feoffees as individuals at that time, and John Davenport hastened home to record in his great Bible his gratitude to God for the decision.[41] In a decree handed down February 13, the barons ordered the feoffees to hold no further assemblies, to make no more ordinances, to present incumbents nominated by the crown to the various advowsons held by them, and authorized the appointment of a commission to investigate the properties acquired by the group. Dependent ministers and lecturers were reduced to poverty.[42] Six months after the decision Davenport and other feoffees were ordered to present Valentine Southerton, the nominee of William Juxon, Bishop-elect of Hereford, to All Saints'

[38] Peter Heylyn, *Cyprianus Anglicus* (1668), p. 211.

[39] William Laud, *Works*, III, 253; IV, 303.

[40] *Ante*, note 27; John Rushworth, *Historical Collections* (1721), Part II, II, 150-152.

[41] Cotton Mather, *Magnalia Christi Americana* (1702), Book III, p. 52.

[42] State Papers, Domestic, Charles I, CCL, no. 57.

in Worcester.[43] A year later criminal proceedings against the feoffees in either the Court of Exchequer or the Star Chamber were still under consideration.[44] The group was held up to ridicule in *The Floating Island,* William Strode's exceedingly poor play produced before the king at Oxford, August 29, 1636.[45] In 1638 certain of the obligations undertaken by the group were assigned to Thomas Turner and John Juxon.[46]

It was during the trial of the company of feoffees for the purchase of impropriations, perhaps in bitterness of spirit as he saw the efforts of more than six years go for naught, that Davenport realized that reformation of the Church of England from within was impossible, and that he could no longer conform to the existing discipline and

[43] *Ibid.,* CCXLV, no. 27.

[44] *Ibid.,* CCLIX, no. 2.

[45] William Strode, *The Floating Island* (London, 1655).

[46] Patent Rolls, Charles I, C. 66: 2839; State Papers, Domestic, Charles I, Docquets, 1637-1638, December 31, 1638. The decision of the Court of Exchequer failed to end the existence of the company of feoffees for the purchase of impropriations. When the Long Parliament assembled, the decree of the Court of Exchequer was brought to its attention. In December, 1640, the House of Commons ordered the committee concerning preaching ministers to consider how the decree might be reversed. At various times in the years which followed the matter came before one or the other of the houses. On March 23, 1646, the House of Commons ordered that the books of the feoffees in the custody of the king's remembrancer, the treasurer's remembrancer, or elsewhere in the Exchequer should be returned to the surviving feoffees in order that they might proceed with their pious work, and on June 10, 1647, the house expressed a desire that the work should be continued. On January 21, 1648, counsel for the feoffees was heard at the bar of the House of Lords, and pleaded that the decree of the Court of Exchequer might be reversed. Favoring reversal, the lords ordered the judges to consider how it might be accomplished. On February 2, 1648, the judges reported that the House of Lords might reverse the decree, and on March 8, 1648, the lords read and passed a judgment condemning the decree of the Court of Exchequer. On March 10, 1648, the records of the Court of Exchequer were brought to the clerk's table, and the seven and one-half page decision was rased by the clerk with his pen. *Commons Journals,* II, 61; IV, 484; V, 204, 519; *Lords Journals,* VI, 154, 161, 162; IX, 657, 658, 671; X, 23, 24, 100, 102, 107.

ceremonies. Despite his denial of 1624, he had become a non-conforming Puritan. A company of non-separating Congregationalists who met in and about London, and under the ministry of John Lothropp entered into a covenant "To Walke togeather in all the Ways of God so farr as he hath made known to Us, or shall make known to us, and to forsake all false Ways," claimed credit for his conversion to non-conformity,[47] but it seems more probable that the writings of William Ames, Paul Baynes, Richard Hooker, Thomas Parker, and Henry Jacob, and the personal efforts of John Cotton and Thomas Hooker were responsible for his change of heart. A conforming Anglican as late as October 2, 1630,[48] two years later John Cotton was cited to appear before the Court of High Commission for non-conformity. Fleeing from Boston in Lincolnshire to London, he was received and concealed by John Davenport. From London he sent his resignation of the rectorship of St. Botolph's at Boston to the Bishop of Lincoln, May 7, 1633.[49] Hooker had preached at Chelmsford and conducted a school at Little Baddow in Essex. Accused of non-conformity, he fled to

[47] Angus Library, Regents Park College, Oxford (in 1933 temporarily housed at New College, Finchley Road, Hampstead, N. W. 3), Gould MS.; Champlin Burrage, *The Early English Dissenters in the Light of Recent Research* (2 vols., 1912), I, 306, II, 302.

[48] Copy of a letter from John Cotton to Samuel Skelton, October 2, 1630, American Antiquarian Society.

[49] "His forced flight from Boston to London for his safety, from persuit of the pursevants sent to apprehend him, I well remember"; wrote Davenport after Cotton's death, "and admire the special providence of God towards my self and some others in it, amongst whom safe retirement and hiding places were provided for him, in and about London." John Norton, *The Life and Death of . . . Mr John Cotton* (1658), p. 32, quoting a manuscript life of Cotton by Davenport which has since disappeared. See also John Cotton to his wife, October 3, 1632, Massachusetts Historical Society *Collections,* 4th series, VIII, 543-544; John Cotton, *The Way of Congregational Churches Cleared* (1648), pp. 23-25; Thomas Hutchinson, *A Collection of Original Papers* (1769), pp. 249-251.

the United Netherlands. Upon the death of John Potts, co-pastor with John Paget of the English congregation at Amsterdam, he was invited to preach at that place, June 22, 1631,[50] but Paget thwarted his efforts to be permanently installed in the vacant office,[51] and he returned to England. While preparing to sail for New England, Cotton and Hooker made their final contribution to the cause of non-conformity in England by converting John Davenport to their views. Convinced that kneeling at the sacrament was plain idolatry, after Christmas, 1632, the vicar of St. Stephen's absented himself from the celebration of the Lord's Supper at the church in Coleman Street.[52]

At this crisis in the religious development of John Davenport, George Abbot, Archbishop of Canterbury, brother of Maurice Abbot of the parish of St. Stephen, and inclined to sympathize with the Puritan cause, died, August 4, 1633. Charles I immediately appointed William Laud to the primacy, and William Juxon, completely under the sway of Laud, to the bishopric of London. The change augured ill for non-conformists.

On Monday, August 5, Davenport left London, ostensibly to visit a friend a few miles from the city. Because of a report that he had fled and that a pursuivant had been sent after him, he remained in concealment. During his enforced idleness he may have written "Christ's Church, and his government of it," a seventy-five page manuscript intended to explain his new views to his parishioners.[53] Throughout his life fearful of the future, he

[50] July 2, 1631, new style. Records of the consistory of the English Reformed Church, Amsterdam, 1628-1700. For permission to examine these records I am indebted to Dr. William Thomson, pastor of the church.

[51] Additional MSS., 6394, fols. 67-72, 146.

[52] *Ibid.*, fols. 144, 178.

[53] Franklin B. Dexter, "Sketch of the Life and Writings of John Davenport," New Haven Colony Historical Society *Papers*, II, 221-222. In the

was convinced by the examination of the churchwardens of St. Stephen's that the new archbishop intended to prosecute him to the utmost, and that a dark cloud was about to descend upon him. Laying his case before a general vestry of his parish, he was advised that it would be best for all concerned if he quietly resigned. This he did, justifying his departure on the grounds that Laud's persecution was directed against him personally and not against the church in general.[54] He left without letters of dismissal and so secretively that it is impossible to tell from the minutes of the vestry just when his connection with the parish of St. Stephen, Coleman Street, came to an end.[55]

Because of the illness of the aged and irascible John Paget, the congregation of English merchants which met in the chapel of the beguines in the Begynenhof off Kal-

summer of 1934 this manuscript could not be found in the library of the American Antiquarian Society.

[54] John Davenport, *An Apologeticall Reply*, pp. 103, 108-110.

[55] Davenport attended a vestry of committees, April 3, 1633. His presence at general vestries April 23, and April 30, 1633, is not recorded, although at the latter meeting he was given £20 to go and come from Bath, and was named a feoffee for the lands of the poor and the almshouse, his name being subsequently crossed out and that of his successor written above it. Of the general vestry at which Davenport laid his case before his parishioners there is no record in the vestry minutes. At a vestry of committees, December 3, 1633, John Goodwin of Raynham in Norfolk, and William Brice, beneficed near Reading, were nominated to stand in election for the vacant vicarage, and at a general vestry on the following day Goodwin was chosen as Davenport's successor. Ejected because of his Independency by the Presbyterians in Parliament in 1645, Goodwin set up an Independent meeting-house in Coleman Street, but later came back to St. Stephen's, bringing his Independent congregation with him. Following the condemnation of Charles I, he pompously set out to offer the sovereign spiritual advice, which, however, was declined. With the Restoration, Goodwin again lost the vicarship of St. Stephen's. His *Obstructours of Justice*, in which he defended the regicides, was ordered to be burned by the hangman, and he himself was ordered to be taken into custody, but, to the surprise of all, according to Bishop Burnet, he escaped punishment. Gilbert Burnet, *History of His Own Time*, I (1724), 163; David Masson, *Milton, passim.*

verstraat in Amsterdam was without a minister. Although Paget had no desire for the presence of one who might outshine him in eminence,[56] and had recently prevented the installation of Thomas Hooker as co-pastor, the congregation sent one Crisp to invite Davenport to come to them.[57] At this time Davenport was looking only for a refuge from the wrath of the new archbishop, and expected soon to return home,[58] and although he had no reason to believe that he would prove more acceptable to Paget than had Thomas Hooker, he relied on the dire need of the congregation, and decided to betake himself to Amsterdam.

By the conduct and contrivance of a Coleman Street merchant named Stone, disguised by a gray suit and an overgrown beard, Davenport crossed the channel, about the middle of November, 1633, in a cloth-ship navigated by one Humphrey. He was met at Harlem by two elders and other members of the Amsterdam congregation. Traveling on horseback to Rotterdam, the party supped with Hugh Peter, formerly lecturer at St. Sepulchre's in London, an active agent of the company of feoffees for the purchase of impropriations, and a member of the Massachusetts Bay Company, who had recently been called to the pastorate of an English church in Rotterdam by those who had assented to a covenant of fifteen articles which Peter had drafted for the church.[59] From Rotterdam the group proceeded to Amsterdam.

For the duration of Paget's illness Davenport preached twice every Sabbath in the Dutch metropolis.[60] He was

[56] Additional MSS., 24,666, fols. 1-3.

[57] State Papers, Holland, CXLVII, fols. 170-171.

[58] John Davenport, *An Apologeticall Reply,* p. 101.

[59] Additional MSS., 6394, fols. 146, 153, 161; State Papers, Domestic, Charles I, CCLII, no. 32; Champlin Burrage, *The Early English Dissenters in the Light of Recent Research,* I, 300-304; II, 271-273.

[60] John Davenport, *An Apologeticall Reply,* p. 15.

soon joined by his wife, and perhaps at this time wrote "the Crowne of a Christian Martyr," or "The Crowne of Christian martyrdome," a peevish pamphlet supposed to have been published at Delft early in 1634 denouncing the constitution of the Church of England.[61] To the former adherents of Thomas Hooker he seemed a suitable candidate for the vacant office of co-pastor.

But the erstwhile vicar of St. Stephen's, Coleman Street, was not destined to find a permanent abode and the quiet for which he craved at Amsterdam. At this time Stephen Goffe, rigid conformist, chaplain to the forces of Sir Horace Vere in the Lowlands, probably to retaliate for the attacks of the English non-conformists in the United Netherlands upon himself, was reporting every move of the English non-conforming clergy in the United Netherlands to Sir William Boswell, and Boswell in turn was passing the information on to Sir Edward Coke in England. With the avowed purpose of gaining delivery "from this plague too," and forcing him to "make for New England, whither Mr Cotton and his sonne borne a shipbord and so caled Sea-borne, and Mr Hooker are safely arrived, (as they say here) by speciall extraordinary prosperous winds," Goffe gave more than usual attention to Davenport. Learning that the one-time adherents of Thomas Hooker desired the installation of Davenport as co-pastor, Goffe visited John Paget and Gerard Vossius at Amsterdam. Making much of the fact that Davenport had stolen out of England without letters of dismissal from his church—at the same time taking steps to see that letters were not sent to him—and of the fact that Davenport had failed to visit the English agent at The Hague, he put Paget and Vossius upon their

61 Additional MSS., 6394, fols. 178, 179; State Papers, Holland, CXLVIII, fols. 45-46; Champlin Burrage, *The Early English Dissenters in the Light of Recent Research,* II, 285.

guard against the non-conformist who had come among them.[62] At the instigation of Goffe, Boswell so shuffled the cards at Amsterdam that Davenport was not likely suddenly to be admitted as minister at that place,[63] and Archbishop Laud wrote to Vossius, "*Si ideo gratus sit vestris Amstelodamensibus, quod Ecclesiae suae et Reformatae desertor sit, fruatur ille fortuna sua, vos illo.*"[64]

Probably as a result of the efforts of Goffe, Paget soon found an unbridgeable chasm between John Davenport and himself on the subjects of baptism and the authority of the classis. Paget advocated the baptism of all children presented for the sacrament during divine service; Davenport would baptize only the children of approved parents.[65] Paget recognized the authority of the Dutch classis; Davenport, that of the congregation. To convince Davenport of his errors, Paget called a meeting of the Dutch ministers at his house, and when Davenport would meet with them neither publicly nor privately—"they sticke not to say His Latine tong is the cause of it," reported Goffe[66]—the ministers constituting the classis of Amsterdam embodied in writing, January 10/20, 1634, the conditions upon which they would admit Davenport as co-pastor of the English church.[67]

Despite the efforts of his opponents, on January 12/22, 1634, the elders of the English church at Amsterdam elected Davenport to the vacant office of co-pastor,[68] in-

[62] Additional MSS., 6394, fols. 176-177; State Papers, Domestic, Charles I, CCLII, no. 55; CCLX, no. 13.

[63] Additional MSS., 6394, fols. 192-193; State Papers, Holland, CXLVII, fols. 201-202.

[64] William Laud, *Works*, VI, 347-348.

[65] Additional MSS., 6394, fols. 179, 192-193.

[66] *Ibid.*, fols. 192-193.

[67] State Papers, Domestic, Charles I, CCLXXXII, no. 68, misdated January 20, 1635.

[68] Records of the consistory of the English Reformed Church, Amsterdam, 1628-1700.

cluding in the call the conditions laid down by the classis. To Davenport this seemed the sign from heaven for which he had been waiting, and perhaps because he did not properly understand the conditions, he at first seemed to assent to them and to accept the call. On January 21/31 the burgomasters of Amsterdam,[69] and on January 27/February 6 the classis of Amsterdam approved the call.[70]

But as Davenport pondered over the conditions, he became less satisfied. This attitude Paget reported to an extraordinary classis which met on February 17/27. The Dutch ministers dispatched three of their number to confer with the co-pastor-elect, but the emissaries accomplished nothing. Supported by Hugh Peter, who made several visits to Amsterdam during the controversy, Davenport laid his refusal to change his views before a meeting of the classis, March 24/April 3, and his resignation of the nomination, April 22/May 2.

As it became increasingly evident that Davenport would not accept the terms forced upon him, his adherents among the merchants, "alleadging the excellency of his guifts, and his discreet and peaceable carriage," desired that he might be admitted as lecturer or assistant pastor,[71] and Davenport expressed a willingness to serve the church in that capacity, but Paget needed and insisted upon a colleague who would share all the burdens of the ministry.

Davenport's supporters next engaged him to preach to them privately, and he held forth to audiences of about a hundred at the home of one Wytacker, an elder of the English church, a mile or two from town, until in the fall

69 Burgomasters' Resolutie-boek, Amsterdam, 1603-1649, p. 102.

70 Nieuwezijds Kapel, Amsterdam, Acta Classis Amstelodamensis, IV, 1631-1645, fol. 35.

71 Additional MSS., 6394, fols. 188, 194.

of 1634 the classis ordered both Davenport and Wytacker to desist.

Withdrawing from Amsterdam, Davenport found employment as assistant to Hugh Peter in the English church which met in a wooden building in the Glashaven at Rotterdam,[72] where Peter was enforcing all the principles of Congregationalism. It was while the two ministers were together at Rotterdam that they persuaded Lyon Gardiner to undertake the construction of a fort and the laying out of a town at the mouth of the Connecticut River in New England for the group of lords and gentlemen to whom Robert Rich, Earl of Warwick, as the patentee of the Council for New England, had granted a hundred and twenty miles of territory to the west of the Narragansett River.[73] When Peter himself departed for New England, Davenport assumed charge of the English congregation in Rotterdam.[74]

The controversy between Davenport and Paget was not terminated by the former's removal from Amsterdam. During his sojourn in the Dutch metropolis, Davenport had written "a trew Report of Passages betweene Mr Paget and me in this business," in which he embodied a translation from the Latin of his letter to the classis of March 24/April 3, and other documents. Obtaining a copy of the manuscript, William Best, an elder of the English church at Amsterdam and an adherent of Davenport, gave it to the world as *A Iust Complaint against an Vniust Doer* (1634),[75] and Paget brought the pamphlet to the attention of the classis of Amsterdam, December 23,

[72] William Steven, *The History of the Scottish Church, Rotterdam*, p. 333.

[73] Massachusetts Historical Society *Collections*, 3d series, III, 136.

[74] J. K. Hosmer, ed., *Winthrop's Journal*, I, 169. Except when otherwise indicated, all references to this work are to this edition. Massachusetts Historical Society *Collections*, 5th series, I, 217-218.

[75] Additional MSS., 24,666, fols. 39-45; Massachusetts Historical Society *Proceedings*, XLIII, 45-68.

1634/January 2, 1635.[76] Against this unauthorized publication, Davenport issued *A Protestation* (1635), also brought to the attention of the classis, January 26/February 5, and Paget, *An Answer to the Unjust Complaints* (1635), the latter a work which the classis of Amsterdam refused to sponsor. Davenport answered with *An Apologeticall Reply* (1636). Probably to end this pamphlet warfare, in April, 1636, Sir William Boswell summoned Davenport to appear before him, perhaps with the intention of silencing him.[77]

Late in 1635 Davenport had sent his wife to England, where she was received into the home of Lady Mary Vere at Hackney.[78] There John Davenport, Jr., was probably born. Disguising himself as a country gentleman, Davenport ignored the summons of the English agent at The Hague, and followed his wife to England.

He found his former parishioners in a sorry plight. In the church, Puritanism had been cowed by the proceedings against the feoffees for the purchase of impropriations, and high-church Anglicanism was rampant. In the state, a series of turbulent parliaments had given way to a government by king and council, which at the moment was arbitrarily exacting funds by writs of ship-money. In an effort to prevent the Eastland Company from being crushed between contending forces in the Thirty Years' War in Germany, Theophilus Eaton had visited Elbing and Danzig in the summers of 1631 and 1633, and unsuccessfully negotiated with the chancellor of Sweden and the magistrates of Danzig. Davenport's boyhood friend was also one of those who had appeared before the Court

[76] Nieuwezijds Kapel, Amsterdam, Acta Classis Amstelodamensis, IV, 1631-1645, fol. 52.

[77] Additional MSS., 6394, fols, 237-238, 244.

[78] John Davenport to Lady Mary Vere, December 15/25, 1635, Additional MSS., 4275, fols. 169-170.

of King's Bench in Michaelmas term, 1635, on a writ of *quo warranto* against the governor, deputy governor, assistants, and freemen of the Massachusetts Bay Company, and disclaimed the charter.[79] One of the undertakers who in 1629 assumed the debts and undertook the management of the joint stock of the company in England, in 1636 Eaton saw the group without funds with which to meet obligations.[80] Truly, longer sojourn in England seemed to have little to offer.

During Davenport's stay in the United Netherlands, he had received glowing accounts of New England from John Cotton.[81] Unable to foresee the changes which the ensuing decade was to usher in in England, Davenport and Eaton organized a company to begin a plantation in the New World. The nucleus of the group was composed of the leaders and their families: John and Elizabeth Davenport, who left their infant son in the care of the noble lady to whom the Long Parliament later entrusted the children of Charles I; Theophilus Eaton, who carried with him all the books of the Massachusetts Bay Company,[82] and the authorization of the grantees of the Earl of Warwick to negotiate with the settlers on the Connecticut River regarding title to their lands;[83] Anne Eaton, daughter of George Lloyd, Bishop of Chester, and widow of Thomas Yale,[84] the second wife of Theophilus Eaton; old Mrs. Eaton, his mother; Samuel and Nathan-

79 C. O. 1: 9, nos. 50, 51; British Museum, Egerton MSS., 2395, fols. 27-29.

80 *Massachusetts Colony Records*, I, 63-66; Massachusetts Historical Society *Collections*, 5th series, I, 484-485.

81 John Davenport, *A Sermon Preach'd at The Election of the Governour, At Boston in New-England, May 19th 1669* (1670), p. 15, reprinted in Colonial Society of Massachusetts *Publications*, X, 6.

82 Frances Rose-Troup, *The Massachusetts Bay Company and Its Predecessors*, p. 104.

83 Egerton MSS., 2648, fol. 1.

84 William Fergusson Irvine, ed., *Marriage Licenses Granted within the Archdeaconry of Chester in the Diocese of Chester*, I, 117.

iel Eaton, his brothers; Mary Eaton, the daughter of his first wife; Samuel, Theophilus, and Hannah, the children of his second wife; Anne, David, and Thomas Yale, the children of Anne Eaton by her former marriage; Edward Hopkins, who on September 5, 1631, had married Anne Yale at St. Antholin's in London;[85] and Richard Malbon, a kinsman of Theophilus Eaton, and perhaps one of the subscribers to the company of feoffees for the purchase of impropriations and a member of the Massachusetts Bay Company.[86] With this nucleus many inhabitants of the parish of St. Stephen, Coleman Street, coalesced: Nathaniel Rowe, sent overhastily and without due consideration by his father, Owen Rowe, who intended to follow;[87] William Andrews, Henry Browning, James Clark, Jasper Crane, Jeremy Dixon, Nicholas Elsey, Francis Hall, Robert Hill, William Ives, George Smith, George Ward, and Lawrence Ward, all with family names found in the accounts of the churchwardens of the parish. Among others who desired to begin life anew in the wilderness across the seas, and who cast in their lots with the emigrants, were Ezekiel Cheever of the parish of St. Antholin, Edward Bannister, perhaps of the parish of St. Lawrence, Old Jewry, and Richard Beach, Richard Beckley, John Brockett, John Budd, John Cooper, Arthur Halbidge, Mathew Hitchcock, Andrew Hull, Andrew Low, Andrew Messenger, Mathew Moulthrop, Francis Newman, Robert Newman, Richard Osborn, Edward Patteson, John Reader, William Thorp, and Samuel Whitehead, probably all from the neighborhood.

The group chartered the *Hector* of London, an almost new vessel of about two hundred and fifty tons burden,[88]

85 Harleian Society *Publications*, VIII, 65.

86 Massachusetts Historical Society *Collections*, 4th series, VI, 344-345; State Papers, Domestic, Charles I, DXV, no. 146 i.

87 Massachusetts Historical Society *Collections*, 5th series, I, 319-321.

88 State Papers, Domestic, Charles I, XVII, no. 117.

which had already made one voyage to Massachusetts Bay.[89] After they had engaged their whole estates in the venture, paid their passage money, and provisioned the vessel, the *Hector* was impressed for the service of the crown. Although the owners petitioned for its release, January 19, 1637,[90] a delay of several months ensued. During this period of enforced waiting, Archbishop Laud learned of Davenport's presence at Braintree and Hackney,[91] but there is no evidence that he made any effort to apprehend him. Early in May the *Hector* was freed.[92] On June 26, 1637, John Winthrop recorded the arrival of the group from London at Boston in New England.[93]

89 *Winthrop's Journal*, I, 181, 182; *Massachusetts Colony Records*, I, 176.

90 C. O. 1: 9, no. 39; State Papers, Domestic, James I, CCXV, 138-139; Charles I, CCCXLIV, no. 52 i; CCCXLVII, no. 10.

91 *Ibid.*, CCCLI, no. 100.

92 On May 10, 1637, Francis Kirby wrote to John Winthrop, "I wrote you lately per the Hector." Massachusetts Historical Society *Collections*, 4th series, VII, 19.

93 *Winthrop's Journal*, I, 223.

CHAPTER II

MASSACHUSETTS BAY

IN Massachusetts Bay John Davenport was welcomed by John Cotton and Hugh Peter; Theophilus Eaton, by associates of the Massachusetts Bay Company; and the group as a whole, by former neighbors and friends. In 1632 and 1633 Davenport had provided a refuge for Cotton in London, and now Cotton received Davenport into his home in Boston. Other members of the company probably met with similar hospitality.

As they surveyed their new environment, the immigrants from England saw much that was new to them. Congregationalism had become an established religion.[1] Without separating from the Church of England, the founders of the Bay Colony had abandoned the ideas of an all-inclusive church and an episcopal hierarchy, and adopted the ideas which in 1648 found expression in the Cambridge platform of church discipline. In each town of the colony a church was formed by a group of saints carefully chosen from the world and united into one body by a holy covenant for the public worship of God and mutual edification one of another. The number of Christians necessary to gather such a church had received much discussion. At the formation of the church at Newtown in 1636, some of the ancient ministers maintained that "Three . . . were too few, because by Matt. xviii. an appeal was allowed from three; but that seven might be a fit number."[2] John Allin, pastor of the church at Dedham,

1 Perry Miller, *Orthodoxy in Massachusetts, 1630-1650* (1933).

2 *Winthrop's Journal,* I, 173.

said, "Butt the number and w^{t} p'sons should l^{t} joine it is not much materiall so thei be such as are living stones; and such as may haue some measure of faithfull care and diseerving to keep the church pure and allso be of that inocency of life as may invite other s^{ts} more willingly to joine to them."[3] In 1630 four individuals entered into covenant at Charlestown and formed the church which became the First Church of Boston. In 1632 and again in 1636 seven entered into covenant at Lynn; in 1636 seven, at Dorchester; and in 1638 eight, at Dedham. In some instances a covenant was quickly arrived at. In other cases individuals met in weekly meetings and related their spiritual experiences and weighed one another's qualifications for church-membership for months before the final step was taken and a church was gathered. Such was the case in the formation of the church at Dedham, under way at the time the Davenport company arrived in the Bay but not completed until the following year. In 1636 the general court of Massachusetts ruled that a church could not be gathered without the approval of the magistrates and elders of a majority of the churches of the colony,[4] but once organized, each congregation was a unit unto itself. Each church chose its own officers: pastor and teacher to carry on the ministry, ruling elder to assist with the government of the church, and deacons to supervise the temporal side of church life, ordained these officers by the imposition of hands, and dismissed them at will, in which case they ceased entirely to be officers of the church until called anew. The doors of the church no longer stood "so wide open that all sorts of people, good and bad, might freely enter." Into their church society the members received only saints who had proved their worthiness and assented to the covenant, and from it they

[3] *Dedham Records, Church and Cemetery, 1638-1845,* p. 3.

[4] *Massachusetts Colony Records,* I, 168.

excluded all who fell from grace. Only those who had been received into the fellowship of the church and the children of members were eligible for baptism, and only members of the church were admitted to the Lord's Supper. Communion of churches or conferences of elders and synods of elders and brethren from several churches was recognized, but no church exercised authority over another.[5]

As the Davenport company arrived on the scene, the system was meeting the first of many onslaughts from within. In 1634 Anne Hutchinson had followed John Cotton from Lincolnshire to New England, and after some hesitation on the part of the congregation, was admitted a member of the church in Boston of which Cotton was teacher. America's pioneer feminist soon instituted weekday meetings at her home to discuss the sermons of the Sabbath,[6] at first without offense. But when she disclosed that John Cotton preached a covenant of grace, and the other ministers of the Bay only a covenant of works, a division appeared. To John Cotton, Governor Henry Vane, John Wheelwright, related to Anne Hutchinson by

[5] For an understanding of the Congregationalism of New England in the seventeenth century, see John Cotton, *A Coppy of a Letter of Mr Cotton of Boston, in New England, sent in answer of certaine Objections made against their Discipline and Orders there, directed to a Friend* (1641); *The Doctrine of the Church, to which is committed the Keyes of the Kingdome of Heaven* (1642); *The Keyes Of the Kingdom of Heaven, . . .* (1644); Richard Mather, *Church-Government and Church-Covenant Discvssed* (1643); Samuel Eaton and Timothy Taylor, *A Defence Of sundry Positions, And Scriptures alledged to justifie the Congregationall-way; . . .* (1645); *A Platform of Church Discipline gathered out of the Word of God* (1649), reprinted in *The Results of Three Synods* (1725), and by Williston Walker in *The Creeds and Platforms of Congregationalism* (1893), characterized by Walker as "the clearest reflection of the system as it lay in the minds of the first generation on our soil"; Perry Miller, *Orthodoxy in Massachusetts, 1630-1650* (1933).

[6] Charles Francis Adams, *Antinomianism in the Colony of Massachusetts Bay, 1636-1638*, pp. 230, 242.

marriage, a majority of the people of Boston, where she was exceedingly helpful in time of sickness, and a minority elsewhere, the theories of the lady were not displeasing, but to the ministers discriminated against, John Winthrop, and the magistrates in general, they were anathema.[7] A fast-day sermon preached by John Wheelwright on Thursday, January 19, 1637, led to an open breach between the factions.[8] On March 9 a general court of the colony found Wheelwright guilty of contempt and sedition,[9] a decision against which the Hutchinsonian faction protested.[10] At the moment of arrival of the Davenport company, this was the status of the quarrel.

To John Davenport the Congregationalism of Massachusetts Bay seemed no radical innovation but the logical outcome of all his previous experiences. He had been elected curate of St. Lawrence's, Old Jewry, and vicar of St. Stephen's, Coleman Street, London, by general vestries of the parishes. He had come into contact with a group of Congregationalists who met in and about London, and under the ministry of John Lothropp entered into a covenant "To Walke togeather in all the Ways of God."[11] He had preached to the congregation of English merchants at Amsterdam who may have entered into a simple covenant.[12] He had opposed the Presbyterianism of John Paget and assisted Hugh Peter, who had enforced a covenant of fifteen articles drafted by himself upon an English church in Rotterdam.[13] The erstwhile

[7] *Ibid.*, p. 243; *Winthrop's Journal,* I, 201.

[8] For Wheelwright's sermon, see Massachusetts Historical Society *Proceedings,* IX, 256-274.

[9] *Massachusetts Colony Records,* I, 189.

[10] Charles Francis Adams, *Antinomianism,* p. 191.

[11] *Ante,* Chapter I, note 47.

[12] Champlin Burrage, *The Early English Dissenters in the Light of Recent Research,* I, 304.

[13] *Ibid.*, pp. 300-303; Additional MSS., 6394, fol. 161.

vicar of St. Stephen's, Coleman Street, not only accepted the Congregationalism of Massachusetts Bay, but readily assumed the rôle of leader in the ecclesiastical life of the colony.

In the midst of the turmoil between the adherents and the opponents of Anne Hutchinson, Davenport pleaded for uniformity. On Thursday, August 17, 1637, he preached on the text, "I exhort you brethren, . . . that there be no division among you . . .; wherein, as he fully set forth the nature and danger of divisions, and the disorders which were among us, . . . so he clearly discovered his judgment against the new opinions and bitter practices which were sprung up here."[14] From August 30 to September 22, he attended the synod of teaching elders which met at Newtown at the country's charge to deal with the controversy, at which gathering eighty-two blasphemous, erroneous, and unsafe opinions were considered and condemned. He may have been responsible for the reconversion to orthodoxy of John Cotton, who while the synod was in session admitted that he had been made a stalking horse by the Hutchinsonian faction, and swung over to the side of the majority.[15] As the elders were about to disperse, Davenport preached on the text, "Nevertheless, whereto we have already attained, let us walk by the same rule, let us mind the same thing."[16]

In November the former vicar of St. Stephen's, Coleman Street, may have attended the trials of Anne Hutchinson "for traduceing the mi^rs and their ministery," and of her adherents for disturbing the peace. If so, he heard John Cotton make a futile attempt to justify his straying disciple, and the general court pronounce sentence of banishment upon Anne Hutchinson, John Wheelwright, and the most ardent of the heretics, and sentence of disfran-

[14] *Winthrop's Journal*, I, 230-231.

[15] *Ibid.*, p. 233.

[16] *Ibid.*, p. 235.

chisement and disarmament upon the less offensive members of the faction.[17]

On Thursday, March 15, 1638, he was present at the trial of Anne Hutchinson before the church at Boston. At this time he had greater influence with her than any other, and wrung from her the acknowledgements, "*I thanke the Lord I have Light.* And I see more Light a greate deale by Mr Damphords opening of it," and, "Now Mr Damphord hath opened it. it is cleare to me. or God by him hath given me Light." It was not Davenport but John Cotton, "as one whose Wordes, by the Blessinge of God, may be of more Respect, and sinke deeper, and soe was likely to doe more good upon the partie offendinge. than any of theas," whom the elders appointed to admonish the unfortunate woman, however, and Davenport listened to his friend preface his remarks with an acknowledgement of his own "sleepines and want of wachfull care over" this lamb of his flock. After the hearing Anne Hutchinson was placed in Cotton's house, where Cotton and Davenport might take pains with her, and throughout the following week the two ministers engaged in theological debate with the misguided woman. On March 22 she was brought before the church for a second hearing. At this time Davenport listened to her acknowledgement of her errors, but when she added that she then thought no differently than she had previously thought, his patience snapped, and he agreed with Cotton that she merited excommunication.[18]

While in Massachusetts Davenport set forth the tenets of Congregationalism in *An Apologie of the Chvrches*

[17] *Massachusetts Colony Records,* I, 207-209, 211-213.

[18] Charles Francis Adams, *Antinomianism,* pp. 225, 297, 299, 310, 315, 317, 332-335; "A Report of the Trial of Mrs. Anne Hutchinson before the Church in Boston, March 1638," Massachusetts Historical Society *Proceedings,* 2d series, IV, 159-191.

in New-England for Chvrch-Covenant . . . Sent over in Answer to Master Bernard, in the Yeare 1639, and *An Answer of the Elders of the Severall Chvrches in New-England unto Nine Positions, Sent over to Them (By divers Reverend and godly Ministers in England) to declare their Judgements therein,*[19] and after leaving the Bay Colony, in *The Power of Congregational Churches Asserted and Vindicated.*[20]

Civil as well as ecclesiastical developments attracted the attention of the new arrivals. At general courts which convened at Boston, August 1, 1637, and at Newtown, September 26 and November 2, 1637, and March 2, 1638, and at meetings of the inhabitants of the various towns of the colony, John Davenport and Theophilus Eaton were probably interested spectators.

Since the arrival of the Winthrop company in 1630, the Massachusetts Bay Company had transformed itself into

19 Thomas Lechford, *Note-Book,* p. 2. ''I writt two manuscripts for Mr Davenporte one in answere to Mr Bernard about the Church Covenant etc. the other an answere to Mr Ball about the Comon prayer booke in E. [1£ 6*s.* 0*d.* Mr Davenport.]'' In the preface to *A Disputation concerning Church-Members and their Children* (1659), Nathaniel Mather claims that although his father Richard Mather did not know Bernard and had had no correspondence with him, he was the author of the first named work, but Lechford's entry, and the fact that both works, the second beyond all doubt that of Davenport, were printed by T. P. and M. S. for Benjamin Allen in 1643, would tend to prove that Davenport was the author. Sent to England in 1638, the manuscripts miscarried, were rewritten, and sent over for a second time in 1639. Richard Mather, *Church-Government and Church-Covenant Discvssed* (1643), pp. 24, 28. John Ball seems to have been the spokesman for the ministers in England, for he wrote the reply to Davenport's second work. After circulating in New England in manuscript form, his queries were expanded and published as *A Friendly Triall of the Grounds Tending to Separation* (1640).

20 Written in reply to John Paget's *A Defence of Church-Government, exercised in Presbyteriall, Classicall, and Synodall Assemblies; According to the Practice of the Reformed Churches* (1641), the manuscript of the last named work was lost at sea, probably in the phantom ship. Rewritten after the lapse of seven years, it was not published until 1672.

the government of a colony. For this, radical departures from the charter obtained from Charles I had been necessary. The nomenclature of the grant of March 4, 1629, had been retained, and there were still governor, deputy governor, assistants, freemen, general courts, and courts of assistants, but the functions of these officers and assemblies differed from the intentions of the framers of the charter. The governor was no longer the chief officer of a trading company, but the governor of a colony, and found himself assisted by a council appointed for life. Freemen were no longer stockholders in the company, but voters and officeholders, and "to the end the body of the comons may be preserued of honest and good men," the general court of May 18, 1631, had "ordered and agreed that for time to come noe man shalbe admitted to the freedome of this body polliticke, but such as are members of some of the churches within the lymitts of the same."[21] The general court was now composed of governor, deputy governor, assistants, and deputies or representatives of the freemen, for as the colony expanded it became increasingly difficult for all freemen to attend. Already looked upon as the supreme legislative and judicial authority in the colony, within a decade after the arrival of the Davenport company in Massachusetts Bay, the general court was described by one of the elders of the colony as "a place of credite and trust for all the greatest affaires of o[r] little cōmon wealth; w[ch] Court is to us as the Parliament is in Englande."[22] In addition to serving as an advisory body to the governor, the court of assistants met at Boston as a great quarter court possessing judicial functions. The right of the company to raise funds by disposing of stock had given way to the right of the colony to collect rates. Beneath this colonial govern-

21 *Massachusetts Colony Records,* I, 87.
22 Additional MSS., 4276, fol. 107.

ment, functioned plantation or town governments reminiscent of the parish organization of England.

The new arrivals found that with true Puritan zeal for the education of youth both colony and town governments were making provision for college and schools. To perpetuate a learned ministry, the general court of Massachusetts Bay on October 28, 1636, appropriated £400 for a school or college, and a year later appointed a committee "to take order for a colledge at Newetowne."[23] On April 13, 1635, the town of Boston agreed "that our brother Philemon Pormont, shalbe intreated to become scholemaster, for the teaching and nourtering of children with us," and on August 6, 1636, forty-five of the wealthier inhabitants of the town pledged £40 6*s*. in amounts varying from the £10 of Governor Henry Vane to the 3*s*. of John Pemberton for "the maintenance of a free school master for the youth with us," and chose Daniel Maude, a graduate of the University of Cambridge, as master. William Witherell undertook the education of the children of Charlestown, and Lionel Chute and John Fiske wrestled with similar duties at Ipswich and Salem.[24] With these projects, not unlike those at one time undertaken by the feoffees for the purchase of impropriations in England, Davenport was in hearty sympathy, and served as one of the first overseers for the college.

The ecclesiastical and civil practices of Massachusetts Bay had recently been embodied in a code of laws framed by John Cotton and at this time under consideration in the colony. There had long been a demand for such a code. The charter had authorized the company "to make lawes and ordiñnces for the good and welfare of the saide

[23] *Massachusetts Colony Records*, I, 217; *Winthrop's Journal*, I, 310-315.

[24] "Boston Records, 1634-1660," Record Commissioners of the City of Boston, *Second Report*, pp. 5, 160; George E. Littlefield, *Early Schools and School-Books of New England*, pp. 55-98; Walter H. Small, *Early New England Schools*, pp. 3-14.

Company, and for the government and ordering of the saide landes and plantac̄on, and the people inhabiting and to inhabite the same, . . . Soe as such lawes and ordinances be not contrarie or repugnant to the lawes and statutes of this our realme of England.''[25] Up to this time the laws were those that had been made by the general court and the court of assistants of the company while still in England, by Governor Endecott and his council in New England under the authorization of the Massachusetts Bay Company, and by the court of assistants and general court after the arrival of the great company headed by Winthrop with the charter in New England. These laws were scattered through the manuscript records of the company and colony. Repeals and revisions were frequent. To discover the law on any subject in force at a given time was a difficult problem. Moreover, situations which were not covered by legislation frequently arose, and the magistrates—for so governor and assistants were coming to be called—dealt with them at discretion.

Before the transfer of the charter to America, a general court of the company appointed a committee of which John Davenport was a member ''for reducing of all former orders into a methode, . . . and to present the same to the next Generall Court, to bee ratyfied and confirmed, in part or in whole, as shalbe then thought fitt; wch are then by the Secretary to bee entered into a faire booke to bee kept for that purpose, according to the vsage and custome of other Companyes,''[26] but that this committee functioned, there is no evidence. Almost five years after the arrival of the Winthrop company in Massachusetts Bay, a general court of March 4, 1635, desired John Winthrop and Richard Bellingham ''to take a vewe of all

25 *Massachusetts Colony Records*, I, 12.
26 *Ibid.*, p. 47.

orders already made, and to informe the nexte Generall Court wch of them they iudge meete to be altered, ebreviated, repealed, corrected, inlarged, or explained.''[27] Two months later the general court added John Haynes and Thomas Dudley to the two men already appointed and instructed the committee to frame a body of laws in resemblance to a Magna Carta, which being allowed by some of the ministers and the general court, should be received for fundamental laws.[28] A year later the general court further enlarged the committee by adding Governor Henry Vane, John Cotton, Hugh Peter, and Thomas Shepard, and turning for inspiration from Magna Carta to the writings of John Wemyss of Lathockar, Fife, Scotland, instructed its appointees ''to make a draught of lawes agreeable to the word of God, wch may be the ffundamentalls of this com̄onwealth, and to present the same to the nexte Generall Court.''[29] The addition of the three ministers produced results, for on October 25, 1636, John Cotton presented to the general court of Massachusetts Bay ''a model of Moses his judicials compiled in an exact method.''

The Cotton code is an excellent illustration of how much and how little the seventeenth-century Puritan meant by the phrase, ''agreeable to the word of God.'' It consisted of ten chapters:

I. Of Magistrates.
II. Of the free Burgesses and free Inhabitants.
III. Of the protection and provision of the Countrey.
IV. Of the right of Inheritance.
V. Of Commerce.
VI. Of Trespasses.

27 *Massachusetts Colony Records,* I, 137.
28 *Ibid.,* p. 147; *Winthrop's Journal,* I, 151.
29 *Massachusetts Colony Records,* I, 174.

VII. Of Crimes.
VIII. Of other Crimes lesse hainous such as are to be punished with some Corporall punishment or Fine.
IX. Of the triall of Causes, whether Civill or Criminall, and the execution of Sentence.
X. Of the causes Criminall betweene our People and Forraine Nations.

Cotton had done little more than embody in written form the existing ecclesiastical and civil organization, laws, and practices of Massachusetts Bay. He had provided for governor, deputy governor, general court, and court of assistants, as did the charter of the Massachusetts Bay Company. He had provided for Congregational churches and a standing council and limited the franchise and the right to hold office to church-members, as was the law in Massachusetts at the time. From the practices of the Bay he departed only in such trivialities as the substitution of the title of "free burgess" for that of "freeman." Unlike the balance of the code, the one chapter dealing with inheritance and the two chapters dealing with crimes were drawn from the Scriptures—the former providing for the division of real property among all male heirs with a double portion to the eldest son, or in defect of male heirs, among all female heirs; the latter making punishable by death the crimes which the Jews so punished in the time of Moses; both being improvements upon seventeenth-century English law. In accord with the practice of the time, the provisions of the code were supported by marginal scriptural citations to prove that they were in harmony with the word of God. After the provision, "The Governor hath power . . . To send out warrants for the calling of the generall Court," occurred the citation, "Iosh.24.1." The verse reads, "And Joshua gathered all the tribes of Israel to Shechem, and called for the elders of Israel, and for their heads, and for their judges, and for their officers; and they presented themselves before God.'' The arrangement accounts for the name, ''Moses his judicials,'' given to the code by John Winthrop, but the analogy between the calling of a general court and the assembling of the tribes of Israel at Shechem is slight, and although it may have convinced the seventeenth-century Puritan that the government of the Bay Colony was in harmony with the word of God, it hardly made the code biblical in the sense that its provisions were drawn from Holy Writ.[30]

The idea of limiting the right to vote and to hold office to church-members was new to John Davenport, and John Cotton and the former vicar of St. Stephen's, Coleman Street, London, seem to have discussed the wisdom of this provision at length. To convince Davenport of the feasibility of the plan, Cotton wrote *A Discourse About Civil Government in a New Plantation Whose Design is Religion.*[31]

The Davenport company left England with the intention of settling in the territory of the Governor and Company of the Massachusetts Bay in New England. The Bay Colony looked upon the group as a potential planta-

[30] *Winthrop's Journal,* I, 196; John Norton, *The Life and Death of . . . Mr John Cotton* (1658), p. 22. A manuscript copy of the Cotton code occurs in British Museum, Sloane MSS., 3448, fols. 16-44. The code was printed in London in 1641 as *An Abstract or* [*sic*] *the Lawes of New England, As they are now established,* and again in London in 1655 as *An Abstract of Laws and Government. Wherein as in a Mirrour may be seen the wisdome and perfection of the Government of Christs Kingdome. Accomodable to any State or form of Government in the world, that is not Antichristian or Tyrannicall. . . .* It was included by Thomas Hutchinson in *A Collection of Original Papers* in 1769; reprinted by the Massachusetts Historical Society in 1798; and included by Peter Force in his *Tracts and Other Papers,* III (1844), no. 9.

[31] See my note, ''The Authorship of a Discourse About Civil Government in a New Plantation Whose Design is Religion,'' *American Historical Review,* XXXVII, 267-269.

tion, and when a £1000 rate was levied on the several towns of the colony in November, 1637, permitted Eaton and his associates to make a voluntary contribution, and when a £1500 rate was levied in the following year, assessed the group £20.[32] Both colony and towns offered the recent arrivals territory upon which to settle: the general court, any unoccupied place;[33] Charlestown, part of its lands;[34] the inhabitants of Newbury, contemplating removal to a more commodious site,[35] their whole town.[36] The Davenport company considered a site beyond Watertown, but they were London merchants, and desired to settle upon a harbor suitable for commerce, and an inland location failed to meet their requirements. The Hutchinsonian controversy added nothing to the attractiveness of the Bay. Finally, the Bay Colony was under attack from England. As Theophilus Eaton either knew or soon learned, the attorney general had been instructed on May 3, 1637, to call for the charter of the Massachusetts Bay Company,[37] and on July 23, 1637, Charles I announced the intention of appointing Sir Ferdinando Gorges governor general of New England.[38]

In 1636 Hugh Peter had visited Saybrook at the mouth of the Connecticut River and doubtless reported the attractions of the place to his friends. During the summer of 1637 the Pequot War made known and available for settlement the territory to the west of Saybrook. "I must extol Qenepiake," wrote Lieutenant Richard Daven-

[32] *Massachusetts Colony Records,* I, 209-210, 231.

[33] John Davenport and Theophilus Eaton to the Governor, Deputy, Assistants, etc., of Massachusetts Bay, March 12, 1638, in the New York Public Library, printed in New York, Public Library, *Bulletin,* III, 393-394; Massachusetts Historical Society *Collections,* 3d series, III, 165-167.

[34] *Ibid.,* 4th series, VI, 94.

[35] *Massachusetts Colony Records,* I, 206.

[36] *Winthrop's Journal,* I, 265.

[37] C. O. 1: 9, nos. 50, 51; Egerton MSS., 2395, fols. 27-29.

[38] C. O. 1: 9, no. 60.

port.[39] "I confess the place and places whither God's providence carried us, that is, to Quillipeage River, and so beyond to the Dutch," reported Captain Israel Stoughton to the governor and council of Massachusetts, "is before this [Pequot], or the bay either, (so far as I can judge,) abundantly . . . considering, 1st, the goodness of the land, 2d, the fairness of the title, 3d, the neighbourhood of Connecticut, 4th, the good access that may be thereto, wherein it is before Connecticut, even in the three forementioned considerations, (for the land Connecticut men so judge,) and, 5th, that an ill neighbour may possess it, if a good do not,—I should readily give it my good word, if any good souls have a good liking to it."[40] Davenport and Eaton knew that this earthly paradise lay within the limits of the grant made by Robert Rich, Earl of Warwick, to a group of friends in England. On the last day of August, 1637, Eaton and several others of the company set out to view it.[41] According to tradition, the explorers were so favorably impressed by the site, that they left several of their number to retain possession of it over the winter,[42] for the season was late, and removal was not feasible before the following spring.

Quickly grasping the vision of a kingdom of Christ on the shores of Long Island Sound, a colony settled by kindred souls, free from the dissensions of Massachusetts Bay, on a harbor suitable for the commerce of London merchants, Davenport and Eaton labored to add to their company. In the Bay Colony pressure of population was beginning to be felt, and they found many who were willing to remove. Among those who undertook either to advance to the frontier with the original company or to fol-

39 Massachusetts Historical Society *Collections*, 5th series, IX, 2.

40 John Winthrop, *The History of New England from 1630 to 1649*, I (1825), 400-401.

41 *Winthrop's Journal*, I, 231.

42 Benjamin Trumbull, *A Complete History of Connecticut*, I (1797), 90.

low soon after were Richard Hull, William Tuttle, and William Wilkes, of Boston; Anne Higginson and her family, Jarvis Boykin, John Chapman, John Charles, Timothy Ford, Thomas James, Benjamin Ling, John Mosse, and Richard Perry, of Charlestown; John Benham, Benjamin Fenn, Thomas Jeffrey, Thomas Kimberley, William Preston, Thomas Sandford, Thomas Trowbridge, and Zachariah Whitman, of Dorchester; John Astwood, of Stanstead Abbey, Hertfordshire, and Roxbury; Thomas Baker, John Burwell, Jasper Gunn, John Hall, John Peacock, William Potter, Edward Riggs, Thomas Uffot, and Joanna and Jacob Sheaffe of Roxbury; Mark Pierce, of Newtown; and Nathaniel Turner, of Lynn.

A recently arrived company headed by Peter Prudden was a notable addition to the group. Perhaps the son of Thomas Prudden of King's Walden, Hertfordshire, and a kinsman of William Thomas of Caerleon, Monmouthshire, Prudden had been admitted as sizar at Emmanuel College, Cambridge, on June 20, 1620, and in 1635 had been offered the post of minister by the Providence Island Company. On May 31, 1637, with fifteen Hertfordshire families—among them Edmund Tapp of Bennington, Hertfordshire, James Prudden, William Fowler, Thomas and Hannah Buckingham, Thomas Welsh, Richard Platt, Henry Stonehill, and William East—he left England, and five weeks after the Davenport company, arrived at Boston. There he may have married Joanna Boyse of Roxbury, who long years later owned land at Edston, Kirby Moorside, and Southfield, Yorkshire. After considering settlement at Dedham, the group cast in their lot with the emigrants to Long Island Sound.[43]

[43] Lillian E. Prudden, *Peter Prudden;* Somerset House, Prerogative Court of Canterbury, 67 Russell (hereafter cited as Somerset House, P.C.C.); New Haven Probate Records, I, Part II, 108-110, 140-141; John and J. A. Venn, *Alumni Cantabrigienses,* Part I, III, 404; Public Record Office, Colonial

Finally, at this time many friends in England were weighing migration to the New World, and Davenport and Eaton probably hoped to attract some of these immigrants to the colony they intended to found.

These gains and expectations were in part offset by the loss of Nathaniel Eaton, Nathaniel Rowe, Edward and Anne (Yale) Hopkins, and John Cotton. Eaton and Rowe remained in Newtown, the former as the unfortunate choice for the first master of the infant collegiate school, which his cruelty and his wife's niggardliness almost wrecked, and the latter as a scholar. Hopkins and his wife turned toward Hartford. Fearful that his ministry in Boston would suffer as an aftermath of the Hutchinsonian controversy, John Cotton considered removal to Quinnipiac, a laboratory where "Moses his judicials" might be applied in all their purity, but was persuaded to remain in Boston.[44]

In the spring of 1638 the group was ready to undertake the voyage to the new plantation. On March 12 Davenport and Eaton wrote "To the much Honored the Governour Deputy and Assistents etc." of Massachusetts Bay, announcing their intention to depart. "Our Desire of staying within this patent was Reall and Strong," they said, "if the eye of Gods providence (to whom we have Com̄itted our Waies especially in so important an enterprise as this, which, we Confess, is farr above our Capacityes) had guided us to a place Convenient for our

Entry Book, III, 199-200; George Sherwood, ed., *American Colonists in English Records,* first series (London, 1932), p. 35, citing Public Record Office, Chancery Bills and Answers, Charles I, B. 93: 34, Barber v. Tapp; *Dedham Town Records, 1636-1659,* pp. 33, 35; Massachusetts Historical Society *Collections,* 4th series, VI, 94; J. H. Tuttle, "Peter Prudden's Company and Colonial Affairs in 1637 and 1638," Colonial Society of Massachusetts *Publications,* XVII, 244-248.

44 John Cotton, *The Way of Congregational Churches Cleared* (London, 1648), pp. 52-54; Narragansett Club *Publications,* II, 81; Thomas Hutchinson, *The History of the Colony of Massachusets-Bay,* I (1760), 63, note.

familyes, and for our freinds.''[45] On March 30, Davenport, Eaton, and many families sailed from Massachusetts Bay for Quinnipiac.[46]

[45] New York, Public Library, *Bulletin,* III, 393-394; Massachusetts Historical Society *Collections,* 3d series, III, 165-167.
[46] *Winthrop's Journal,* I, 265.

CHAPTER III

STAKING OUT A COLONY

THE vessel carrying the Davenport company and the recruits gained in Massachusetts Bay skirted Cape Cod, entered Long Island Sound, passed the fort commanded by Lyon Gardiner at the mouth of the Connecticut River, and before the middle of April, 1638, entered the harbor at Quinnipiac. The region was claimed by the Dutch of New Netherland but it also lay at the western end of the grant of Robert Rich, Earl of Warwick, to friends of John Davenport and Theophilus Eaton in England.

Until a town could be laid out at Quinnipiac, in 1640 named New Haven, more symmetrical than was usually the case in seventeenth-century New England, and houses erected, some of them pretentious enough in architecture and furnishings for Coleman Street merchants, the immigrants found shelter in pits or cellars dug into the ground, encased, floored, and roofed with timber, and in some cases partitioned into rooms.[1]

With the Congregationalism and civil government of Massachusetts Bay, John Davenport and Theophilus Eaton were in hearty sympathy. At the moment of depar-

[1] *New Haven Colonial Records, 1638-1649,* pp. 31, 32, 46, 47, 70; *New York Colonial Documents,* I, 368. See also Michael Wigglesworth, "Autobiography," *New England Historical and Genealogical Register,* XVII, 137-139, reprinted in Edward E. Atwater, *History of the Colony of New Haven,* Appendix I. "Winter approaching we dwelt in a cellar partly under ground covered with earth the first winter, But I remember that one great rain brake in upon us and drencht me so in my bed being asleep that I fell sick upon it; but the Lord in mercy spar'd my life and restored my health."

ture from the Bay Colony a copy of "Moses his judicials" seems not to have been available, but to guide the group in gathering churches and establishing governments in the towns they proposed to found on Long Island Sound, Davenport apparently carried with him Cotton's *Discourse About Civil Government in a New Plantation Whose Design is Religion,* and long years later was responsible for its publication for the guidance of another group of planters,[2] and as soon as possible John Winthrop forwarded a transcript of the Cotton code to Quinnipiac.[3]

On a day of extraordinary humiliation soon after arriving at their new home the whole assembly of free planters entered into a solemn covenant "thatt as [in] matters thatt Concerne the gathering and ordering of a Chur. so Likewise in all publique offices wch concerne Cuill order as Choyce of magistrates and officers makeing and repealing of Lawes devideing allotmts of Inheritance and all things of Like nature we would all of vs be ordered by those Rules wch the scripture holds forth to vs." To the New England Puritan of 1638, fresh from Massachusetts Bay, this statement could mean only the adoption of the frame of government and code of laws drafted by John Cotton, at the moment under consideration in the Bay. The agreement to adopt the code "was Called a plantatiō Couent to distinguish itt frō [a] Chur. Couent wch Could nott att thatt time be made a Chur nott being then gathered butt was deferred till a Chur. might be gathered according to god."[4]

The planters of Quinnipiac thus accepted a definite and written frame of government and code of laws some nine

2 See my note, "The Authorship of a Discourse About Civil Government in a New Plantation Whose Design is Religion," *American Historical Review,* XXXVII, 267-269.

3 *New Haven Colonial Records, 1653-1665,* p. 518.

4 *Ibid., 1638-1649,* p. 12.

months before the three towns on the Connecticut River adopted the eleven fundamental orders which have sometimes been called the first written constitution, and awaited only the gathering of a church and the admittance of church-members as freemen to put the government outlined by Cotton into operation. Until such a government could be organized, power or trust for managing the public affairs of the plantation was committed to several individuals whose names were not recorded for posterity.[5]

Between Saybrook and the Dutch settlement at New Amsterdam the coast stretched unoccupied. The Davenport company was without a patent from the crown upon which to base a claim to this territory. Of this deficiency, John Davenport, after his experience with the company of feoffees for the purchase of impropriations, could not have been unaware. Of it the leaders of the group became increasingly conscious as the years went on. Davenport and Eaton knew that the region lay within the limits of the grant of the Earl of Warwick to a group of lords and gentlemen in England with whom they were upon terms of friendship. Had they left England with the intention of settling at Quinnipiac, they would undoubtedly have asked for and received the authorization of these friends to settle within the limits of their grant. But since they had arrived at Quinnipiac without authorization, they probably relied upon their friendship with the holders of the title, knowing that they could receive authorization from them if need arose. Meanwhile they remedied their lack of title as best they could by acquiring the Indian rights to the soil.

In their letter to "the Governour Deputy and Assistents etc." of Massachusetts, announcing their intention to depart from the Bay, Davenport and Eaton had said,

[5] *New Haven Colonial Records, 1638-1649*, p. 20.

"we . . . have sent letters to Coñectacutt for a speedy transacting the purchase of the parts about Quillypiock from the Natives which may pretend title thereunto."[6] The negotiations for the purchase of territory begun before the Davenport company left Massachusetts were uncompleted when the group arrived at Quinnipiac. It was not until November 24, 1638, that "Articles of Agreement betweene Theophilus Eaton and John Davenport and others English Planters att Quinopiocke on the one partye and Momaugin the Indian Sachem of Quinopiocke and Sugcogisin Quesaquauch, Caroughood, Wesaucucke and others of his Counsell on the other partye," were signed. At this time Thomas Stanton, official interpreter of Connecticut, served as intermediary. In consideration for the promise of protection and the free gift of "Twelve Coates of english trucking cloat[h], Twelve Alcumy spoones, Twelve Hatchetts, twelve hoes, two dozen of knives, twelve porengers and four[e] Cases of ffrench knives and sizers," Momaugin and his company transferred to the English "all th^r Right title and interest to all the land rivers and ponds, trees with all the libertyes and appurtenances belonging unto the same in Quinopiocke to the utmost of their bounds East, West, North, South." The Indians reserved only planting ground on the east side of the harbor, to be laid out by the English, and the right to hunt and fish within the limits of Quinnipiac, subject to the regulations of the English.[7]

Soon after this first acquisition of territory, Mantowese, son of the Indian sachem living at Mattabezeck, approached Theophilus Eaton and voluntarily offered to surrender to the planters of Quinnipiac title to a much larger area of land. On December 11, 1638, he conveyed to Theophilus Eaton, John Davenport, and sundry other

[6] Massachusetts Historical Society *Collections*, 3d series, III, 165.

[7] *New Haven Colonial Records, 1638-1649*, pp. 1-5.

English planters at Quinnipiac land surrounding the first purchase and extending eight miles to the east and five miles to the west of the Quinnipiac River, and north for a distance of ten miles. Again the Indians reserved planting land on the river and the right to hunt, fish, and kill beaver. In compensation Mantowese received a gift of "Eleven coates made of Trucking cloth, and one Coate for himselfe of English cloth, made up after the English mañer." This time John Clarke of Wethersfield served as interpreter.[8] Robert Cogswell, Roger Knapp, and James Love, who may have been squatters on the soil, renounced all right to any and every part of the territory. Thomas Moulener, originally of Ipswich, Suffolk, England, sold his rights to land at Totoket within the limits of the purchase to the planters of Quinnipiac, reserving only a lot for himself when a people should settle there. In 1639 he repurchased part of a neck of land, where he settled and became a thorn in the flesh, first of the planters of Quinnipiac, and later of the settlers of Totoket, until the latter group bought out his rights in 1651.[9]

On May 20, 1645, a third purchase of territory was made, extending north to a tree marked H on the Connecticut highway, east to a great hill to the west of Mattabezeck, and west to Tuncksus Hill.[10]

Although the lands surrounding the harbor of Quinnipiac were ample for a single plantation, the leaders of the group dreamed of a colony that would stretch along the coast from the settlement of the grantees of the Earl of Warwick at the mouth of the Connecticut River to Delaware Bay and include part if not all of Long Island.

[8] *New Haven Colonial Records, 1638-1649,* pp. 5-7; Massachusetts Historical Society, Winthrop MSS., XIII, 92; Massachusetts Historical Society *Collections,* 4th series, VII, 518.

[9] *New Haven Colonial Records, 1638-1649,* pp. 47, 84, 122; Branford Records, I, 215.

[10] Massachusetts Historical Society, Winthrop MSS., XIII, 92.

The settlers and their friends proceeded to acquire title to as much of this territory as they could.

Fifteen months after the arrival of the Davenport company at Quinnipiac, a group of friends under the leadership of Henry Whitfield reached the new plantation on Long Island Sound in the first vessel to sail directly from England to Quinnipiac. On August 23, 1639, negotiations with Shaumpishuh, sister of Momaugin, disclosed the fact that she was the sole owner of the territory from "Tuckshis to Oiockocommock River,"[11] and was willing to dispose of Menunkatuck lying between Kuttawo and Oiockocommock rivers to the newly arrived friends of the settlers of Quinnipiac. Meeting in Robert Newman's barn at New Haven, the Whitfield company agreed that "the whole lands called Menuncatuck shall bee purchased for vs all," the deed and writing to be drawn in the names of Henry Whitfield, Robert Kitchel, William Chittenden, John Bishop, John Caffinch, and William Leete, but all members of the group to pay their proportionate share of the cost of purchasing and settling the plantation of Menunkatuck.[12] On September 29, 1639, Shaumpishuh conveyed the territory to the six purchasers in return for "12 Coates 12 fathō of wompom 12 glasses 12 payer of shooes 12 hatchetts 12 paire of stockings 12 Hooes 4 Kettles 12 Knives 12 Hatts 12 porringers 12 spoones and 2 English coates," with which she professed "her selfe to be fully payed and satisfied."[13] The Indians agreed to remove from Menunkatuck and settle at Kuttawo beyond the limits of the purchase.

In the territory thus acquired, the Whitfield company settled the plantation of Menunkatuck, in 1643 named Guilford. As opportunity offered, they rounded out their boundaries by additional purchases from the natives. On

[11] Massachusetts Historical Society, Leete MSS.

[12] Guilford Records, B, 6.

[13] *Ibid.*, pp. 1-2; Leete MSS.

September 20, 1641, Henry Whitfield bought from Weekwash of Passquishank "all the land called the Neck lying beyond the East River in Menuncatuck wch reacheth unto Tuckshishoag." The compensation was a fathom of wampum and the usual assortment of clothing, which the town at a later date repaid to Whitfield.[14] The rights of Weekwash to this territory were not undisputed, however, and on December 17, 1641, this flaw in the title was cleared up by a third Indian deed by which Uncas the Mohegan transferred to the English planters of Menunkatuck the land between the East River and Tuckshishoag, the shore and Connecticut path to the sea.[15]

On October 22, 1645, George Fenwick, representative of the grantees of the Earl of Warwick, transferred to the town of Guilford as a gift the land between Tuckshishoag and the Hammonassett River, title to which area Fenwick had already acquired from Uncas the Mohegan.[16] Fenwick had previously agreed to convey to the River Colony the rights of the grantees of the Earl of Warwick to the region to the east of the Connecticut River, so far as it lay in his power to do so.[17] It seems probable that he intended to convey to the settlers of New Haven and their friends the rights of the grantees of the Earl of Warwick in the territory to the west of the river, not included in his promise to Connecticut, but the intention was never expressed.

Just as the colony established by John Davenport was coming to an end, the town of Guilford acquired additional territory by the purchase by William Leete and Samuel Kitchel from Uncas the Mohegan and Ahaddon, his son, of land between the East and Hammonassett

[14] Guilford Records, B, 6. [15] *Ibid.*, pp. 2-3.
[16] *Ibid.*, pp. 4-5.
[17] *Connecticut Colonial Records,* I, 266-270.

rivers to the north of the territory previously acquired, a purchase subsequently accepted by the town.[18]

The small group headed by Peter Prudden that had removed with the Davenport company to Long Island Sound soon determined to found a third plantation to the west of Quinnipiac. On February 12, 1640, William Fowler, Benjamin Fenn, Edmund Tapp, Zachariah Whitman, and Alexander Bryan, in trust for the group, bought from the Indians the territory between the East or Indian River and the Housatonic, the shore and Paugassett, at first known as Wepowaug and later as Milford. Like the town of Guilford to the east, in 1655, 1659, 1660, and 1661, the town of Milford to the west of New Haven rounded out its boundaries by additional purchases from the natives.[19]

In the spring of 1642 Stephen Goodyear, John Wakeman, and Mathew Gilbert, merchants of New Haven, acquired land at Paugassett to the north of Milford. In 1653 Goodyear added to the original purchase. In 1654 the first proprietors of Paugassett sold their rights to a group of Milford men. In the following year the new proprietors placed their purchase under the jurisdiction of the New Haven Colony. In 1657, 1659, 1660, 1661, and 1664, the village was rounded out by further purchases from the natives.[20]

In the spring of 1640 James Forrett, agent of William Alexander, Earl of Stirling, was at Quinnipiac. Stirling

18 Guilford Records, B, 20; Leete MSS.

19 Edward R. Lambert, *History of the Colony of New Haven*, pp. 85-88; Milford Land Records, I, 36, 55, 57, 58, 72-73. Mention of the first deed occurs only in Lambert. He gives the date as February 12, 1639, old style, which he says would be February 23, 1639, new style, but which would actually be February 12/22, 1640, new style.

20 *New Haven Colonial Records, 1638-1649, 1653-1665, passim; Derby Records, 1655-1710*, pp. 3, 9-10, 60-64; Samuel Orcutt and Ambrose Beardsley, *The History of the Old Town of Derby*, pp. xxviii-xxix, 2-15.

held Matowacks or the Isle of Stirling, more commonly known as Long Island, of the Council for New England *per gladium comitatus,* more specifically "by findeing foure able men conveniently armed and arrayed for the warre to attend vppon the Governor of Newe England for the publique service within ffourteene Dayes after any warninge given." His agent had already made two grants of territory on Long Island to a group of individuals from Lynn in Massachusetts Bay, under which they had begun a plantation at the western end of Long Island but been driven off by the Dutch. With John Davenport and Theophilus Eaton assisting, Forrett at this time negotiated a third grant of land on Long Island to the Lynn men. Under it they attempted a settlement at Schout's Bay, and after again suffering expulsion at the hands of the Dutch, settled the town of Southampton on the southeastern arm of Long Island, on December 13, 1640, perfecting their title by acquiring the Indian rights to the soil.[21]

At a time when transportation was largely by water, Long Island was more accessible than land in the interior on the mainland, and the planters of Quinnipiac took advantage of the presence of Forrett to gain a foothold across the Sound. As a town they bought the northeastern arm of Long Island, a region at first known as Yennicock and later as Southold.[22] Similarly, Mathew Sunderland and Richard Jackson acquired title to Hashamomack nearby, over which, on February 24, 1663, Southold

[21] C. O. 1: 8, no. 56; *New York Colonial Documents,* XIV, 627-628; *Southampton Records,* I, 9-12. See also my article, "The Earl of Stirling and the Colonization of Long Island," *Essays in Colonial History,* pp. 74-95.

[22] The deed from James Forrett to the planters of Quinnipiac is not extant. For evidence that the title was acquired by the town from Forrett, see *New Haven Colonial Records, 1638-1649,* p. 463; *New York Colonial Documents,* III, 197-198; *Acts of the Privy Council, Colonial,* 1613-1680, no. 942.

extended its jurisdiction.[23] In addition to the purchase from Forrett, the rights of the natives to the soil were acquired.

In February, 1640, the Earl of Stirling died, and his agent was stranded without money or supplies in New England. On May 18, 1641, to obtain funds with which to return to Scotland, Forrett sold the island between the eastern arms of Long Island of which he had previously taken possession for himself to Stephen Goodyear, and probably at about the same time, a small island nearby, to Robert Carmand. Carmand in turn disposed of his island to Goodyear.[24] On August 30, 1641, Goodyear offered Forrett's Island to New Haven, but perhaps because the plantation already had many irons in the fire, and the island in the hands of Goodyear was quite safe for New England Congregationalism, New Haven did not accept it at this time.[25] On June 9, 1651, Goodyear disposed of both islands to Thomas Middleton, Thomas Rous, and Constant and Nathaniel Sylvester in return for sixteen hundred pounds of good, merchantable, Muscovado sugar,[26] and when the purchasers proved themselves quite out of sympathy with the religious ideals of New Haven, the colony lost little time in claiming jurisdiction over the islands.[27]

About to return to Scotland, on July 29, 1641, Forrett gave a mortgage deed covering the whole of Long Island not otherwise disposed of to George Fenwick of Saybrook, John Haynes, Samuel Wyllys, and Edward Hop-

[23] *Southold Records,* I, 112, 115-117, 168-170, 208-209, 354; II, 276.

[24] *East-Hampton Records,* I, 96-99.

[25] *New Haven Colonial Records, 1638-1649,* p. 57.

[26] *East-Hampton Records,* I, 96-99.

[27] C. O. 1: 15, no. 31, p. 5; Connecticut State Library, Robert C. Winthrop Collection of Connecticut Manuscripts, II, 249; *Plymouth Colony Records,* X, 247.

kins of Connecticut, and Theophilus Eaton, Stephen Goodyear, and Thomas Gregson of New Haven, who acted "for the good of the countrey" for their respective colonies, in return for a loan of £110 to be repaid in three years, or in default of payment, the title to Long Island to vest in the mortgagees.[28] The loan was never repaid. Fenwick sold out the rights of the grantees of the Earl of Warwick to Connecticut, and the New Haven Colony and Connecticut, as successors to the Earl of Stirling, claimed the rights of the Earl of Stirling in Long Island. With the support of the New England Confederation,[29] representatives of the two colonies proceeded to buy up the Indian title to the soil, and to promote the settlement of the island. In 1646 Theophilus Eaton bought a tract of land adjoining Cow Bay and the neck of land subsequently known as Eaton's Neck on the northern shore of Long Island.[30] On April 29, 1648, Theophilus Eaton, governor of the New Haven Colony, and Edward Hopkins, governor of Connecticut, bought East Hampton from the natives.[31] On May 6, 1648, Theophilus Eaton, governor, Stephen Goodyear, deputy governor, and Richard Malbon, captain of the artillery company at New Haven, acquired title to the land from Wading Creek or Paucuckatux to Plum Isle, including the island.[32] On March 14, 1649, Theophilus Eaton and Stephen Goodyear, as governor and deputy governor of the New Haven Colony, acquired title to Ocquebanck,[33] and a week later, to Matti-

28 Office of the Secretary of State, Hartford, Connecticut Colonial Records, I, 319; *Connecticut Colonial Records,* II, 93.

29 *Plymouth Colony Records,* IX, 104.

30 Office of the Secretary of State, Albany, Deeds, II, 237, 249-250; *Huntington Records,* I, 42-44, 49-51; New Haven Town Records, 1662-1678, reverse, p. 3.

31 New York Deeds, II, 92-94, 191; *East-Hampton Records,* I, 2-4.

32 New York Deeds, II, 207-209, 214; *Southold Records,* I, 249-251; II, 6-7.

33 New York Deeds, II, 210-213.

tuck.[34] In 1658 the New Haven Colony disposed of both Ocquebanck and Mattituck to the town of Southold for £7.[35] In 1649 William Wells of Southold and Richard Woodhull of Southampton purchased lands at Corchauge, Mattituck, and Ocquebanck from the natives. When questioned by a general court for the jurisdiction at New Haven, May 30, 1649, Wells announced his willingness to resign his interest to the colony. On October 21, 1658, he bought out the rights of Woodhull, taking the deed in his own name but alleging that he acted in behalf of Southold, and on July 2, 1667, after the New Haven Colony had come to an end, he resigned his own rights at Corchauge, Mattituck, and Ocquebanck to the plantation of Southold.[36] In 1653 protégés of the New Haven Colony from Sandwich in the colony of New Plymouth acquired title to Oyster Bay and Huntington on Long Island,[37] and on April 4, 1655, individuals of Southold purchased the locality variously known as Setauket, Ashford, Cromwell Bay, and Brookhaven from the natives.[38] In the years which followed, the settlers of Oyster Bay, Huntington, and Setauket extended their boundaries by additional purchases from the Indians.

In the summer of 1640, Captain Nathaniel Turner set out to explore the mainland toward New Netherland. On July 1, 1640, on behalf of the planters of Quinnipiac, he bought all the lands belonging to Ponus, sagamore of Toquams, and to Wascussue, sagamore of Shippan, a piece of planting ground reserved by Ponus only excepted. For this acquisition he paid twelve glasses, twelve

34 *Brookhaven Records,* I, 76-77.

35 *New Haven Colonial Records, 1653-1665,* pp. 233, 302.

36 *Ibid., 1638-1649,* p. 463; *Southold Records,* I, 5, 204-205, 229-230, 262-263, 266-268; *Southampton Records,* I, 79.

37 New York Deeds, II, 219-220, 252; *Oyster Bay Records,* I, 670-671; *Huntington Records,* I, 1-4.

38 New York Deeds, II, 183-184; *Brookhaven Records,* I, 1-2.

knives, and four coats immediately, and agreed to send twelve coats, twelve hoes, twelve hatchets, twelve glasses, twelve knives, four kettles, and four fathom of white wampum within a month.[39] According to explanatory deeds of August 10, 1655, and January 7, 1668, the Turner purchase extended eight miles from east to west and sixteen miles inland.[40] Within this purchase the plantation of Toquams, Rippowams, or Stamford was settled. On March 24, 1646, the original purchase was augmented by land to the east between Five Mile River and Pine Brook, acquired from Piamikin, sagamore of Roatan.[41]

On July 18, 1640, a few weeks subsequent to the Turner purchase, Robert Feake and Daniel Patrick of Watertown in Massachusetts Bay bought the land to the west of Toquams between Asamuck and Tatomuck rivers. At the same time Feake's wife, Elizabeth Fones, widow of Henry Winthrop, acquired title to the neighboring neck of land subsequently known as Elizabeth's Neck.[42] In this territory Feake and Patrick founded the small settlement of Greenwich. Although in 1641 Feake placed the settlement under the jurisdiction of New Haven,[43] probably to gain the protection of an older colony against the Indians, on April 9, 1642, Patrick submitted to the jurisdiction of New Netherland.[44] By the Hartford award of 1650, the boundary between the New Haven Colony and New Netherland was fixed at the west side of Greenwich Bay, and

[39] Stamford Records, B, 30; E. B. Huntington, *History of Stamford, Conn.*, pp. 94-95.

[40] Stamford Records, B, 30-32; Huntington, *History of Stamford, Conn.*, pp. 97-99.

[41] Stamford Records, A, 343; *New Haven Colonial Records, 1653-1665*, pp. 104-107; Huntington, *History of Stamford, Conn.*, pp. 95-96.

[42] Greenwich Land Records, I, 455; Spencer P. Mead, *Ye Historie of Ye Town of Greenwich*, pp. 5-6.

[43] *New Haven Colonial Records, 1653-1665*, p. 144; *Plymouth Colony Records*, X, 14.

[44] *New York Colonial Documents*, II, 144.

the New Haven Colony promptly claimed Greenwich, but the award was not ratified by the States General of the United Netherlands until 1656, and meanwhile the Dutch colony continued to exercise jurisdiction over the settlement.[45] In May, 1655, Stamford complained of the situation to the general court of the New Haven Colony,[46] and dissatisfied with the reply of Greenwich, in the following May the colony sent Richard Law and Francis Bell of Stamford to Greenwich to demand the submission of the settlement.[47] It was not until October 6, 1656, however, that the inhabitants of Greenwich finally agreed to accept the government of the Puritan commonwealth and became part of the town of Stamford.[48]

After the purchase of Toquams, Captain Nathaniel Turner may have continued along the coast to Delaware Bay and River, for in later years the New Haven Colony always traced its title to the Delaware region back to 1640. In this fertile valley the English found the colonists of two other nations. On the basis of the voyage of Henry Hudson in the *Half Moon* in 1609, the Dutch claimed the Delaware, by them called the South River. Their several attempts to found colonies in the region had met with scant success, however, and in 1640 they held only Fort Nassau, near the mouth of Little Timber Creek, on the east side of the river.[49]

In 1637 Chancellor Axel Oxenstierna of Sweden chartered the New Sweden Company.[50] In the same year the company sent Peter Minuit, formerly in the employ of the Dutch West India Company, and twenty-four colo-

[45] Massachusetts Historical Society *Proceedings*, 2d series, VI, 12; *Laws and Ordinances of New Netherland*, 1638-1674, pp. 215-217.

[46] *New Haven Colonial Records, 1653-1665*, p. 144.

[47] *Ibid.*, p. 176.

[48] *Ibid.*, pp. 215-216; Stamford Records, I, 94.

[49] E. B. O'Callaghan, *History of New Netherland* (2 vols., 1848).

[50] Amandus Johnson, *The Swedish Settlements on the Delaware, 1638-1664* (2 vols., 1911).

nists in the *Kalmar Nyckel* and *Grip* to begin a colony in America. Forced to stop at Medemblik for repairs, on December 21/31, 1637, Minuit sailed from there, and in the following March, just as the Davenport company were preparing to leave Massachusetts Bay for Quinnipiac, arrived in the South Bay. On April 26/May 6, 1638, Director General Kieft and the council of New Netherland protested against this invasion of the territory of the Dutch West India Company,[51] but Minuit disregarded the protest and in the name of the New Sweden Company took possession of the territory below Fort Nassau. Purchasing the lands between Duck Creek and the Schuylkill on the west side of the river from the Indians, he erected Fort Christina on Christina Creek, twenty-five miles below Fort Nassau. In June Minuit sailed away to lose his life at St. Christopher. On April 17, 1640, the men left at Fort Christina were about to remove to New Amsterdam when Peter Hollender Ridder and additional Swedish colonists appeared upon the scene. Ridder bought the lands from the Schuylkill to the falls at Trenton and from Duck Creek to Cape Henlopen on the west bank and from Racoon Creek to Cape May on the east side of the Delaware from the Indians.

In the spring of 1641 a small company sent out by Captain Nathaniel Turner and George Lamberton of New Haven entered this area of international conflict.[52] They bought the lands between Racoon Creek and Cape May on the eastern shore and perhaps other lands on the west bank from the Indians.[53] To the original purchase, Lamberton added, on April 19, 1642, land at the junction of the Delaware and Schuylkill rivers, opposite the Dutch fort.[54]

[51] *New York Colonial Documents,* XII, 19.

[52] *Ibid.,* II, 144.

[53] *Winthrop's Journal,* II, 56-57.

[54] Johnson, *The Swedish Settlements on the Delaware, 1638-1664,* I,

The rights of the New Haveners to the Delaware were first challenged by one Miles, agent of Sir Edmund Plowden. On June 21, 1634, Thomas, Lord Wentworth, deputy general of Ireland, acting in the name of Charles I, had granted to Plowden Long Island, by this grant to be called the Isle of Plowden, and forty leagues square of territory on the adjacent continent. The grant was to be held *in capite* as of the crown of Ireland, and Plowden was created earl palatine or governor of the province of New Albion thus created. Just as the New Haveners had recognized the right of the Earl of Stirling to Long Island, so, when they learned through Miles that they were trespassing upon Plowden's manor of Watcessit, they recognized his right to the Delaware region, and took an oath of allegiance to the king and obedience to the earl palatine.[55]

At its greatest extent the New Haven Colony stretched from the Hammonassett River on the east to the western boundary of Milford, and from the eastern boundary of Stamford to the western boundary of Greenwich, and inland for a distance of ten miles at Guilford; twenty at New Haven; and sixteen, at Stamford. The colony included the northeastern arm of Long Island, and claimed jurisdiction over the small islands between the northern and southern arms. Individuals of the colony held title from the Indians to lands on the northern shore of Long Island and to tracts on both sides of Delaware River. Be-

211. Although a protest sent by the English, presumably to the Swedes, states that the purchase of the lands on the Schuylkill took place April 19, 1642, Johnson believes that the purchase was made in 1641. The Dutch did not protest until 1642, however, and it seems probable that that is the correct date of the English invasion.

[55] Ebenezer Hazard, *Historical Collections,* I, 160-169; Beauchamp Plantagenet, *A Description of the Province of New Albion* (1648), p. 23; reprinted by Peter Force, *Tracts and Other Papers,* II, no. 7, p. 25; "Plowden's New Albion," New York Historical Society *Collections,* 1869, pp. 213-222; Amandus Johnson, *The Instruction for Johan Printz* (1930), p. 217.

tween Milford and Stamford, Connecticut wedged its way down to the sea, and exercised jurisdiction over the towns of Stratford, Fairfield, and Norwalk, thus separating the holdings of the New Haven Colony on the northern shore of Long Island Sound into two parts.

For these lands the colony held no patent from the crown. For its right to possess the lands it had acquired from George Fenwick, representative of the grantees of the Earl of Warwick, and from James Forrett, agent of the Earl of Stirling, and perhaps for its right to possess the lands to which the agent of Sir Edmund Plowden had recognized its title, it might have made out a case. But the hodge-podge of Indian deeds by which the greater part of the lands of the colony were held would have received no recognition outside of New England, and would never have stood the scrutiny of an English court of law. Nor would the recital of the grant of the territory between the fortieth and the forty-eighth parallels by the crown to the Council for New England in the charter of Charles I to the Governor and Company of the Massachusetts Bay in New England have prevailed in an English court, where it was known that the settlers of Massachusetts Bay had themselves disavowed the grant to the Council for New England by going over the head of the Council to obtain a grant from the crown, and that the Council for New England had handed back its rights to the crown to enable Charles I to deal with just such non-separating Congregationalists as those who had established the New Haven Colony. But to flaunt in the faces of the directors general of New Netherland and New Sweden when they claimed that their aggressive English neighbors were trespassing upon their territories, a copy of the dubious charter to the Governor and Company of the Massachusetts Bay in New England served very well.[56]

[56] *Winthrop's Journal*, II, 160-161.

CHAPTER IV

SETTLERS OF THE OUTLYING PLANTATIONS

FOUNDED at a time when England seethed with dissatisfaction because of the high-church Anglicanism of William Laud and the personal government of Charles I, the New Haven Colony attracted many settlers from Old England and New.

Robert Seely, at one time a resident of the parish of St. Stephen, Coleman Street, London, may have been responsible for the first group of recruits. In company with Sir Richard Saltonstall, also of the parish of St. Stephen, Coleman Street, he had crossed the Atlantic with the Winthrop fleet in 1630. After spending some time at Watertown in Massachusetts Bay, he had bought the adventurer's rights of William Bassum in Wethersfield, the town on the Connecticut River settled from Watertown, and migrated to that place. His service as lieutenant in the campaign against the Pequots probably gave him a knowledge of the territory along Long Island Sound and he may have reported his findings in Wethersfield. At any rate, to a goodly number at Wethersfield the territory on the Sound seemed far more attractive both objectively and subjectively than the inland plantation already stirring with discontent; and Robert Seely, Edmund Sherman, a native of Dedham, England, John Sherman, his son, and John Livermore, his son-in-law, John Clarke, Abraham Bell, Andrew Benton, John Fletcher, John Gibbs, George Hubbard, Richard Miles, Thomas Tibbals, Thomas Topping, and Robert Treat, all from the town on the Connecticut River, soon joined the first arrivals at Quinnipiac.

The founders of the colony on Long Island Sound next entered into negotiations with Ezekiel Rogers and a small group of twenty families, most of them of good estate, who early in the summer of 1638 arrived in Massachusetts Bay, the forerunners of a larger group expected from England.

The son of Richard Rogers, lecturer at Wethersfield, Essex, England, Ezekiel Rogers held the degrees of bachelor and master of arts from Christ's College, Cambridge.[1] After serving as chaplain in the family of Sir Francis and Lady Joan Barrington, the latter the aunt of Oliver Cromwell, at Hatfield Broad Oak, Essex, he was presented by his patron to the rectorship of St. Peter's at Rowley in Yorkshire. On February 21, 1621, he was admitted to the thirteenth-century church standing in open country eight miles northwest of Kingston-upon-Hull.[2] Serving a congregation drawn from the neighboring hamlets of Bentley, Hunsley, Riplingham, Risby, and Little Weighton,[3] he "liued plentifully and not basely" for a period of seventeen years.[4] Embracing the principles of non-separating Congregationalism, he apparently met with no molestation as long as Tobie Matthew, George Montaigne, and Samuel Harsnett held the see of

1 John and J. A. Venn, *Alumni Cantabrigienses,* Part I, III, 478.

2 Registrar of the Diocese, York, Institutions 1606-1627, fol. 277.

3 A. N. Cooper, "How Rowley in Yorkshire Lost Its Population in the 17th Century, and How Rowley in Massachusetts was Founded," East Riding Antiquarian Society *Transactions,* XV, 85-100. The author supposes Rowley in Yorkshire to have been depopulated by the exodus of the Rogers company to Massachusetts Bay, but an examination of the transcripts of the parish registers of Rowley for the years 1620-1625 and 1630-1640 in the office of the Registrar of the Diocese, York (in part printed by J. Henry Lea, "Transcripts of the Lost Registers of Rowley, Co. York, England," Essex Institute *Historical Collections,* XLIV, 305-312), indicates that even in Rogers' day Rowley drew its congregation from the neighboring hamlets.

4 Egerton MSS., 2650, fol. 334.

York. With the advent of Richard Neile, conditions changed, however, and "for Refusing to Reade that accursed Booke that allowed sports on Gods holy Sabbath,"[5] he was suspended. He had been appointed to the living at Rowley for life, and desired to nominate his successor, but was put off with a promise of £200 for repairs that he had made to the parsonage, a debt which Sir Thomas Barrington later repudiated.[6] Despite the efforts of Archbishop Neile over a period of two years to reclaim him to orthodoxy, he gathered a small company of Yorkshire adherents and set out for London. In the spring of 1638 he resigned his living at Rowley from aboard ship sailing for New England.[7]

Probably in response to the invitation of Davenport and Eaton, some of the members of the Yorkshire company embarked from Massachusetts Bay for Long Island Sound in the fall of 1638. After running aground at Aquidneck,[8] they arrived at Quinnipiac. Although the group undoubtedly intended to found a plantation separate from but under the jurisdiction of the colony taking form on Long Island Sound, the first arrivals were assigned homelots in the western part of Quinnipiac.

Rogers himself tarried in the Bay Colony and seems to have been more impressed by offers there made to him than he was by the reports from those of his company

5 *The Probate Records of Essex County, Massachusetts,* I, 331-336.

6 Egerton MSS., 2646, fols. 104-105, 109-110, 163-164; 2648, fols. 6-7, 74, 84-85; 2650, fols. 333-334. The last two letters are printed in Essex Institute *Historical Collections,* LIII, 216-219.

7 State Papers, Domestic, Charles I, CCCXLV, no. 85; CCCCXII, no. 45. Rogers' resignation is recorded under date of May 24, 1638, Registrar of the Diocese, York, Institutions 1632-1660, fol. 243. The Yorkshire men were in Massachusetts Bay, June 27, 1638, Thomas Lechford, *Note-Book,* pp. 1, 208.

8 Michael Wigglesworth, "Autobiography," *New England Historical and Genealogical Register,* XVII, 137-139, reprinted in Edward E. Atwater, *History of the Colony of New Haven,* Appendix I; *Winthrop's Journal,* I, 291.

who had preceded him to Long Island Sound. Consulting with the elders of Massachusetts, he was released from his agreement to follow Davenport and Eaton to Quinnipiac on the grounds that the settlers of Quinnipiac were not living up to their promises. But when Rogers sent a pinnace to Long Island Sound to bring back those of his company who had preceded him to Quinnipiac, Davenport and Eaton stayed the pinnace, and sent a messenger with letters "which wanted no arguments, though some truth,"[9] to persuade Rogers to come to them. Once again he consulted the elders of the Bay Colony, and once again he was freed from any obligation to proceed to Quinnipiac. In March, 1639, the general court of Massachusetts Bay granted Rogers and his company "8 miles every way into the countrey, where it may not trench vpon other plantations already setled,"[10] The group founded the plantation of Rowley between Ipswich and Newbury, and were thus lost to the colony on the Sound. Some of those already at Quinnipiac, however, among them Thomas Fugill,[11] Robert and Thomas Johnson from Kingston-upon-Hull,[12] John Ponderson,[13] and Edward Wigglesworth, remained in the new plantation on Long Island Sound.

During the second summer of the Davenport company at Quinnipiac, three ships sailing directly from London brought a great company from England to the new col-

[9] *Winthrop's Journal,* I, 298.

[10] *Massachusetts Colony Records,* I, 253.

[11] In 1624 he held lands at Kirk Ella near Rowley, Yorkshire; in 1631 served in the family of Sir Richard Darley at Buttercrambe, ten miles northeast of York; and in 1637 buried a son at Rowley. Yorkshire Archaeological Society *Record Series,* LVIII, 242; "The Autobiography of Thomas Shepard," Colonial Society of Massachusetts *Publications,* XXVII, 372; Registrar of the Diocese, York, Transcript of the Rowley Parish Register, 1637.

[12] John Langdon Sibley, *Biographical Sketches of Graduates of Harvard University,* I, 123; F. C. Johnson, *Rev. Jacob Johnson* (1904), p. 2.

[13] Thomas Lechford, *Note-Book,* pp. 1, 208.

ony. In the first vessel came George Fenwick, one of the group of lords and gentlemen to whom the Earl of Warwick had granted the territory along the Sound, and his wife, the Lady Alice Boteler, not to settle at Quinnipiac but to take up their residence at Saybrook at the mouth of the Connecticut River.[14] At this time the small son whom John and Elizabeth Davenport had left with Lady Mary Vere at Hackney more than two years before was brought to his parents by a maid-servant.[15] Henry Whitfield, son of Thomas and Mildred Manning Whitfield of the manor of East Sheen and West Hall, Mortlake, Surrey, since 1616 rector of St. Margaret's at Ockley in Surrey, headed a company to augment the colony on the Sound. The leader was accompanied by his wife, Dorothy, the daughter of Thomas Sheaffe,[16] canon of Windsor, and granddaughter of Thomas Sheaffe of Cranbrook in Kent, his sons John and Nathaniel, and his daughters Dorothy, Sarah, Abigail, Mary, and Rebecca. Other members of the group were William and Jane (Lutman) Dudley, Thomas and Jude (Bowell) Norton, and John and William Stone from Whitfield's parish of Ockley in Surrey;[17] William and Joanna (Sheaffe) Chittenden, the former probably baptized at Marden near Cranbrook,[18] the latter the kinswoman of Dorothy Whitfield; John and Mary Mepham, friends and possibly relatives of George Fenwick; the wealthy John Bishop, Thomas Jones, Abraham Crutten-

14 Egerton MSS., 2646, fols. 181, 182, 240; 2648, fol. 1; Connecticut Historical Society *Collections*, XXIV, 1-5.

15 John Davenport to Lady Mary Vere, September 28, 1639, Additional MSS., 4275, fol. 171.

16 Somerset House, P. C. C., 38 Coventry.

17 St. Margaret's, Ockley, Surrey, Transcript of the Parish Register. For permission to examine this transcript, I am indebted to Mr. H. C. Martin, Rector. See also Alfred Ridley Bax, "The Church Registers and Parish Account Books of Ockley, Co. Surrey," *Surrey Archaeological Collections*, X, 20-78.

18 Alvan Talcott, *Chittenden Family*.

den, Francis Chatfield, Thomas Naish, and Thomas Cooke, probably all from Cranbrook in Kent or its vicinity;[19] John and Thomas Jordan of Lenham, Kent; Robert and Margaret (Sheaffe) Kitchel, the latter a kinswoman of both Dorothy Whitfield and Joanna Chittenden, John Hoadley, and William Hall, all from Rolvenden, a short distance to the southeast of Cranbrook; Henry Kingsnorth from Staplehurst, Kent, a short distance to the north; Francis Bushnell of Horsham in Sussex; William Leete, yeoman of Keyston in Huntingdonshire; and Ann Payne, whom Leete had married at Hail Weston, Huntingdonshire, August 1, 1636;[20] Leete's servants, William Barnes, Thomas Hunt, Elizabeth Fox, and Edward Jones, the latter of Wellingborough in Northamptonshire and newly engaged;[21] Henry Doude, Richard Guttridge, John Hughes, John Parmelee, and William Plane. With the exception of George Fenwick, the heads of families entered into a covenant on June 11, 1639, while still on board ship, "to plant our selves in new England and if it may be in the Southerly pt about Quinnipyock."[22]

In the two vessels which followed came Samuel Desborough of Eltisley in Cambridgeshire, related to Oliver Cromwell by the marriage of his brother to Jane Cromwell, and probably himself already married to Dorothy Whitfield;[23] John Stevens, perhaps from Ockley; Jasper Stillwell of Dorking nearby;[24] John Scranton, William Boreman, Alexander Chalker, John Johnson, Thomas

19 St. Dunstan's, Cranbrook, Kent, Parish Register, 1559-1662. For permission to examine this register I am indebted to Mr. H. T. Swingler, Vicar. See also William Tarbutt, *The Annals of Cranbrook Church* (1870-1875).

20 Joseph Leete, *The Family of Leete* (London, 1906).

21 Leete MSS.; Thomas Lechford, *Note-Book,* pp. 427-428.

22 Leete MSS.

23 "Papers of General Desborough 1651-1660," Egerton MSS., 2519.

24 John E. Stillwell, *The History of Lieutenant Nicholas Stillwell, Progenitor of the Stillwell Family in America* (1929).

French, Thomas Betts, all with family names found at Cranbrook;[25] Thomas Relf, and John, Samuel, and Thomas Caffinch from Tenterden, a short distance to the southeast of Cranbrook; and possibly David and Joshua Atwater of Royton in the parish of Lenham and Ashford, and Ralph Dayton of Ashford, Kent.

Acquiring the Indian title to Menunkatuck,[26] strikingly similar to the rolling hills of Surrey and Kent from which they came, the Whitfield company founded the plantation of Menunkatuck or Guilford, in its symmetry resembling New Haven. The group soon lost Thomas Naish and his family, the Caffinches, the Atwaters, and Ralph Dayton to New Haven, but received valuable additions in the persons of Joanna and Jacob Sheaffe and John Higginson. Joanna Sheaffe was the mother, and Jacob Sheaffe, the twenty-two year old brother of Joanna Chittenden. Although originally from Cranbrook in Kent, at this time they came from Roxbury in Massachusetts Bay. John Higginson was the son of Francis Higginson, first teacher at Salem. Probably prepared for the ministry by Thomas Hooker of Hartford, he had already served as schoolmaster at Hartford, as clerk to the synod which gathered at Newtown in the summer of 1637, and as preacher at Saybrook.[27]

The small group headed by Peter Prudden that had coalesced with the Davenport company in Massachusetts Bay and migrated with them to Quinnipiac drew toward the plantation on Long Island Sound Sarah (Bryan) Baldwin, widow of Sylvester Baldwin of Aston Clinton, Buckinghamshire, who in the summer of 1638 died on board the *Martin* on his way to New England; her two

25 St. Dunstan's, Cranbrook, Kent, Parish Register, 1559-1662.

26 Leete MSS.

27 John Higginson, *Our Dying Saviour's Legacy of Peace* (1686), preface addressed "To the Church and People of God at Salem; also at Guilford and Say Brook"; Massachusetts Archives, X, 102, 185-186.

sons and four daughters; Alexander Bryan, a native of Aylesbury in Buckinghamshire, kinsman of Sarah Baldwin; John Baldwin, Francis Bolt, and others from Hertfordshire and Buckinghamshire. Increasing rapidly in numbers, the group determined to found a third plantation to the west of Quinnipiac, an enterprise in which they were joined by Benjamin Fenn, Thomas Sandford, and Zachariah Whitman of the Dorchester contingent at Quinnipiac; Andrew Benton, John Fletcher, George Hubbard, Richard Miles, John Sherman, Thomas Tibbals, Thomas Topping, and Robert Treat of the Wethersfield group; and John Astwood, Thomas Baker, John Burwell, Jasper Gunn, Edward Riggs, and Thomas Uffot of the Roxbury recruits. Early in 1640 the group followed Thomas Tibbals, who had served in the Pequot War, westward to Wepowaug, and laid out the town of Milford on the banks of Mill River and West End Brook.[28]

On January 26, 1640, Stephen Goodyear, merchant taylor, owner of messuages and tenements near Paul's Chain, London, was licensed to carry two hundred and fifty passengers to New England in the *St. John of London.* Among those he brought to augment the colony on the Sound at this time may have been John Evance, who had married Anna Yong at St. Stephen's in Coleman Street, May 2, 1624; Luke Atkinson, William Davis, William Gibbons, Nathaniel Merriman, Richard Merriman,

[28] Charles Candee Baldwin, *The Baldwin Genealogy* (1881); *Supplement* (1889); *Massachusetts Colony Records,* I, 235; Milford Land Records, I, 134-135. Edward R. Lambert, *History of the Colony of New Haven,* p. 85, says that the ''settlement of the town was commenced in 1639.'' He bases this assertion upon the fact that the first Indian deed is dated February 12, 1639, old style, without seeming to realize that this would be February 12, 1640, new style. Connecticut State Library, Milford First Congregational Church Records, I, 1, indicates that the removal took place between February 9, 1639/40, when Hannah Buckingham joined the church at New Haven, and March 8, 1639/40, when William East joined at Milford.

Thomas Morris, Adam Nicolls, Robert Pigg, James Russell, William Russell, Anthony Thompson, John Thompson, and John Walker, all with family names found at St. Stephen's, Coleman Street; William Gibbard, who owned property at Tanworth, Warwickshire; and Thomas Gregson of London.[29]

In the summer of 1637 John Youngs, son of Christopher Youngs, vicar of St. Margaret's, Reydon, Suffolk County, to which was attached the chapel of St. Edmund, Southwold, with his wife Joan, his sons John, Thomas, and Joseph, and his daughters Anne, Rachel, and Mary, migrated from England to Massachusetts Bay. Joining members of his family already settled at Salem, on August 14, 1637, John Youngs was admitted an inhabitant of the town. Three years later, perhaps at the suggestion of Hugh Peter, at the time filling the office of pastor in the church at Salem, he gathered a small company, the nucleus of which was undoubtedly drawn from Salem, and migrated to the colony on Long Island Sound. Assigned to the recently acquired northeastern arm of Long Island, the group was joined by individuals drawn from Southampton on Long Island and Salem in Massachusetts Bay in the settlement of the town at first called Yennicock and later Southold after Youngs' English home. Unlike the settlers of Guilford and Milford, Stamford and Branford, the settlers of Southold neither themselves acquired title to their lands nor immediately repaid to the plantation of Quinnipiac the amount that had been spent in acquiring title to the land upon which they settled. Until 1649 the ultimate title to the lands of Southold rested in the town of New Haven, and until 1658 the

29 Public Record Office, P. C. 2: 51, p. 262; Henry F. Waters, *Genealogical Gleanings in England* (1901), I, 271; II, 888-889; Thomas Lechford, *Note-Book*, p. 315; Grace Goodyear Kirkman, *Genealogy of the Goodyear Family* (1899).

ultimate title to Ocquebanck and Mattituck rested in the New Haven Colony.[30]

Wethersfield continued to seethe with unrest. On October 30, 1640, probably at the invitation of John Davenport, Richard Denton, bachelor of arts of St. Catharine's, Cambridge,[31] and a group of between twenty and thirty malcontents deputed Andrew Ward and Robert Coe to treat with New Haven about the plantation of Toquams or Rippowams, recently purchased by Captain Nathaniel Turner from the Indians.[32] On November 2, 1640, Ward and Coe and Richard Gildersleeve came to an agreement with Robert Feake and Daniel Patrick regarding the boundary between the Turner purchase and Greenwich.[33] On November 4, 1640, at New Haven, the two deputies agreed to settle a plantation under the jurisdiction of New Haven, to accept the form of government established at New Haven, to repay £33 which New Haven had expended in acquiring title to the region from the Indians, and to reserve a fifth of the intended plantation for a period of one year for colonists expected at New Haven. Twenty Wethersfield men next bound themselves under pain of forfeiture of £5 to remove with their families to Rippowams, Denton, before May 16, 1641, and the others, before the end of the following November.[34] Twenty-nine individuals agreed to raise a hundred bushels of corn at three shillings the bushel to be sent to New Haven toward the purchase price of the plantation. In the spring of 1641 the Denton company migrated to the south and settled the plantation of Toquams, Rippowams,

[30] Selah Youngs, *Youngs Family* (1907); "Town Records of Salem 1634-1659," Essex Institute *Historical Collections,* IX, 54; *New Haven Colonial Records, 1638-1649,* p. 463; *New Haven Colonial Records, 1653-1665,* pp. 233, 302.

[31] John and J. A. Venn, *Alumni Cantabrigienses,* Part I, II, 34.

[32] *New Haven Colonial Records, 1638-1649,* p. 45.

[33] Greenwich Land Records, I, 451.

[34] Stamford Records, I, 5.

or Stamford. Denton and more than a fourth of the inhabitants of the new town soon wearied of the strictest of the Puritan commonwealths, however, and crossing the Sound, they joined John Carman of Roxbury in Massachusetts Bay and Robert Fordham of Cambridge and Sudbury in settling Hempstead on Long Island under the jurisdiction of New Netherland. From that place some of the group pressed westward to Flushing, Middelburgh, and Rustdorp. Stamford also lost heavily to Greenwich on the mainland, from 1642 to 1656 also under the jurisdiction of New Netherland.

The short-lived plantations on the Delaware seem to have been settled without external assistance. In the spring of 1641 Captain Nathaniel Turner and George Lamberton sent out the initial company of twenty families or sixty persons, probably from New Haven. As the vessel carrying the colonists passed Manhattan Island, Director General Kieft of New Netherland protested, but when Robert Cogswell, master of the bark, assured him that the company had been instructed to interfere with neither Dutch nor Swedes, and that the English intended to select a site over which the United Netherlands had no authority, Kieft not only permitted the expedition to proceed but wrote to Jan Jansen van Ilpendam, commissary at Fort Nassau, instructing him to hold good correspondence with the English.[35] Disregarding their statement to the Dutch governor, the New Haveners headed for the Delaware and added to the already complicated international situation by beginning a settlement at Varkens Kill. In the following year they extended their activities to the junction of the Delaware and Schuylkill rivers. The Dutch soon realized that they were nursing vipers. On May 5/15, 1642, the council at New Amsterdam resolved to expel the English from the Schuylkill in the quietest

[35] *New York Colonial Documents,* II, 144.

manner possible, and a week later sent Jan Jansen van Ilpendam to carry out the resolution.[36] Duly executing his commission, the Dutch commissary seized Lamberton's bark and carried men and goods to New Amsterdam. Upon their release at that place, the unsuccessful settlers of a plantation at the junction of the Delaware and Schuylkill rivers made their way back to New Haven.

The English families at Varkens Kill lingered on. Although they suffered severely from sickness,[37] they met with no active opposition from the Swedes under Peter Hollender Ridder. But peaceful relations with their Scandinavian neighbors came to an end, February 15, 1643, when Johan Printz arrived as the successor of Ridder with instructions to bring the English on the Delaware under Swedish rule. Urged on by Jan Jansen van Ilpendam, Printz forced the English on the Delaware to take an oath of allegiance to Sweden or to depart. To overawe those who remained, he built Fort Elfsborg just below Varkens Kill. Charging Lamberton with plotting with the Indians to cut off the Swedes, he imprisoned him, and when proof of the charge was not forthcoming, on July 10, 1643, fined him for trading on the Delaware.[38]

Samuel Eaton was a member of the original Davenport company. Educated at Magdalen College, Cambridge, holder of the degrees of bachelor and master of arts, preacher at West Kirby in Cheshire until suspended in 1631, he had spent some time in Holland and then accompanied his elder brother Theophilus to Boston and New Haven.[39] In seventeenth-century New England every minister was the potential founder of a plantation. Perhaps

[36] New York State Library, New York Colonial MSS., IV, 123, 124; *New York Colonial Documents,* XII, 23.

[37] *Winthrop's Journal,* II, 70-71.

[38] *New Haven Colonial Records, 1638-1649,* p. 106; Amandus Johnson, *The Swedish Settlements on the Delaware, 1638-1664* (2 vols., 1911); *The Instruction for Johan Printz* (1930).

[39] John and J. A. Venn, *Alumni Cantabrigienses,* Part I, II, 83.

as early as the summer of 1639 Samuel Eaton had a separate settlement in mind, for he took no part in the gathering of the church at Quinnipiac. After the establishment of a plantation government at Quinnipiac, he received a grant of Totoket, lying between Quinnipiac and Menunkatuck, for such friends as he intended to bring over from England, upon the conditions that it be settled under the jurisdiction of New Haven and given a government identical with that of New Haven.[40]

Eaton proceeded to England, and probably with John Cotton's "Moses his judicials" in mind, on the afternoon of Sunday, January 3, 1641, preached at St. John's Church in Chester, at about the same time at Knutsford, a great market town twenty-five miles to the northeast,[41] and in the following August, at Barrow, Cheshire,[42] in favor of a petition at the time circulating among the common people of Cheshire, in which complaint was made of civil and ecclesiastical abuses, episcopacy was denounced, the ecclesiastical organization of New England was advocated, and parliament was urged to follow the revealed will of God and make the "Morall Doctrine of the Prophets and Apostles" the canons of Old England. He either failed to attract a group of settlers for New England, or with the gathering of the Long Parliament, decided to remain in England. There he furthered the cause of Congregationalism by preaching to the parliamentary garrison at Chester and serving as teacher to the Church of Jesus Christ at Dukinfield in the parish of Stockport, Cheshire, and later as pastor to the combined Churches of God in Dukinfield and Stockport.[43] Silenced in 1662, he died at Denton in Lancashire, January 9, 1665.

40 *New Haven Colonial Records, 1638-1649,* pp. 40, 45.

41 Sir Thomas Aston, *A Remonstrance against Presbytery* (1641), pp. 1-6.

42 State Papers, Domestic, Charles I, CCCCLXXXIII, no. 20; Historical Manuscripts Commission, *Fourth Report,* Appendix, p. 55.

43 State Papers, Domestic, Interregnum, LXXIV, no. 27.

In the two decades which followed, the towns on the Sound continued to draw recruits from the colonies to the north. In 1644 Totoket was granted for a second time to William Swayne "and some others of Weathersfeild, they repaying the Chardge, wch is betwixt 12. and 13l and Joyning in one Jurisdiction wth Newhaven."[44] William Swayne and his sons Samuel and Daniel, Robert Rose, and other inhabitants of Wethersfield migrated to Long Island Sound and founded the plantation of Totoket or Branford. Without the customary minister, in the fall of 1644 the group was joined by John Sherman of Milford. He had been educated at St. Catharine's College, Cambridge,[45] and preached to the settlers of Totoket until 1647, when he was called to the pastorate of the church at Watertown in Massachusetts Bay. After his departure, Abraham Pierson, a native of Yorkshire, and graduate of Trinity College, Cambridge,[46] who had migrated from England to Massachusetts Bay, from Lynn in Massachusetts Bay to Southampton on Long Island, and from Southampton to Branford,[47] and who had yet another long trek before him, undertook the preaching of the gospel at Totoket. About 1651 Jasper Crane and others of New Haven took up their residence in the new plantation to the east.

In the spring of 1653, probably in response to the invitation of John Davenport and Theophilus Eaton, William Leveridge, bachelor and master of arts of Emmanuel College, Cambridge,[48] rector at Great Livermere, Suffolk, England, and pastor of the church at Sandwich

44 *New Haven Colonial Records, 1638-1649,* p. 200.

45 John and J. A. Venn, *Alumni Cantabrigienses,* Part I, IV, 62.

46 *Ibid.,* III, 330.

47 An examination of the records of Southampton and Branford indicates that Abraham Pierson brought no one with him from Southampton to Branford. Of the inhabitants of Branford, only Robert Rose had lived in Southampton for a brief period in 1644 and 1645.

48 John and J. A. Venn, *Alumni Cantabrigienses,* Part I, III, 78.

in the colony of New Plymouth, migrated to Long Island in the ship *Desire,* Samuel Mayo owner and John Dickinson master. With Samuel Mayo and Peter Wright he purchased lands at Oyster Bay.[49] To settle a plantation under the protection of the New Haven Colony at that place, he drew some adherents from Southold and others from Hempstead, who, because of tenths soon due upon their crops, were only too glad to escape from under the jurisdiction of New Netherland. Perhaps to meet objections of the Dutch to the settlement of the English at Oyster Bay,[50] Leveridge and other inhabitants of the town moved eastward, and again augmented from Hempstead and Southold, founded the plantation of Huntington, also under the protection of the New Haven Colony.

At about the same time inhabitants of Southold, Southampton, and towns on the mainland joined in the settlement of the town between Southold and Huntington variously known as Setauket, Ashford, Cromwell Bay, and Brookhaven.

For more than a decade Paugassett to the north of Milford remained unsettled, the property of the New Haven merchants who had purchased the region from the Indians. In 1654 the original proprietors disposed of their rights to Richard Baldwin and others of Milford,[51] and settlers from Milford moved to the north. In 1655 the New Haven Colony extended its jurisdiction over the region, and about 1660, after the objections of Milford had been overcome, the colony's only inland settlement was organized as a village.[52]

49 *Plymouth Colony Records,* X, 91; Howland Delano Perrine, *The Wright Family of Oysterbay, L. I.* (1923), p. 33.

50 New York Colonial MSS., V, 394; VI, 6, 23, 25, 26; XII, 53; *New York Colonial Documents,* II, 160; XIV, 311, 313-314, 384; *Oyster Bay Records,* I, 628, 671-673.

51 *Derby Records, 1655-1710,* p. 3.

52 *New Haven Colonial Records, 1653-1665,* pp. 77, 148, 156, 178, 221-222, 298, 377.

But despite this gradual increase in population, Samuel Eaton's failure to gather a company of settlers in Cheshire in 1641 was prophetic. Almost coincident with the founding of the New Haven Colony in America the Long Parliament assembled in England. In 1647 the non-separating Congregationalists rose to power in the mother country and no longer sought a refuge from Anglicanism and arbitrary government across the seas. The movement from Old England toward New England gave way to a counter migration from the New World toward the Old, and the colony on Long Island Sound ceased to grow by leaps and bounds.

CHAPTER V

THE CONGREGATIONAL WAY

AT Quinnipiac and the plantations settled in its vicinity, the ecclesiastical system of Massachusetts Bay was carried to its logical conclusion. The organization of churches preceded the establishment of town governments, and from the beginning the right to participate in the civil affairs of both colony and towns—to vote for all officers and to hold all offices—was restricted to church-members.

There was never a time without services for the worship of God. On the first Sabbath at Quinnipiac John Davenport preached in the morning on the text, "Then was Jesus led up of the spirit into the wilderness to be tempted of the devil,"[1] and Peter Prudden, in the afternoon on, "The voice of one crying in the wilderness, Prepare ye the way of the Lord, make his paths straight,"[2] the choice of texts perhaps indicating the reverend founders' first impression of their new heaven and new earth.

But the formal organization of churches took place only after prolonged inward searching of hearts. For this purpose the planters of Quinnipiac were "Cast into seuerall priuate meetings wherein they thatt dwelt nearest together gaue their accounts one to another of Gods Gracious worke vpon them and prayed together and conferred to their mutuall Edifficatiō," and thus learned to know one another and the most approved among them. After fourteen months they were ready to proceed further. On June 4, 1639, they agreed to choose twelve or

1 Matthew 4. 1. 2 Matthew 3. 3.

more to begin the foundation work of a church. Actually they chose only Theophilus Eaton, John Davenport, Robert Newman, Mathew Gilbert, Richard Malbon, Nathaniel Turner, Ezekiel Cheever, Thomas Fugill, John Ponderson, William Andrews, and Jeremy Dixon, probably because eleven exhausted the supply of individuals sufficiently close to sainthood to take part in the gathering of a church. And even to one of these, probably Richard Malbon, accused of profiteering, exception was taken.[3] Of the eleven, Theophilus Eaton, John Davenport, Robert Newman, Mathew Gilbert, Thomas Fugill, John Ponderson, and Jeremy Dixon made satisfactory professions of their faith,[4] and on August 21 or 22, 1639, entered into covenant,[5] and thus gathered the First Church of Christ at Quinnipiac. To their fellowship the "pillars" soon admitted Nathaniel Turner, William Andrews, and Ezekiel Cheever.[6]

[3] *New Haven Colonial Records, 1638-1649,* pp. 15-17.

[4] *The Profession of the Faith of that Reverend and worthy Divine Mr J. D. sometimes Preacher of Stevens Coleman-street. London.* (London, 1642), reprinted in John Cotton, *The Covenant of Gods free Grace* (London, 1645), pp. 34-40, is probably more detailed than the professions of the other six pillars, and illustrates how close were the Puritans to the Anglicans on questions of faith, how far apart on questions of church organization and government.

[5] According to Cotton Mather, *Magnalia Christi Americana* (1702), Book III, p. 93, the church at New Haven was gathered on August 21, 1639, the day preceding the gathering of the Milford church, but the traditional date is August 22, 1639. The covenant occurs in the second person plural, the form in which it was offered to those about to unite with the church. Connecticut State Library, New Haven, First Church Records, I, 1. It became the model for the covenants in use in the churches in the plantations along the sound. Although not the covenant in use in the church in Boston in Massachusetts Bay, it was sent to England by John Cotton as a model of the covenants in use in the churches of New England. It was published in *A Coppy of a Letter of Mr Cotton of Boston, in New England, sent in answer of certaine Objections made against their Discipline and Orders there, directed to a Friend* (1641), pp. 5-6, and probably from that source was paraphrased by Thomas Lechford in *Plain Dealing: Or, Newes from New-England* (1642).

[6] *New Haven Colonial Records, 1638-1649,* p. 20.

From 1639 until his departure from New Haven in 1668 John Davenport served as pastor of the first church of the colony. Five years after the gathering of the church, William Hooke, bachelor and master of arts of Trinity College, Oxford,[7] and pastor of the church at Taunton in the colony of New Plymouth, was ordained as teacher and filled that office in the church at New Haven until 1656. Samuel Eaton, son of Theophilus Eaton, a graduate of Harvard College in 1649 and a fellow of the college from 1650 to 1653,[8] would probably have carried on the work of Davenport and Hooke at New Haven had not his untimely death in July, 1655, prevented. In 1658 and 1659 Richard Blinman, bachelor of arts of New Inn Hall, Oxford,[9] and preacher at Pequot from 1650 to 1658, assisted Davenport. From 1659 until Davenport's departure in 1668, Nicholas Street, bachelor of arts of Pembroke College, Oxford,[10] and master of arts of Emmanuel College, Cambridge, filled the office of teacher in the church at New Haven, and then succeeded to the office of pastor. From 1644 to 1650 Robert Newman functioned as ruling elder. During the existence of the New Haven Colony, Robert Newman, Mathew Gilbert, John Wakeman,

[7] Joseph Foster, *Alumni Oxonienses*, 1500-1714, II, 741; Samuel Hopkins Emery, *The Ministry of Taunton*, I, 63-155; Charles Ray Palmer, "Rev. William Hooke, 1601-1678," New Haven Colony Historical Society *Papers*, VIII, 56-81. Hooke was married to Jane Whalley, sister of Edward Whalley and cousin of Oliver Cromwell, for whose hand Roger Williams had besought her aunt, Lady Joan Barrington, in vain. Egerton MSS., 2644, fols. 204, 275.

[8] John Langdon Sibley, *Biographical Sketches of Graduates of Harvard University*, I, 171-172.

[9] Joseph Foster, *Alumni Oxonienses*, 1500-1714, I, 139; Frances Manwaring Caulkins, *History of New London, Conn.* (1852), pp. 111-117; S. Leroy Blake, *The Early History of the First Church of Christ, New London, Conn.* (1897), pp. 55-90; Massachusetts Historical Society *Collections*, 4th series, VII, 490.

[10] Joseph Foster, *Alumni Oxonienses*, 1500-1714, IV, 1435; John and J. A. Venn, *Alumni Cantabrigienses*, Part I, IV, 174; Samuel Hopkins Emery, *The Ministry of Taunton*, I, 156-170.

Richard Miles, William Peck, and Roger Alling served the church at New Haven as deacons.[11]

Churches were similarly organized for the other plantations on the Sound. On August 22, 1639, Peter Prudden, William Fowler, Edmund Tapp, Zachariah Whitman, John Astwood, Thomas Buckingham, and Thomas Welsh entered into a covenant identical with that of the first church of the colony with the intention of gathering a church for the plantation they intended to found at Wepowaug. Before removing from Quinnipiac the "pillars" of this second church admitted Richard Miles, James Prudden, Joanna Prudden, Richard Platt, Francis Bolt, and Hannah Buckingham to their fellowship. On Wednesday, April 8, 1640, after the settlement at Wepowaug was under way, the brethren returned to Quinnipiac for a day of solemn humiliation and the ordination of Peter Prudden as pastor.[12]

The death of Peter Prudden in 1656 was followed by an interregnum of four years in the pastorate of the church at Milford, for as the first generation of ministers died or removed it became increasingly difficult to fill their places. Then Roger Newton, sizar of King's College, Cambridge, in 1636,[13] and trained in theology by Thomas Hooker of Hartford, was chosen as pastor. On June 10, 1645, Zachariah Whitman was nominated for the office of ruling elder. In the presence of the elders from the church at New Haven and the pastor and a messenger from the church at Stratford, on June 26 he was ordained.[14] At

11 Franklin Bowditch Dexter, *Historical Catalogue of the Members of the First Church of Christ in New Haven, Connecticut*, pp. 1-5.

12 Connecticut State Library, Milford First Congregational Church Records, I, 1. Probably because the church records are difficult to decipher, Edward R. Lambert, *History of the Colony of New Haven*, p. 101, erroneously gives the date of Prudden's ordination as Saturday, April 18, 1640.

13 John and J. A. Venn, *Alumni Cantabrigienses*, Part I, III, 253.

14 Connecticut State Library, Milford First Congregational Church Records, I, 158.

various times Zachariah Whitman, Benjamin Fenn, George Clarke, Sr., John Fletcher, and Jasper Gunn held the office of deacon in the second church of the colony.

According to tradition, on October 21, 1640, before departing from New Haven, the small company which settled the plantation of Yennicock or Southold on Long Island gathered themselves into a church estate, and chose John Youngs as their pastor.[15]

Richard Denton, Andrew Ward, Robert Coe, and Jonas Weed, a majority of the church at Wethersfield, were among the settlers of Toquams, Rippowams, or Stamford, and there is no evidence that reorganization of the church was considered necessary. If the church were gathered anew, the reorganization took place before October 27, 1641, when delegates from Rippowams appeared at a general court at New Haven. After the removal of Denton in 1644, John Bishop, probably educated in England, was chosen as pastor, and held the office until his death fifty years later.

The Whitfield company came to America that they "might settle and uphold all the ordinances of God in an explicite congregationall Church way," but it was not until the late spring of 1643 that Henry Whitfield, John Higginson, Samuel Desborough, William Leete, Jacob Sheaffe, John Mepham, and John Hoadley, the customary "seven pillars," gathered a church and chose Henry Whitfield as pastor and John Higginson as teacher.[16] After the departure of Whitfield in 1650, Higginson filled the office of pastor until he himself left Guilford in 1659. In the interregnum which followed, John Cotton, Jr., and John Bowers, both graduates of Harvard College, served as supplies, and Increase Mather, a graduate of Harvard College and master of arts of Trinity College,

[15] Benjamin Trumbull, *A Complete History of Connecticut*, I (1797), 117.
[16] Guilford Records, B, 7-8.

Dublin, was called to the vacant pastorship but declined the office. Finally, in 1664, Joseph Eliot, also a graduate of Harvard College, responded to the call of the church at Guilford, and the town again had a duly ordained minister.[17] Men annually chosen to order the ministers' maintenance performed the functions of deacons in the most easterly of the towns of the colony on the Sound.

Totoket or Branford was also settled by "men of Congregationall prrinciples," who first engaged John Sherman of Milford to preach to them, and after Sherman's departure for Watertown in 1647, Abraham Pierson of Southampton on Long Island. But probably because of the paucity of saints, it was not until some time after November 4, 1650, that the inhabitants of Branford gathered a church and ordained Pierson as their pastor.[18]

Although the first planters at Quinnipiac all desired "thatt they may be admitted into Chur. ffellowp according to Christ as soone [as] God shall fitt them therevnto,"[19] and the group was probably representative of a majority of the first settlers of the other towns of the colony, the membership of the churches was never large. The mere desire to unite with the church was not sufficient to gain one admittance to the company of God's elect. The doors of the church were carefully guarded, and evidence of conversion and a satisfactory and usually public profession of faith were required of all adherents.

The worship of God occupied much of the time of the seventeenth-century Puritan. Although actual membership of the churches might be limited, in the early years the attendance of both brethren and non-members, men, women, and children, was expected at the services on the Sabbath, in the morning at nine o'clock and in the after-

17 John Langdon Sibley, *Biographical Sketches of Graduates of Harvard University,* I, 192-193, 410-470, 496-508, 530-533.

18 Branford Records, I, 31, 319.

19 *New Haven Colonial Records, 1638-1649,* p. 13.

noon at two, and on days of humiliation and thanksgiving, and by the colony laws of 1656 it was made compulsory. The beat of the drum—bells belong to a later era—called the congregation together. A prayer by the pastor was followed by the reading of the Scriptures, a psalm from *The Whole Booke of Psalmes Faithfully Translated into English Metre,* published at Cambridge in Massachusetts Bay in 1640, the congregation probably making up in earnestness for what the Puritan version of the songs of David lacked in rhythm and music, a sermon perhaps two hours long, a prayer, and the benediction. In towns where pastor and teacher were supported by voluntary contributions, at the close of the afternoon service the heads of families or their representatives, brethren and non-members alike, moved to the front of the assembly and deposited their offerings before the deacons. On the recommendation of the commissioners of the United Colonies of New England,[20] the New Haven Colony ordered that each person pledge himself to give a specified amount toward the support of the ministers, and if he refused, that he be rated by authority and the amount collected by the civil government,[21] but in the town of New Haven complaints continued that some gave nothing and others, insufficient and bad wampum, until in desperation a general court ordered the inhabitants to contribute silver and bills and more of them.[22] At Guilford, where the inhabitants annually chose three men to levy and collect a rate for the ministers' maintenance, and at Branford, where they carried two pounds of butter for each milch cow in their possession, and beef, pork, Indian corn, wampum, wheat, and peas to an amount that had been agreed upon to the pastor, a public contribution was probably

20 *Plymouth Colony Records,* IX, 20.
21 *New Haven Colonial Records, 1653-1665,* p. 588.
22 *New Haven Town Records, 1649-1662,* p. 98.

not the practice. Once a month, after the departure of non-members from the morning service, the sacrament of the Lord's Supper was celebrated, the ministers and ruling elders sitting at the table and the brethren in their accustomed places. As occasion arose baptism of those about to be received into the church and of the children of members occurred at the close of the afternoon service.

In addition to the services of the Sabbath, on every third day or Tuesday the brethren of the church at New Haven assembled to manage the affairs of the church and to elect officers, the male members voting by upraised hands. On every fourth day or Wednesday brethren and non-members came together to listen to a lecture resembling the sermons of the Sabbath. At neighborhood meetings sermons and lectures were repeated and questions propounded and discussed for mutual edification.

Until the first meeting-houses were erected, services were held out of doors or in Robert Newman's barn at New Haven, in Whitfield's house at Guilford, and in Sherman's house at Branford. In 1640 a structure fifty feet square surmounted by a tower and turret was completed at New Haven at a cost of £500.[23] In the following year a meeting-house forty feet square was built at Milford.[24] Before 1646 an edifice of stone with thatched and clayed roof had been erected at Guilford.[25] And probably at equally early dates similar structures appeared in the other towns of the colony.

For these rude meeting-houses the deacons of the churches and the officers of the towns prepared seating plans, a custom not unknown in England.[26] On one side

[23] *New Haven Colonial Records, 1638-1649*, p. 25.

[24] Milford Land Records, I, 3.

[25] Guilford Records, A, 6.

[26] *New Haven Colonial Records, 1638-1649*, pp. 302-304; *New Haven Town Records, 1649-1662*, pp. 176, 242, 266, 270-274, 505, 510-513. For references to seating plans in churches in England, see Alfred Ridley Bax,

of the house the men of the congregation were placed according to dignity, age, and estate, and on the other, the women. Soldiers took their places near the door. Boys were assigned to seats where they might be under the surveillance of an older person, and scholars of the town and colony school, to a scholars' bench. The deaf were seated well to the front.

A logical outcome of the theory that the saints were in covenant with God was the contrasting belief that the least godly were in league with the devil. About 1653 John Davenport himself preached "That a froward discontented frame of spirit, was a subject fitt for the Devill to worke vpon,"[27] probably with the result of stimulating accusations of witchcraft against troublesome old women and men in disrepute with their neighbors. Individuals suspected of practicing the black art were haled before the civil authorities. Some were ordered to give bond for their good behavior, others, to meddle only with their own business, and all to remain away from the contribution at the close of the Sabbath afternoon service.[28] But in the New Haven Colony these children of Satan never paid the ultimate penalty of death.

As in the colonies of Massachusetts Bay and Connecticut, so in the colony on Long Island Sound the ideal of uniformity was never abandoned. Because New England was "but a little body, and soon overrun and shaken with any distemper,"[29] because they who tolerated false doctrines were more guilty than they who accepted

"The Church Registers and Parish Account Books of Ockley, Co. Surrey," *Surrey Archaeological Collections*, X, 22-23; R. Garraway Rice, "Horsham Churchwardens' Account Book," *Sussex Notes and Queries*, I, 139-142.

27 *New Haven Colonial Records, 1653-1665*, p. 29.

28 *New Haven Town Records, 1649-1662*, pp. 249, 256-257; *New Haven Colonial Records, 1653-1665*, p. 31.

29 John Norton, *The Heart of New England Rent at the Blasphemies of the present Generation* (London, 1660), p. 82.

them,[30] and because the New England Puritan was his brother's keeper in a very real sense, and seldom evaded his responsibilities, individuals out of sympathy with Congregationalism met with neither toleration nor understanding. Alone or with one or two of the brethren, the upholder of orthodoxy visited one suspected of falling from grace and pointed out the failings that had come to his attention. If this did not result in visible repentance and reform, the case was laid before the brethren, and the erring brother or sister questioned in a private meeting of the church. If the backslider remained defiant, charges were prepared by the elders and laid before the congregation at the close of the Sabbath afternoon service. In the ensuing arguments both brethren and non-members participated. The debate often lasted until dusk fell, and was sometimes adjourned until the next lecture day or until the following Sabbath afternoon. At its conclusion the elders declared their judgment and held forth light, and the brethren voted, usually as the elders had advised. Sentence of censure or excommunication was pronounced by the pastor. A repentant brother returned to the fold in a similar way.

In the church at New Haven "the Golden Snuffers of the Sanctuary" were employed almost overmuch,[31] and the list of those censured and excommunicated includes the names of one of the "seven pillars" of the church, the wife of the governor of the colony, and the first schoolmaster of the town. Of the trial of Thomas Fugill before the church, there is no record, but of the ordeals of Anne Eaton and Ezekiel Cheever, detailed accounts have been preserved.

30 Nathaniel Ward, *The Simple Cobler of Aggawam in America*, reprint of the edition of 1713 in Peter Force, *Tracts and Other Papers*, III (1844), no. 8, p. 9. See also Thomas Hutchinson, *A Collection of Original Papers* (1769), pp. 401-402.

31 Cotton Mather, *Magnalia Christi Americana* (1702), Book III, p. 55.

Convinced by Lady Deborah Moody,[32] and Andrew Ritor's *A Treatise on the Vanity of Childish-Baptisme* (London, 1642), and the same author's *The Second Part of the Vanity and Childishnes of Infants Baptisme* (London, 1642), that infant baptism was unlawful and that she herself was unbaptized, Anne Eaton early formed the habit of departing from the assembly when the sacraments of baptism and the Lord's Supper were administered, and soon absented herself from all services. When the questions of the brethren and the arguments of the elders proved without avail, she was called before the church on a Sabbath afternoon, July 14, 1644, after the contribution, and publicly admonished by Davenport. Although she strove over a period of nine months, she failed to convince the elders of her repentance, and on a Sabbath afternoon, April 20, 1645, and on the following lecture day she was again haled before the congregation. At the latter meeting, by the unanimous vote of the brethren, in the presence of elders from the neighboring churches, she was excommunicated from the company of God's elect.[33] Although in seventeenth-century New England the expulsion of the archangels from heaven represented no greater tragedy, after the lapse of three hundred years it is possible to see the humor in the excommunication of the first lady of the colony, who knew the walled city of Chester and its cathedral, from the £500 church in the center of seventeenth-century New Haven by those who had crossed the Atlantic to avoid religious persecution.

Ezekiel Cheever had served as one of the eleven chosen

[32] Lady Deborah Moody passed through New Haven on her way from Massachusetts Bay to Gravesend on Long Island.

[33] Connecticut State Library, New Haven First Church Records, I, 17-22, printed as "Mrs. Eaton's Trial," New Haven Colony Historical Society *Papers*, V, 133-148, where the dates are erroneously given as August 14, 1644, and May 20, 1645, days which did not fall upon Sunday.

to take part in the founding of the church at New Haven but a similar fate awaited him. Probably not without cause, the first schoolmaster of the town objected to the domination of the elders at New Haven and refused to vote with a majority of the brethren to clear them of a charge of partiality. Because of "his opinion and his stiffness in maintaining it," and his "overweening conceit of his own sufficiency," he was called without warning before the congregation at the conclusion of the afternoon service, May 20, 1649, and censured and "cast out of the body, till the proud flesh be destroyed, and he be brought into a more member-like frame."[34] His departure for Ipswich in Massachusetts Bay in the following year is not difficult to understand.

Malcontents never admitted to the privileged inner circle were beyond the reach of the brethrens' censure and excommunication, and answered for their lese-majesty to colony and town. Among these were Bamfield Bell, who scoffed "the Holy Bretheren that will Lye for Advantadge";[35] Lucy Brewster, who accused the brethren of going "two And two together, and writt down what scandelous Persons say, and soe Hurrey them, and Compare their wrighteings," and drew an analogy between going to the contribution and going to the high altar;[36] Mrs. Moore, who held pastors and teachers to be the work of men, and maintained, "A vayle is before the eyes of mjnisters and people in this place, and till that be taken away, they Cannot be turned to the Lord";[37] Mrs. Leach, the daughter of Mrs. Moore; and Luke Atkinson, who spoke slurringly of Davenport.[38]

[34] Yale University Library, The Trial of Ezekiel Cheever before the Church at New Haven, printed in Connecticut Historical Society *Collections*, I, 22-51.

[35] *New Haven Colonial Records, 1638-1649*, p. 173.

[36] *Ibid.*, p. 244.

[37] *Ibid.*, p. 253.

[38] *Ibid.*, pp. 279-280.

The kingdom of Christ on the shores of Long Island Sound was soon called upon to deal with greater evils than scoffers. Of grave countenance, plain apparel, and few words, devoid of all respect for magistrates and elders, and imbued with the doctrine of the inner light, Mary Fisher and Ann Austin arrived at Boston from Barbados in July, 1656.[39] Resorting to a law against heretics, on July 11 a council of the Bay Colony ordered the books in the possession of the two women to be burned by the public hangman and them themselves to be kept close prisoners until deported to the place whence they came. The banishment of Mary Fisher and Ann Austin did not dam the flood, however, for they were merely the forerunners of a host of missionaries of the sect founded by George Fox, who saw in New England a fruitful field for their endeavors, and continued to swarm through the Puritan colonies.

In response to the recommendation of Massachusetts Bay to the New England Confederation in September, 1656, that Quakers be barred from New England,[40] the New Haven Colony forbade Quakers, ranters, and other heretics to enter its territory.[41] Nevertheless, Nathaniel Sylvester, one of the proprietors of Forrett's or Shelter Island, turned the island into a haven of refuge for the persecuted sect. There the disciples of Fox gathered strength to face the torments meted out to them by God's elect, and from that place they invaded the outlying towns of the colony on the Sound.[42]

In August, 1657, Robert Fowler, master of the *Wood-*

[39] John Norton, *The Heart of New England Rent at the Blasphemies of the present Generation* (London, 1660); Rufus M. Jones, *The Quakers in the American Colonies* (1911).

[40] *Plymouth Colony Records,* X, 155-158.

[41] *New Haven Colonial Records, 1653-1665,* p. 217.

[42] *An Account of Some of the Labours, Exercises, Travels and Perils, by Sea and Land, of John Taylor* (London, 1710), pp. 5-8.

house, carried Humphrey Norton to Newport. In the following February Norton appeared at Southold, on his way to New Netherland. Accused of traducing John Youngs, pastor of the church at Southold, and reviling the magistrates and government of the New Haven Colony in the meeting-house at Southold on the Lord's day, he was carried to New Haven. After a frivolous examination he was clapped into a cold, open prison. There he received neither fire nor candle, and wore irons "linked to a great lump of wood" day and night for a period of twenty-one days. On March 10, 1658, he was brought before a plantation court to which William Leete and Benjamin Fenn, magistrates of Guilford and Milford, had been added to approximate a court of magistrates. In this assembly Davenport answered questions which Norton had previously put to him in writing, but the prisoner was given no opportunity to reply. At the end of a two-day trial the culprit was sentenced to be whipped, branded, fined £10, and banished. He was immediately led forth to the stocks, and in the presence of a great crowd summoned by the beat of a drum, stripped to the waist and given thirty-six stripes. Next a pan containing burning coals and an iron was brought, and the letter "H" for heretic was burned into the hand of the prisoner still held fast in the stocks, "in malice . . . his right hand to hinder him from Writing." To proffers of salves, Norton replied that he "could not suffer a dog to lick his sores." Unwilling to pay the fine, he returned to prison, but two days later one Yoss, a baker at New Amsterdam, appeared before the magistrates at New Haven and agreed to pay £6 13*s.* 4*d.* in wampum within a month. New Haven accepted this amount in lieu of nothing, and Norton betook himself to further persecution at Plymouth and Boston.[43]

[43] Humphrey Norton, *New England's Ensigne* (London, 1659), pp. 50-52;

William Brend, Mary Weatherhead, one who on a meeting day cried, "Wo be unto you, for Humphrey Norton's sake, Wo be unto you," and other disciples of Fox appeared at New Haven, but were quickly driven away and deprived of the privilege of suffering. Somewhat later the literature in the possession of Edward Barnes, a mariner and Quaker of feeble intellect, was confiscated, and he himself was hastily put aboard his vessel and deported.[44]

After its experience with Humphrey Norton and his friends, in May, 1658, the New Haven Colony passed legislation against Quakers modeled on the laws of Massachusetts Bay of October 14, 1656, and October 14, 1657.[45] To lose no penny of profit which might accrue to the merchants of the colony through trade with the proprietors of Shelter Island, however, the New Haven law permitted Quakers to enter the colony to dispatch their lawful business, and imposed a penalty of only £50, half the amount of the penalty imposed by Massachusetts, on those who brought Quakers within the limits of the colony for any other purpose. In September, 1658, the New England Confederation recommended the death penalty for that "accursed and permisious sectt of heritiques . . . comonly called Quakers,"[46] but perhaps beginning to realize the futility of persecution, the New Haven Colony failed to respond. In May, 1660, a final law against Quakers permitted the towns to enforce the law of May, 1658, or to inflict a penalty of £5 for the first offense and £10 for the second.[47]

New Haven Town Records, 1649-1662, pp. 339-343; *New Haven Colonial Records, 1653-1665,* p. 233.

[44] *Ibid.,* p. 276.

[45] *Ibid.,* pp. 238-241; *Massachusetts Colony Records,* III, 415-416; IV, Part I, 277-278, 308-309.

[46] *Plymouth Colony Records,* X, 212.

[47] *New Haven Colonial Records, 1653-1665,* p. 363.

Despite these precautions, the teachings of George Fox received some acceptance in the outlying towns of the colony. For harboring Quakers and possessing Quaker literature, Richard Crabb of Greenwich was fined £30 and required to give bond of £100 for good behavior.[48] For accepting the teachings of Fox, Arthur Smith of Southold was whipped and required to give bond of £50 for good behavior.[49] For permitting Quakers to assemble in his home, and "saying that they were the honestest and most godly people that were now in the world," and worse treated in the New Haven Colony than elsewhere—a statement which was probably correct until Massachusetts in desperation began to inflict the death penalty—John Budd, Sr., a member of the church at Southold, was fined £15.[50] But all attempts to bring Nathaniel Sylvester of Shelter Island, the harborer of the sect, before the general court of the colony met with failure.[51]

Coincident with this attack from without came a movement for a more liberal Congregationalism from within. Before the arrival of the Davenport company in Massachusetts Bay there was dissatisfaction with the limitation of the privilege of baptism to the children of those in full communion with the church. As the second generation in New England grew to maturity, murmurs against the rigidities of the Congregational order grew louder. Without the religious experiences of their fathers, the children of the founders were less articulate, and few of them could qualify for full membership in the church. Yet the founders desired baptism for their grandchildren, and baptized persons who had not yet entered into full communion with the church desired the privileges of church-members, the right to participate in civil affairs for themselves, and baptism for their children. Some of the clergy

[48] *New Haven Colonial Records, 1653-1655,* pp. 242-247.

[49] *Ibid.,* pp. 291-292.

[50] *Ibid.,* pp. 412-415.

[51] *Ibid.,* pp. 364, 380, 412.

saw that the limitation of baptism to the children of those in full communion with the church could result only in adult baptism. As early as December 16, 1635, John Cotton and the ruling elders of the church at Boston advised the baptism of the grandson of a Dorchester church-member although the parents of the child had not been admitted to full membership in the church. In time the practice took on varied forms. Some ministers baptized children if one or both of the parents were members of the church; others, if the grandparents were members.[52] With the hope of arriving at some uniformity of practice, the general court of Massachusetts Bay called a synod to meet at Cambridge, September 1, 1646, to draft a form of government for the churches of New England.[53] In preliminary drafts Richard Mather and Ralph Partridge embodied the principle of a wider baptism,[54] but the opposition was sufficiently strong to prevent the inclusion of the principle in the platform of church-government adopted at Cambridge in 1648.[55] The movement continued to gather force, however, and in 1654 the churches of Salem and Lynn, and a little later the churches of Dorchester and Roxbury accepted the Half-Way Covenant. In 1656 the church at Ipswich put the principle into practice.

In May, 1656, a petition praying for an enlargement of the privilege of baptism came before the general court of

52 Increase Mather, *The First Principles of New-England* (Cambridge, 1675); Henry Martyn Dexter, *The Congregationalism of the Last Three Hundred Years, as Seen in Its Literature* (1880), pp. 467-518; Williston Walker, *The Creeds and Platforms of Congregationalism* (1893), pp. 238-239; Perry Miller, "The Half-Way Covenant," *New England Quarterly*, VI, 676-715.

53 Massachusetts Archives, X, 187-189.

54 American Antiquarian Society, Richard Mather, Modell of church-governmt. 1648; Ralph Partridge, On Church Government.

55 *A Platform of Church Discipline gathered out of the Word of God* (1649); reprinted in *The Results of Three Synods* (1725); and in Williston Walker, *The Creeds and Platforms of Congregationalism* (1893).

Connecticut, and the legislature of the River Colony appointed a committee to draft questions on the problem to be submitted to the colony's confederates.[56] To the twenty-one queries of Connecticut, Massachusetts Bay responded by calling a conference of clergy.[57] From June 4 to June 19, 1657, elders of Connecticut and Massachusetts Bay debated the question at Boston. A majority of the gathering concluded that the baptized children of church-members were themselves members and therefore subject to the discipline of the church and, if they owned the covenant, regardless of whether or not they had been admitted to full communion with the church, they transmitted the right of baptism to their children. These conclusions Richard Mather sent to his sons, Samuel, Nathaniel, and Increase, in Europe, and Increase Mather gave them to the world as *A Disputation concerning Church-Members and their Children* (London, 1659).[58] But under Congregationalism each church was at liberty to accept or reject these conclusions as it pleased.

In an attempt to arrive at a more definitive settlement, on December 31, 1661, the general court of Massachusetts Bay called a synod of elders and brethren of the churches of the colony to meet at Boston on the second Tuesday of the following March to consider: 1. Who are the subjects of baptism? 2. Whether according to the word of God there ought to be a consociation of churches, and if so, what should be the nature of it?[59] Giving but scant attention to consociation, the delegates to the synod of 1662 concentrated on the question of baptism. At their first session a majority of those present drafted seven propo-

56 *Connecticut Colonial Records*, I, 281.

57 *Massachusetts Colony Records*, III, 419; IV, Part I, 280.

58 American Antiquarian Society, note by Increase Mather on copy of Richard Mather, Answer to 21 Questions.

59 American Antiquarian Society, letter General Court of Massachusetts to the Church at Roxbury, December 31, 1661.

sitions in favor of baptizing the children of all baptized persons who had accepted the covenant even though they had not been admitted to full communion with the church, and the group adjourned.[60] At a second session in June, the propositions were accepted and the delegates again adjourned to gather scriptural precepts to support the conclusions at which they had already arrived. At a final session in September, a majority of the delegates reiterated their former conclusion that baptized persons who owned the covenant had the right to present their children for baptism. On the order of the general court of Massachusetts Bay, the conclusions of the synod were published as *Propositions concerning the Subject of Baptism and Consociation of Churches* (Cambridge, 1662) and recommended to the churches of the Bay Colony. The acceptance or rejection of the principles was again optional with the congregations, however, and the decisions of the synod of 1662 were no more definitive than had been those of the assembly of 1657.

With the rigidities of the Congregational order, Richard Denton, pastor of the church at Stamford in the New Haven Colony, soon found himself out of sympathy. "Blind of one Eye," but "not the least among the Seers of our Israel,"[61] he saw that the limitation of baptism to the children of those in full communion with the church would become less feasible as time went on, and that the system could not outlive the generation of the founders. With a following drawn from Stamford, he crossed the Sound in 1644, and took part in the founding of Hempstead on Long Island under the jurisdiction of New Netherland. There he freely administered the sacrament of baptism.[62]

60 Massachusetts Historical Society *Collections*, 4th series, VIII, 179.

61 Cotton Mather, *Magnalia Christi Americana* (1702), Book III, pp. 95-96.

62 *Documentary History of New York*, III, 107.

Peter Prudden, pastor of the church at Milford, also accepted the idea of a wider baptism. As early as 1651 he maintained that the children of church-members were themselves members, and whether or not they had entered into full communion with the church, possessed the right to present their children for baptism.[63] He never put the principle into practice, however, and died just as the issue was becoming vital.

To John Davenport and a majority of the ministers of the New Haven Colony, the idea of accounting all baptized persons as church-members and, even though they had not been admitted to full communion, of according them ecclesiastical and civil privileges, was anathema. Davenport attended the synod which convened at Cambridge, September 1, 1646, "and observed with greife that the Tempter was tempting us."[64] When the commissioners of the United Colonies of New England assembled at New Haven a week later, his influence can be seen in their recommendation that the colonies of New England check spreading error and growing corruption in church and state by holding fast to the original rules and patterns, guarding the doors of God's house, admitting only those effectually called to the churches, and restricting baptism to members and their children.[65] In reply to a writing on the subject of baptism sent by a minister of the Bay Colony to a minister of the New Haven Colony, he prepared "An Essay for Investigation of the Truth,"

63 *Propositions concerning the Subject of Baptism and Consociation of Churches* (Cambridge, 1662), preface; Increase Mather, *The First Principles of New-England* (1675), pp. 25-26.

64 Davenport says "a general synod met in Cambridge, in the yeare 1645," but it was in 1646 that the synod convened. American Antiquarian Society, copy of John Davenport, A Vindication of the Treatise entituled Another Essay for Investigation of the Truth. The original manuscript was given by the society to William B. Sprague.

65 *Plymouth Colony Records,* IX, 81.

and sent it to the ministers in and about Boston.[66] To the twenty-one questions of Connecticut, he also prepared answers, and with the approval of Governor Eaton and the magistrates of the colony, forwarded them to the Bay, but at the same time he persuaded the general court of the colony to reply that the petition to the general court of Connecticut did not merit a meeting of the elders of New England and should have been dealt with as had been Child's petition in Massachusetts Bay.[67] Although not a member of the synod of 1662, he visited Boston between the second and third sessions, probably carrying with him "A Reply To the 7 Propositions Concluded by the Synod, Sitting at Boston, June 10: 1662 in Answear to the first Question, vizt Whoe are the Subject[s] of Baptisme,"[68] and, at the request of Increase Mather for an opinion on the subject of consociation,[69] a longer opinion supplemented by one from his colleague, Nicholas Street, on both subjects before the synod. "Christ doth not allow the Churches to provide for a succession by setting up a Meer Membership of adult persons, that are visibly unfit for Church-communion in all Ordinances. Such irregular bringing of men into membership, will unavoidably bring in the corrupting of Religion, which will end in Apostacy," Davenport maintained. "New England Christians are of all Christians in the world most miserable and foolish," Street added. "We have suffered many things in vain, in leaving such a Countrey for this; our Estates, Friends, Comforts there, to enjoy God, and Christ, and our consciences in the Congregational way, in a low afflicted condition in the Wilderness,

66 American Antiquarian Society, copy of John Davenport, A Vindication of the Treatise entituled Another Essay for Investigation of the Truth.

67 American Antiquarian Society, Rev. Mr Davenport's Answer to the 21 Questions; *New Haven Colonial Records, 1653-1665*, pp. 195-198.

68 American Antiquarian Society.

69 Massachusetts Historical Society *Collections*, 4th series, VIII, 189.

for so many years together; and now we must lose those things which we have wrought, and may return to our former state when we please: which the Lord preserve us from." On the first afternoon of the third and final session Davenport sat with the synod and, mistaking courtesy for conviction, was carried away by his skipper and favorable winds believing that he had brought the members to his point of view.[70] But after his departure John Norton prevented Increase Mather from reading the opinions of Davenport and Street to the gathering, and a majority of the delegates voted to adhere to their original conclusions. When the general court of Massachusetts Bay authorized the publication of the decisions of the synod, Increase Mather laid the opinions of Davenport and Street before the legislature. Gaining the consent of the general court not to hinder their publication,[71] Davenport's influential young adherent gave them to the world as *Another Essay for Investigation of the Truth* (Cambridge, 1663). When Richard Mather and Jonathan Mitchell replied with *A Defence of the Answer and Arguments of the Synod Met at Boston in the Year 1662* (Cambridge, 1664), Davenport prepared "A Vindication of the Treatise entituled Another Essay for Investigation of the Truth," and "The third Essay containing a Reply to the Answer unto the other Essay," and sent them to Increase Mather. In manuscript Davenport's writings circulated among the elders of the Bay Colony,[72] but probably because Increase Mather soon switched sides in the controversy and lost interest in propagating the ideas of the conservative faction, they remained unpublished. To

[70] American Antiquarian Society, John Davenport, The third Essay containing a Reply to the Answer unto the other Essay printed In Defense of the Synods Booke.

[71] Massachusetts Historical Society *Collections*, 4th series, VIII, 205.

[72] *Ibid.*, 3d series, X, 60; Increase Mather, *The First Principles of New-England* (1675), Postscript, p. 2.

the spiritual leader of the New Haven Colony the desertion of his young and vigorous ally was a cruel blow, but thinking back over the preceding twenty-five years, he could see no flaw in the ecclesiastical system adopted by the planters of Quinnipiac, June 4, 1639, and to the end he continued to oppose all modifications of the original rules and patterns.

CHAPTER VI

MOSES HIS JUDICIALS

AT the meeting at which they chose eleven of their number to lay the foundations for a church, the free planters of Quinnipiac, rapidly approaching a time when they would have a body of saints who could qualify as free burgesses and officeholders, reiterated their acceptance of "Moses his judicials," the code of laws prepared by John Cotton for Massachusetts Bay.[1] This frame of government provided for governor, deputy governor, assistants, a general court composed of these officers and deputies to represent the towns, a court of assistants, a secretary and ministers of justice for every court, a treasurer, and town governments. Although quite suitable for Massachusetts Bay six years after the transfer of the charter to America, such a government was far too complex for the infant plantation of Quinnipiac. After the gathering of a church, August 21 or 22, 1639, the code could be applied in part, however, and on October 25, 1639, the "seven pillars" met as a civil court and instituted a plantation government.[2] All former grants of power were recalled. Nathaniel Turner, William Andrews, and Ezekiel Cheever, who had been admitted to the recently gathered church at Quinnipiac, and Samuel Eaton, John Clarke, Robert Seely, John Chapman, Thomas Jeffrey, and Richard Hull, members of other approved churches, were received as free burgesses and assented to the freeman's charge. Commenting upon

[1] *New Haven Colonial Records, 1638-1649,* pp. 11-15.
[2] *Ibid.,* pp. 20-21.

John Cotton's scriptural citations regarding the kind of men who should be chosen to public office, John Davenport preached the New Haven Colony's first election sermon. The sixteen free burgesses of the plantation chose Theophilus Eaton as magistrate, Robert Newman, Mathew Gilbert, Nathaniel Turner, and Thomas Fugill as deputies to assist the magistrate, Thomas Fugill as public notary, and Robert Seely as marshal, and agreed to elect new officers annually in the last week of October. In the years immediately following some changes were made. In 1640 the title of public notary gave way to that of secretary.[3] In 1641 a second magistrate, and in 1642 a treasurer were elected.[4] Functioning not only as officers of a single plantation or town but as governor, deputy governor, and assistants of a colony, the magistrates and deputies nevertheless hesitated to use the titles of colonial officialdom until additional towns had been settled under the jurisdiction of the first plantation. The more important business of Quinnipiac was transacted in meetings attended by all free burgesses and planters; the less important business, in meetings of the magistrates and deputies. Although resembling the town meetings of Massachusetts Bay, the assemblies of free burgesses and planters were called "general courts" because the planters of Quinnipiac were copying the colonial government outlined in the Cotton code. Gatherings of magistrates and deputies were designated simply as "courts." In the formative years, the general court met frequently; the magistrates and deputies, usually on the first Wednesday of the month.

Acquiring title to the lands of Menunkatuck without assistance from New Haven, the Whitfield company at first remained independent of outside control. Until a church could be gathered the group entrusted civil power

[3] *Ibid.*, p. 44. [4] *Ibid.*, pp. 58, 78.

for the administration of justice and preservation of peace to Robert Kitchel, William Chittenden, John Bishop, and William Leete,[5] and for a period of four years took no further action, probably because they had come directly from England to Long Island Sound and were without the Massachusetts Bay experiences of their friends at Quinnipiac.

Some weeks subsequent to the organization of a government at Quinnipiac, the Prudden company, not yet removed to Wepowaug, agreed to accept the written word of God as their guide in the plantation which they intended to found, and thus laid the foundations for a government akin to that of the mother plantation. Although like the settlers of Quinnipiac, they limited the right to hold office to church-members, they granted the franchise to all free planters. They made provision for general courts to meet when necessary, and particular courts to meet every six weeks. Naming William Fowler, Edmund Tapp, Zachariah Whitman, John Astwood, and Richard Miles as judges, they authorized them to try all causes between man and man and to punish all offenses and misdemeanors.[6] Like the planters of Menunkatuck, the group acquired title to the land upon which they settled without the assistance of New Haven, and for a time remained independent of outside control.

Before entering into negotiations with New Haven, on October 19, 1640, the Wethersfield men who purchased Toquams, Rippowams, or Stamford, from New Haven,

[5] Guilford Records, B, 7-8.

[6] Milford Land Records, I, 1-2. Free planters were settlers entitled to share in the lands of the town. Edward R. Lambert, *History of the Colony of New Haven*, pp. 89-90, is again in error when he says that all free planters were church-members. Connecticut State Library, Milford First Congregational Church Records, I, 1, proves conclusively that at the time an agreement regarding a plantation government was made the church gathered for Milford had only nine members.

chose Richard Denton, Mathew Mitchell, Andrew Ward, Thurston Raynor, and a fifth individual, probably Robert Coe, to order the common affairs of their intended plantation and its inhabitants, and to determine differences "according to equitie, peace, love, convenience and . . ."[7] In November, 1641, after the removal had taken place, they named Mathew Mitchell, Thurston Raynor, Andrew Ward, John Whitmore, Richard Law, and Richard Crabb to order the town's occasions, and a year later, John Underhill, Mathew Mitchell, Andrew Ward, and Robert Coe. Unlike the settlers of Menunkatuck or Guilford and Wepowaug or Milford, the planters of Stamford acquired title to their lands through New Haven, and agreed to join with New Haven in the form of government there established. Journeying to the mother plantation, on October 27, 1641, Andrew Ward and Francis Bell were admitted members of the general court at that place. At this assembly Thurston Raynor was named constable for Rippowams, and after he had received his charge from the general court at New Haven and testified his acceptance thereof, he was authorized "to order such busines as may fall in thatt towne according to God for the next Ensueing year." On April 6, 1642, Mathew Mitchell and John Whitmore represented Rippowams in the general court at New Haven at which their plantation received the name of Stamford. Deputies from Stamford attended the general court of elections at New Haven, October 26, 1642, at which Andrew Ward was chosen constable for Stamford for the ensuing year. On April 5, 1643, John Underhill and Richard Gildersleeve brought to the general court at New Haven the request of the free burgesses of Stamford that they might have a magistrate and the nomination of either Mathew Mitchell or Thurs-

[7] The last word is illegible. Stamford Records, I, 5-6; *New Haven Colonial Records, 1638-1649,* p. 85.

ton Raynor for the office. The general court confirmed Raynor as magistrate, to be assisted by the four men chosen to order the town's occasions, until the next general court of elections at New Haven.[8] Stamford now had a government of magistrate, four deputies, and a constable, resembling the government of New Haven, but the plantation was subordinate to New Haven, for the magistrate and constable had been chosen not by the free burgesses of the town but at a general court at New Haven to which Stamford sent only two representatives.

The plantations settled in the territory acquired from the agents of the Earl of Stirling and Sir Edmund Plowden were likewise subordinate to the mother plantation. On April 6, 1642, a general court at New Haven appointed Thomas Tuttle constable at Yennicock or Southold on Long Island, "to order the affayres of thatt Plantatiō the time being till some further course be taken by this Court for the settling a magistracie there according to God."[9] Fifteen months later Stephen Goodyear was instructed "to write to the Inhabitants of Yenycott to Lett them know the Equity of the proceedings of this Court in rateing all men Impartially according to their accom̄odations wthin the Libertyes of this Plantation and thatt itt will be expected thatt the same Rule be attended vnto by them there allso."[10] On August 30, 1641, a general court at New Haven voted that the sundry plantations in Delaware Bay, purchased by particular persons at their own charge, for the advancement of the public good in way of trade and also for the settling of churches and plantations in those parts, should be settled in combination with the town of New Haven.[11]

At this stage in the evolution of a colonial government

[8] *New Haven Colonial Records, 1638-1649*, pp. 45, 58, 69, 78-79, 85, 199.
[9] *Ibid.*, p. 70.
[10] *Ibid.*, p. 97.
[11] *Ibid.*, pp. 56-57.

the plantation-colony of New Haven was invited to join a confederation of the Puritan colonies of New England. Such a confederation had first been proposed in August, 1637, soon after the arrival of the Davenport company in New England, when representatives of the towns on the Connecticut River visited the Bay Colony in connection with the Pequot War and the Hutchinsonian controversy. At this time five proposals made by some of the assistants of Massachusetts Bay proved acceptable to the magistrates and people of Connecticut, but a sixth, providing for the reference of intercolonial disputes to commissioners to be appointed by the colonies, the decision of a majority of the commissioners to be accepted as final, met with opposition. In May, 1638, John Haynes, William Pynchon, and John Steele of Connecticut laid before the general court of Massachusetts Bay at Newtown revised articles providing for the reference of intercolonial disputes to commissioners, the decision of the latter to be accepted as final only if unanimous. The Bay Colony seized upon this opportunity to advance its claim to Agawam or Springfield, most northerly of the river towns. The delegation from Connecticut assented to the claim, but Massachusetts demanded the assent of the general court of the colony. When the latter continued to exercise jurisdiction over Agawam, Governor Winthrop protested and received a harsh reply from Roger Ludlow. The conflicting interests of the two governments, the claim of the Bay Colony to Agawam, the belief of the River Colony that Massachusetts was discouraging emigration to Connecticut, and the refusal of Connecticut to be bound by a treaty which Massachusetts Bay had signed with Miantonomo, chieftain of the Narragansetts, on the eve of the Pequot War, interrupted further negotiations.[12]

[12] Massachusetts Archives, II, 196-203; "Rev. Thomas Hooker's Letter," Connecticut Historical Society *Collections*, I, 1-18; *Winthrop's Journal*, I,

Lying on the outskirts of New England, in territory claimed by New Netherland, and without the support of the neighboring colonies, Connecticut could not long hold out, however, and on the occasion of a visit of John Haynes and Thomas Hooker to Boston in May, 1639, a motion for confederation was again laid before the general court of Massachusetts Bay. Roger Ludlow, Thomas Welles, and Thomas Hooker of Connecticut next visited George Fenwick at Saybrook and won the assent of the representative of the grantees of the Earl of Warwick to the project. Fenwick informed John Winthrop that he and the lords he represented desired to promote mutual defense and peace, and Haynes reported to the Bay Colony that Fenwick would join with the two Puritan colonies in an agreement regarding offensive and defensive war.[13]

Probably because of diversity of interests, negotiations proceeded slowly, and information regarding them is fragmentary. In October, 1640, a letter of Edward Hopkins and John Haynes of Connecticut, Theophilus Eaton of New Haven, and William Coddington and William Brenton of Aquidneck, perhaps on the subject of confederation, was before the general court of Massachusetts Bay. The legislature authorized Governor Dudley to reply to Hopkins, Haynes, and Eaton, but refused to deal with the outcasts at Aquidneck.[14]

Almost two years later propositions prepared by Connecticut and New Haven, supported by letters of Theophilus Eaton to the governor of Massachusetts Bay and

231-232, 287-291; *Massachusetts Colony Records,* I, 216; *New Haven Colonial Records, 1653-1665,* p. 5.

[13] *Winthrop's Journal,* I, 301-302; *Connecticut Colonial Records,* I, 30, 31; Thomas Hutchinson, *A Collection of Original Papers* (1769), pp. 107-108.

[14] *Massachusetts Colony Records,* I, 305.

of John Haynes to Thomas Shepard and John Wilson,[15] were before the general court of Massachusetts Bay, and were referred to a committee consisting of the magistrates of the colony in and near Boston and the deputies of Boston, Charlestown, Cambridge, Watertown, Roxbury, and Dorchester.[16] After revising the proposals of Connecticut and New Haven, the committee sent them to New Plymouth, Connecticut, and New Haven, but omitted the province of Sir Ferdinando Gorges, for "they ran a different course . . . both in their ministry and civil administration."

Connecticut responded by appointing John Haynes and Edward Hopkins, March 27, 1643, to go to the Bay either to bring about a confederation of Massachusetts Bay, Connecticut, and New Haven, or to begin negotiations for the union of the Bay Colony and Connecticut.[17] In the execution of their mission, Haynes and Hopkins were joined by George Fenwick of Saybrook. Without authorizing its delegates to enter into a formal alliance, New Plymouth appointed Edward Winslow and William Collyer to treat with Massachusetts regarding confederation.[18]

Important though confederation was to Massachusetts Bay, Connecticut, and New Plymouth, to New Haven it was vital. The plantation—in 1642 it could hardly be called a colony—and its outlying settlements lay in territory claimed by New Netherland, within a short sail from New Amsterdam, and in its efforts to gain a foothold on Delaware Bay and River, it had already clashed with the

15 *Connecticut Colonial Records,* I, 68; John Haynes to Thomas Shepard or John Wilson, undated, American Antiquarian Society.

16 *Massachusetts Colony Records,* II, 31; *Winthrop's Journal,* II, 82, 98-99.

17 *Connecticut Colonial Records,* I, 82.

18 *Plymouth Colony Records,* II, 53.

Dutch, who claimed that region, and the Swedes, who had established themselves there.

After obscure negotiations between Theophilus Eaton and Massachusetts Bay and Connecticut, on April 6, 1643, a general court at New Haven "ordered thatt Mr Eaton and Mr Gregson as Comissioners for this Jurisdictiō of Newhaven shall goe wth other Comissioners for other Plantatiō^{s} into the Bay of Massacusetts to treate about a Gen^{rll} Combinatiō for all the Plantations in New England, and to conclude and determine the same as In their wisdome they shall see cause for the Exalting of Christs Ends and advancing the Publique Good in all the Plantations. And allso thatt Mr Goodyeare o^{r} Pasto^{r} the fower Deputyes together wth Georg Lamberton Robt Newman and Tho. ffugill shall meete and advise wth them before they Goe the better to p^{r}pare them for thatt Greate and weighty busines And more ouer thatt If any of the members of the Court or of the Plantatiō have any thing of weight to suggest for consideratiō they are desired to repaire to the comittee or any one of them to cast in whatt Light they can." Several weeks later, "The Comissioners aforesaid desired the Court now to propound any thing to them thatt they would have considered of in reference to the foremenc̄oned Combinatiō and thatt If any of them had any Light to cast in to them, thatt they would att this time Impart itt because the time of their goeing drew neare; butt the whole Court seemed to rest satisfied in the wisdome and ffaithfullnes of those wch they had chosen and Intrusted for thatt great busines and therefore had nott thought of any thing butt whatt they thought had beene considered off and would be provided for by those Intrusted."[19]

On May 10, 1643, representatives of New Plymouth, Connecticut, and New Haven were in Boston and the gen-

[19] *New Haven Colonial Records, 1638-1649,* p. 87.

eral court of Massachusetts Bay appointed John Winthrop, Thomas Dudley, Simon Bradstreet, William Tynge, Edward Gibbons, and William Hauthorne to confer with them.[20] After several meetings the group agreed upon articles of confederation. Immediately approved by the general court of Massachusetts Bay, the agreement was signed by the secretary of that colony and the commissioners of Connecticut and New Haven; but without the authorization of New Plymouth to append their signatures at this time, Edward Winslow and William Collyer did not sign the articles until September 7, 1643.[21]

The articles of confederation brought into existence the United Colonies of New England, more commonly known as the New England Confederation. In the words of the negotiators, this was a firm and perpetual league of friendship and amity for offense and defense, mutual advice, and succor upon all just occasions, both for preserving and propagating the truth and liberties of the gospel and for mutual safety and welfare.[22] Provision was made for annual meetings of two commissioners from each of the four colonies on the first Thursday in September, the meeting in September, 1643, to be at Boston, the successive meetings to be at Hartford, New Haven, Plymouth, and again at Boston, and then, beginning once more at Boston, the five-year cycle was to be repeated. Three magistrates of any jurisdiction might call extraordinary meetings of the commissioners of the four colonies to consider, treat, and conclude all affairs belonging to the confederation. For the passage of acts of the United Colonies, the vote of six of the eight commissioners was necessary. For the reception by any one of the

[20] *Massachusetts Colony Records,* II, 35.

[21] *Ibid.,* pp. 36, 38; *Plymouth Colony Records,* II, 56; IX, 8, 9; *Winthrop's Journal,* II, 98-99.

[22] *Plymouth Colony Records,* IX, 3-8; *New Haven Colonial Records,* 1638-1649, pp. 98-104; *Winthrop's Journal,* II, 100-105.

colonies of plantations lying beyond its limits in 1643, and for the union of any two of the colonies to form one government, the consent of the confederation was required.

On July 6, 1643, Theophilus Eaton and Thomas Gregson informed the general court at New Haven of the successful outcome of the negotiations in Boston. The articles of confederation were read, approved, and confirmed. The general court ordered copies to be sent to the several plantations of the jurisdiction and chose Eaton and Gregson to represent New Haven at the meeting of the commissioners of the United Colonies to be held at Boston in the following September.[23]

The formation of the New England Confederation forced the plantations of Guilford and Milford to the east and west of New Haven, each with its independent plantation government, to cast in their lot with New Haven, for only in this way could they gain the protection afforded by confederation. It also forced the plantation-colony of New Haven to differentiate between colony and town affairs and to superimpose a colonial government upon the already established plantation or town government.

Guilford was the first to act. To qualify for inclusion in the New Haven Colony, the Whitfield company agreed, ordered, and concluded that only such planters as were also members of the church should be and be called freemen, and that freemen only should have the power to elect magistrates and deputies and all other officers. On or before June 19, 1643, the customary "seven pillars" gathered themselves into a church estate. The feoffees in trust for purchasing the plantation resigned up their right into the hands of the church. The four men to whom the direction of civil affairs had been temporarily entrusted de-

[23] *New Haven Colonial Records, 1638-1649*, pp. 96, 97.

clared their office at an end. At last enjoying a government controlled by church-members and identical with that of the mother plantation, Menunkatuck or Guilford sent William Leete and Samuel Desborough to represent it at the general court which convened at New Haven, July 6, 1643.[24]

At the first meeting of the commissioners of the United Colonies of New England at Boston in September, 1643, "It was graunted and ordered That the Towne of Milford may be receiued into Combinac̄on and as a member of the Jursdicc̄on of New Hauen, if New Hauen and Milford agree vpon the termes and condic̄ons among themselues." The plantation of Milford promptly entered into negotiations with Theophilus Eaton. Six non-church-members who had been admitted as freemen at Milford caused difficulties, but after it had been agreed that they might continue to vote in town elections, and for deputies to represent the town in the general court at New Haven, but should take no part in colonial affairs, the brethren at New Haven admitted Milford to the New Haven Colony.[25]

Meanwhile, a differentiation between plantation and colony affairs was gradually taking place. On April 6, 1642, a general court at New Haven "ordered thatt every first wednesday in Aprill and every wednesday in the Last whole weeke in october shall be a Genrll Court held att Newhaven for the Plantations in Combination wth this towne,"[26] but even after this date some wavering in procedure persisted. On October 26, 1642, the court of elections at New Haven failed to differentiate between officers of the colony and officers of the town.[27] Although the gathering at New Haven on July 6, 1643, to which

[24] Guilford Records, B, 7-8; *New Haven Colonial Records, 1638-1649*, p. 96.

[25] *Plymouth Colony Records*, IX, 10; *New Haven Colonial Records, 1638-1649*, pp. 110-111.

[26] *Ibid.*, p. 70.

[27] *Ibid.*, pp. 78-79.

Eaton and Gregson reported the formation of the New England Confederation, and at which representatives of Guilford appeared, was distinctly labeled, "a Genrll Court held att Newhaven for the Plantations wthin this Jurisdictiō," and ordered copies of the articles of confederation to be sent to Stamford, Guilford, and Yennicock, assessed Stamford £5, Guilford £5, and Yennicock £2 toward the expenses of the confederation, and devoted itself entirely to the affairs of the colony,[28] on October 23, 1643, the church-members of the town of New Haven admitted Milford to the jurisdiction. Three days later, at a meeting designated "A Genrll Court of Elections held att Newhaven for this Jurisdictiō the 26th of October 1643," not only governor, deputy governor, secretary, and marshal for the colony were elected for the first time, and magistrates for New Haven, Milford, and Stamford, but also deputies to represent New Haven and Guilford at meetings of the general court for the jurisdiction, officers later chosen by the freemen of the respective towns.[29]

On October 27, 1643, this ambiguity between the affairs of the plantation and the affairs of the colony disappeared. At that time a general court composed of governor, deputy governor, magistrates, and deputies from New Haven, Milford, Guilford, and Stamford assembled at New Haven and outlined a frame of government for the colony. For the first time in five and one-half years the trading-company organization of the Cotton code could be applied in something like its entirety. In provisions drawn in part verbatim from the code, the New Haven fundamental orders reasserted the limitation of the right to vote and to hold office to church-members. These orders provided for governor, deputy governor, assistants or magistrates, treasurer, secretary, and marshal,

[28] *New Haven Colonial Records, 1638-1649,* pp. 96-97.

[29] *Ibid.,* pp. 110-112.

to be annually chosen by the free burgesses of the colony. To the governor, deputy governor, or two magistrates was given the power to call special sessions of the general court. To the general court were assigned legislative and judicial powers. To the court of magistrates were given original jurisdiction in the more important civil and criminal cases, and appellate jurisdiction over cases which had originated in the particular courts of the various towns, sentence to pass by the vote of the major part of the magistrates present and to be subject to revision by the general court of the colony. Beneath this superstructure provision was made for the already existing plantation or town governments.[30]

Although the Cotton code made no provision for separate gatherings of the freemen to elect officers, nevertheless from 1643 to 1647 a general court of elections for the jurisdiction of New Haven assembled on the day preceding the October meeting of the general court. Thereafter it met on the same day that the general court convened in May. After an election sermon by one of the elders of the colony,[31] the free burgesses or their proxies proceeded with the choice of officers for the jurisdiction for the ensuing year. Despite annual elections, there was little rotation in office. Year after year a limited number of free burgesses filled the various offices of trust. During the existence of the New Haven Colony only three individuals held the office of governor; four, the office of deputy governor; six, the office of secretary; five, the office of treasurer; and two, the office of marshal.

In neither the Cotton code, drafted before the United Colonies of New England had come into existence, nor in

30 *Ibid.*, pp. 112-116. See my article, "John Cotton and the New Haven Colony," *New England Quarterly*, III, 82-94.

31 Probably John Davenport, although in the spring of 1654 Peter Prudden was asked to preach the election sermon. *New Haven Colonial Records, 1653-1665*, p. 66.

the New Haven fundamental orders of 1643, based upon that code, was provision made for commissioners to represent the colony at meetings of the New England Confederation. At the general court at which the fundamental orders were adopted, Theophilus Eaton and Thomas Gregson with Richard Malbon as alternate were named to represent the colony at the meeting of the New England Confederation at Hartford in September, 1644, or Stephen Goodyear and Thomas Gregson with Malbon as alternate if the meeting were held sooner and farther away.[32] To remedy the omission of all mention of commissioners from the fundamental orders, on October 21, 1644, a general court for the town of New Haven directed its secretary to advise the plantations of the colony that commissioners would be chosen by the freemen of the colony at the ensuing court of elections for the jurisdiction.[33] Thereafter two commissioners and one or two alternates to represent the colony at meetings of the New England Confederation were annually chosen in the court of elections for the jurisdiction.

In practice the general court of the New Haven Colony was composed of governor, deputy governor, magistrates, and two deputies from each plantation. In harmony with the fundamental orders of 1643, from 1643 to 1647 it convened in regular session in April and October. In 1648 these semiannual meetings gave way to an annual session which convened on the last Wednesday in May and sat until all business was concluded. At these gatherings the deputies of the central towns were usually present, but those from Stamford and Southold were often absent. Although infrequent in the middle period of the colony's history, in the early years and after the restoration of Charles II to the throne of England special sessions of the general court were numerous.

[32] *New Haven Colonial Records, 1638-1649*, pp. 117-118.
[33] *Ibid.*, p. 147.

As a legislative body, the first general court of the New Haven Colony to meet after the adoption of the fundamental orders of 1643 enacted "thatt the Judiciall Lawes of God as they were delivered by Moses and as they are a fence to the morrall Law being neither Typicall nor Ceremoniall nor had any referrence to Canaan shall be accounted of morrall Equity and Genrlly binde all offendrs and be a rule to all the Courts in this Jurisdictiō in their proceeding against offendors till they be branched out into perticulars hereafter."[34] Up to this time the settlers of Guilford and Milford may have been working out their own systems of legislation, but by this order the legislation of the Cotton code was extended over all towns of the colony. At every meeting of the general court, sometimes on its own initiative, sometimes on the initiative of the New England Confederation, the legislation of the Cotton code was added to and amended. These new laws are scattered through the records of the colony. Losing confidence in the integrity of Thomas Fugill, in 1645 the town of New Haven made an attempt to codify the law,[35] but for another ten years the colony took no steps in that direction. Finally in 1654 and 1655 a general court for the jurisdiction desired Governor Eaton "To view ouer The Lawes of this Jurisdiction, and draw vp those of them, wch he thinkes will be most necessary To Continew as lawes here, and Compyle them Together fitt to be printed." Never original in its law-making, the colonial legislature authorized the governor to consult the Massachusetts code of 1648 and an edition of the Cotton code which had appeared in London in 1655.[36] In preparing a compilation, Eaton retained the outline of government of the Cotton code as it had been adapted to the needs of the New Haven Colony, but drew heavily on the Massachu-

[34] *Ibid.*, p. 130. [35] *Ibid.*, pp. 155, 191-219.
[36] *Ibid.*, *1653-1665*, pp. 146-147, 154-155, 186, 559-616.

setts code of 1648 for general legislation. Twice approved by the general court of the jurisdiction, the resulting manuscript was sent to Edward Hopkins, who had returned to London in 1651, to be printed. In the summer of 1656 five hundred copies of *New-Haven's Settling in New-England. And Some Lawes for Government:* (London, 1656) were received in the colony and distributed among the towns. Two hundred copies went to New Haven, eighty to Milford, seventy to Stamford and Greenwich, sixty to Guilford, fifty to Southold, and forty to Branford. Thereafter ignorance of the law was without excuse.

Also in its legislative capacity, the general court of the jurisdiction authorized rates for the support of the colonial government. As early as July, 1643, the plantation of New Haven assessed part of the charges arising from the formation of the New England Confederation on Stamford, Guilford, and Southold, probably roughly in proportion to population.[37] After the formation of a colonial government, October 27, 1643, both ordinary and extraordinary expenses of the jurisdiction were met by rates levied by the general court of the colony on the towns and the proprietors of Paugasset in proportion to the population of males between sixteen and sixty and the value of estates.[38] Falling to £100 in 1659 and rising to £500 in 1663, the amount thus apportioned was usually £150 or £200 a year. To this revenue the colony added the income derived from fines imposed by the general court and the court of magistrates of the colony, licenses for drawing wines and liquors, the duty authorized May 30, 1655, on wines and liquors distilled in the colony or brought from any other place than England for sale in the colony or its harbors, and its share of the tribute collected by the New England Confederation from the Indians.[39]

[37] *New Haven Colonial Records, 1638-1649,* p. 97.

[38] *Ibid., passim; ibid., 1653-1665, passim.*

[39] New Haven, Office of the Town Clerk, A Booke Conteyning The Ac-

As a judicial body, the general court of the jurisdiction was the highest court in the colony. Before it came the most important civil and criminal cases and appeals from the court of magistrates. When functioning in a judicial capacity magistrates and deputies sat together but decisions required the consent of a majority of each group.

In practice the court of magistrates was composed of governor, deputy governor, one or two magistrates from New Haven, one or two magistrates from Milford, a magistrate from Guilford, a magistrate from Stamford in the early years of the colony's history, and one from Branford in the later years, four of whom constituted a quorum. Until the abolition of the October general court in 1647, the court of magistrates convened in regular session at one o'clock on the Monday preceding the April and October meetings of the general court. Thereafter it met on the Monday preceding the May meeting of the general court, on the afternoon of the third Wednesday in October, and in special session as need arose.

Beneath the superstructure erected by the fundamental orders of 1643, town governments functioned, the government of the plantation of Quinnipiac serving as a model for the governments of the other towns of the colony. Magistrates and deputies to the general court of the jurisdiction served as the connecting links between central and local governments. The former were nominated by the towns but elected in the general court of elections for the jurisdiction. The latter were chosen by the freemen of the towns to represent the towns in the general court of the colony. Two, three, or four deputies, chosen by the freemen of the respective plantations of New Haven, Milford, and Guilford, and by the general court of elections for the jurisdiction for the subordinate plantations of

counts of Newhaven Jurisdiction began the 3[d] mo. 1652; *New Haven Colonial Records, 1653-1665, passim.*

Southold, Stamford, and Branford, constituted a plantation or town court. The deputies chosen by the freemen of the towns to represent the towns in the general court of the jurisdiction and the two, three, or four deputies who constituted the plantation court in each town must not be confused. One title served to designate two sets of officials exercising quite different functions because the Cotton code was first adapted to the plantation of Quinnipiac, and the government of that plantation became the model for the governments of the other towns of the colony, and was later superimposed over those plantations as the government of the New Haven Colony. A secretary kept a record of town meetings, particular courts, grants and transfers of land, births, marriages, and deaths, and the brands and earmarks of horses and cattle. A treasurer received rates levied for the maintenance of colony and town governments, the ministers, and the town schools. At Guilford this officer was assisted by men to order the ministers' maintenance in the early years and by assessors in the later years. A marshal summoned free burgesses and planters to town meetings, served warrants, levied attachments, inflicted punishments, and inspected fire ladders. Townsmen rendered town meetings less frequent. A trained band guarded the safety of each settlement, at New Haven augmented by an artillery company reminiscent of the Artillery Company which drilled just beyond the Wall, not far from Moorgate in London. Fence-viewers and overseers of the highways complete the list of officers who concerned themselves solely with town affairs.

Summoned by notices left at their homes by the marshal, and by the beat of the drum a half hour before the meeting, all free burgesses and planters attended gatherings variously called general courts for the town or plantation at New Haven, Guilford, and Milford, general town meetings at Stamford, town meetings at Southold, and general meetings or town meetings at Branford. These assemblies convened in the meeting-houses, at New Haven on Mondays at eight o'clock in the morning, at Guilford on Thursdays.

The magistrate or magistrates, or commissioners who functioned as magistrates within the limits of the town, and the two, three, or four deputies sat as a town, plantation, particular, monthly, or quarterly court, with jurisdiction over petty civil and criminal cases. Occasionally such a court was augmented by two or three magistrates from other towns and thus elevated to the rank of a court of magistrates or of a plantation court extraordinarily assisted. At other times it disappeared entirely before a constable and marshal or two constables chosen in the general court of the jurisdiction to order the civil affairs of a particular town. At New Haven this lowest unit in the judicial hierarchy came together on the first Tuesday of the month. In other towns of the colony such courts met from four to eight times a year.

In all courts of the New Haven Colony trial by jury was abolished. This noteworthy departure from the Cotton code was made not because the decision of questions of fact by twelve men of the locality was without biblical authorization, but "upon some reasons urged by Mr. Eaton (a great reader and traveller) against that way."[40] In a colony that accepted the "Rules wch the scripture holds forth" as its fundamental law, and limited freedom to church-members, a jury of non-church-members would have been an anomaly. Yet some of the towns of the colony were so small, and the church-members so few, that after the elimination of interested parties and officers, a jury of twelve church-members could not have been im-

40 William Hubbard, "General History of New England," Massachusetts Historical Society *Collections*, 2d series, V-VI, 320.

paneled. Yet despite the abolition of trial by jury, the decisions of the courts never represent the conclusions of one man. A comparison of the article entitled "Courts for Strangers" in the New Haven code of 1656 with the provision in the Massachusetts code of 1648 from which it was derived indicates that in the lowest unit of the judiciary the functions of a jury were performed by the town deputies.

From the rule limiting the right to vote and to hold office to church-members, first laid down in the Cotton code, included in the plantation covenant adopted soon after the arrival at Quinnipiac and again in the agreement of June 4, 1639, and reiterated in the fundamental orders of 1643, the New Haven Colony never departed. Both by the Cotton code and in practice planters were permitted to express opinions on questions touching their temporal estates. On May 30, 1655, a general court for the jurisdiction agreed that if a freeman qualified to serve as chief military officer in a plantation were not available, another might be chosen.[41] But with these exceptions the colony held fast to the original pattern. On May 28, 1656, the general court of the jurisdiction reiterated that on questions of weighty trust and concernment only freemen of the towns might vote.[42]

This rigid limitation of the right to vote and to hold office in colony and towns to church-members who had been admitted as free burgesses or freemen by the towns gave the colony on Long Island Sound a franchise more narrow than that of Massachusetts Bay, where non-church-members were at first admitted as freemen by the colony and permitted to participate in the conduct of the affairs of the towns, and far more narrow than that of Connecticut, where freemanship was not specifically lim-

[41] *New Haven Colonial Records, 1653-1665,* p. 145.
[42] *Ibid.,* p. 177.

ited to church-members and where all approved inhabitants of the towns voted in town meetings. During the years when the New Haven Colony was in being, only two hundred and fifty-eight probable members, almost half of them women, have been listed for the church at New Haven.[43] Throughout the ministry of Peter Prudden about a hundred and fifteen, the same proportion of them women, seem to have been admitted to the church at Milford.[44] During the existence of the New Haven Colony twenty-five was the greatest number of freemen to participate in a single election at Guilford, and at a time when the planters numbered sixty, the number of freemen seems not to have exceeded twenty-eight, and at other times was as low as sixteen. In 1669, five years after the New Haven Colony had come to an end and the bars had been let down, New Haven boasted only ninety-one freemen, Milford forty-six, Guilford thirty-six, Stamford eight, and Branford eight.[45] Too much must not be read into these final figures, however, for in 1666 and 1667 an exodus of malcontents from within the limits of the former New Haven Colony had taken place.

Because of the narrow franchise and the limited number of office-holders, discontent smoldered in the outlying towns of the colony. As early as 1645 Francis Chatfield was haled before a particular court at Guilford because he had expressed much, in a sinful passion, against the government of the place.[46] By 1653 some of the inhabitants of Southold had grown "weary of that way of Civill Gouerment, wch they haue for Diuers yeares (and wth much Comfort and safty) liued vnder," and sent an ob-

43 Franklin Bowditch Dexter, *Historical Catalogue of the Members of the First Church of Christ in New Haven, Connecticut.*

44 Connecticut State Library, Milford First Congregational Church Records, I.

45 *Connecticut Colonial Records*, II, 518-526.

46 Guilford Records, A, 1.

noxious petition to the general court at New Haven and disturbed the peace of the colony.[47] The following year found John Youngs, Jr., son of the pastor of the church at Southold, dissatisfied because he had not the right to vote for military officers and in open rebellion against the colony.[48] On May 30, 1655, Southold sent no deputies to the general court for the jurisdiction. In the following year some of the inhabitants of the town on Long Island evinced marked disrespect for law and order. In 1659 they refused to take an oath of fidelity to the colony. In 1654 Nathaniel Sylvester, one of the proprietors of Forrett's or Shelter Island, complained of the tyranny of the government of the New Haven Colony, and although at that time he expressed sorrow and craved the pardon of the general court, a few years later he was harboring Quakers, slandering the government of the colony, and claiming to be beyond the jurisdiction of the town of Southold and both Old and New England.[49] Dissatisfied because he had no share in the government of the colony and town and believed himself to be deprived of justice and cut off from appeal to England, in 1654 Robert Bassett headed a rebellion at Stamford. In 1662 individuals of the most westerly town were demanding the right to choose persons to manage their prudential affairs.[50]

Nevertheless, the privileged inner circle of the New Haven Colony urged "that all planters would make it their serious endeauour to come in by the doore to enjoy all priuilidges, and beare all burdens equall wth themselues, according to our foundation setlements, and vniuersally professed ends, And that there may be noe

[47] *New Haven Colonial Records, 1653-1665,* p. 17.

[48] *Ibid.,* pp. 51-52, 93-94, 143, 177, 285, 302, 313.

[49] *Ibid.,* pp. 92-93, 364; *Southold Records,* I, 468.

[50] *New Haven Colonial Records, 1653-1665,* pp. 47, 54-57, 58-66, 94-95, 452.

disorderly or vncomely attempts to climbe vp another way," and refused to commit their "more weighty ciuill or military trusts, into the hands of either a crafty achitophell, or a bloody Joab."[51]

[51] *Ibid.*, p. 404.

CHAPTER VII

FOR THE SERVICE OF GOD IN CHURCH AND COMMONWEALTH

TAUGHT to read the Scriptures, future inhabitants of the New Haven Colony would be able to lay law-book and Bible side by side and discover the excellencies of the ecclesiastical and civil governments established by the founders. In the Old Testament precept, "one from among thy brethren shalt thou set king over thee: thou mayest not set a stranger over thee, which is not thy brother,"[1] they would find authorization for the delegation of civil power to church-members. In the order, "Hear the causes between your brethren, and judge righteously between every man and his brother, and the stranger that is with him,"[2] might be discovered justification for the judicial hierarchy. By the command, "Thou shalt not suffer a witch to live,"[3] they would see that the death penalty for those in covenant with the devil was rendered inevitable. In the proverb, "A whip for the horse, a bridle for the ass, and a rod for the fool's back,"[4] they would find sanction for the whippings so frequently administered on the orders of the particular courts. To equip the on-coming generation with this rudimentary knowledge and to train leaders for the service of God in church and commonwealth, an educational system was indispensable.

Among the first settlers of Quinnipiac was the twenty-one year old Ezekiel Cheever. Educated at Christ's Hos-

1 Deuteronomy 17. 15.
2 *Ibid.*, 1. 16.
3 Exodus 22. 18.
4 Proverbs 26. 3.

pital and Emmanuel College, Cambridge, he already possessed a library of Latin authors, and was quite capable of instructing the youth of the town.[5] As early as 1639 and 1640 he was directing the studies of Michael Wigglesworth and possibly Charles Higginson, son of the first teacher at Salem in Massachusetts Bay, and somewhat later, of the children of Thomas Trowbridge and others.[6] Perhaps he had a competitor in Thomas James, also of Emmanuel College, Cambridge, who had joined Davenport and his followers in Massachusetts Bay and removed with them to Quinnipiac.[7] In 1645 Mark Pierce offered to teach writing and arithmetic to the children of New Haven,[8] and in 1651 Goodwife Wickham was conducting a school for girls.[9]

Soon assuming responsibility for providing education for the children of the town, on February 25, 1642, the free burgesses of New Haven "ordered thatt a ffree Schoole shall be sett vp in this towne," and appointed John Davenport, Theophilus Eaton, and Stephen Goodyear, the first two educated at the Free Grammar School in Coventry, a committee to consider the yearly allowance to be made to a schoolmaster from the town treasury and the necessary rules and orders for the school.[10]

Abandoning his private school, Ezekiel Cheever served as the first master of the town school at New Haven.

[5] John and J. A. Venn, *Alumni Cantabrigienses,* Part I, I, 328; Register of the Commissary Court of London, 1629-1634, fol. 147, printed in Henry F. Waters, *Genealogical Gleanings in England* (1901), I, 87-88.

[6] Michael Wigglesworth, "Autobiography," *New England Historical and Genealogical Register,* XVII, 137-139, reprinted in Edward E. Atwater, *History of the Colony of New Haven,* Appendix I; *New Haven Colonial Records, 1638-1649,* pp. 30, 124.

[7] John and J. A. Venn, *Alumni Cantabrigienses,* Part I, II, 462; Thomas Lechford, *Plain Dealing: Or, Newes from New-England* (1642), p. 43, reprinted in Massachusetts Historical Society *Collections,* 3d series, III, 98.

[8] *New Haven Colonial Records, 1638-1649,* p. 156.

[9] *New Haven Town Records, 1649-1662,* p. 88.

[10] *New Haven Colonial Records, 1638-1649,* p. 62.

After his removal to Ipswich in 1650, William Janes undertook the instruction in elementary subjects of such children as were sent to him by their parents and masters, but soon departed to become schoolmaster at Wethersfield. In November, 1651, the town employed Thomas Hanford to teach Latin, but he became discouraged with the task, and left to take up the ministry at Norwalk. For a time John Davis, son of William Davis of New Haven, and "one of the best accomplished persons for learning, as ever was bred at Harvard College," carried on the work. Finally, after Governor Eaton had negotiated with Joseph Rowlandson of Ipswich, the only graduate of Harvard College in the year 1652, and William Janes had offered to return from Wethersfield to teach reading and writing, and the town had considered the advisability of maintaining both Latin and elementary or English schools, in 1653 John Bowers, a graduate of Harvard College in 1649 and schoolmaster at Plymouth, was induced to come to New Haven to conduct the school. When a colony school was established at New Haven in 1660, the town school was discontinued, but after the abandonment of the colony school in 1662, it was revived under Recompense Osborn and George Pardee.[11]

Coincident with the town school, private instruction in elementary subjects probably continued to be offered, for the school at New Haven was intended to be a Latin school for the preparation of boys for college, and sank to the level of an elementary school, offering instruction in reading, writing, arithmetic, and good manners, only for brief intervals when a grammar schoolmaster was not available.

The town of New Haven paid the salary of a schoolmaster capable of preparing boys for college and part of the salary of a teacher of elementary subjects. Until 1644

[11] *New Haven Colonial Records, 1638-1649, passim; New Haven Town Records, 1649-1684, passim.*

Ezekiel Cheever received £20 a year, and from 1644 to 1650, £30. Janes received £10 in addition to what he collected from the parents and masters of the children he taught. Hanford received £20 a year and his chamber and diet at Joshua Atwater's, thirty shillings toward traveling expenses, and time off to visit his friends during harvest. During his first year and a half at New Haven Bowers received £20 a year and his living with Thomas Kimberley, and after December 11, 1654, £38.

During the early years of the plantation of Guilford John Higginson, teacher of the church, also served as schoolmaster. In 1654 James Cornish was imparting knowledge to the youth of the town. From 1656 to 1660 Jeremiah Peck, a student at Harvard College from 1653 to 1656, taught at Guilford. In the period between 1660 and 1665 John Bowers may have combined teaching with preaching. The schoolmasters were paid in part by rates for school charges and town occasions levied upon the inhabitants of the town, and in part by the parents and masters of the children they taught. In 1646 guardians of children were assessed four shillings a student a quarter. In 1654, "the pay being all to bee levyed vpo~ the scholars," they paid thirteen shillings a head. As the cost of education mounted, the litigious Benjamin Wright refused to pay for one of the children he sent to school "because some of them stayed at home while the other went."[12]

Only fragmentary information regarding education in other towns within and under the influence of the New Haven Colony is extant. At Milford John Sherman, Jasper Gunn, and Richard Bryan are all credited with having taught school, and in 1657 the colony commended the town for the provision it made for education.[13] At Stam-

[12] Guilford Records, B, 14, 163.

[13] *New Haven Colonial Records, 1653-1665,* pp. 219-220.

ford Richard Mills was schoolmaster in 1663.[14] At Huntington Jonas Holdsworth taught children in return for a house, land, diet, and £25 the first year, £35 the second and third, and £40 the fourth year, plus anything that he might collect from students who came from beyond the limits of the town.[15]

Schools functioned the year round, and hours were long—from eight to eleven o'clock in the morning, and from one to four or five o'clock in the afternoon.

Few books for elementary and grammar-school use were available. In addition to a horn-book and primer, each family possessed a Bible and possibly one or more of *The Whole Booke of Psalmes Faithfully Translated into English Metre* (Cambridge, 1640), John Cotton's *Spiritual Milk for Boston Babes* (Cambridge, 1656), and John Davenport and William Hooke's *A Catechisme containing the Chief Heads of Christian Religion* (London, 1659). These works probably sufficed for instruction in reading and spelling. Although not published until 1709, Ezekiel Cheever's Latin Accidence may have existed in manuscript form. In addition, the school at New Haven possessed some books, for in 1652 a chest in which to keep them was necessary. In 1658 this school library was enlarged by the books suitable for the use of a Latin school sent to the town as the gift of a friend of William Gibbard in England.[16]

Just as the early church services were conducted in the homes of the ministers, so the earliest schools may have been conducted in the homes of the masters, but before 1651 a schoolhouse had been erected at New Haven and in 1671 the schoolhouse at Guilford was undergoing repairs. No description of these early centers of learning has been preserved but they were probably crude edifices.

14 Stamford Records, I, 32.

15 *Huntington Records*, I, 8-10.

16 Thomas Goddard Wright, *Literary Culture in Early New England, 1620-1730* (1920); *New Haven Town Records, 1649-1662*, pp. 112, 349-350.

With the publication of a code of laws in 1656, the New Haven Colony undertook the supervision of the education of the youth of the colony. The code authorized the deputies or constables of the towns to see that all children and apprentices were taught to read the Scriptures and other good and profitable books in the English tongue and to understand the main grounds and principles of religion.[17] In the following year the colony ordered each town to maintain a school, the grade unspecified, the salary of the master to be paid one-third by the town and two-thirds by those benefited.[18] In 1660 the colony added writing to the minimum of education required of "sonnes of all the Inhabitants, within this Jurisdiction."[19]

Some of the founders of the New Haven Colony desired more than a Latin school education for their sons, and responded readily to the suggestion of Thomas Shepard, pastor of the church at Cambridge in Massachusetts Bay, to the commissioners of the United Colonies in session at Boston in September, 1643, that every family able and willing to do so annually contribute the fourth part of a bushel of corn or its equivalent for the maintenance of the poor scholars at Cambridge.[20] Thereafter college corn was regularly collected in the towns of New Haven and Guilford.

To the college at Cambridge the settlers of the colony on the Sound sent their more promising sons. Among the graduates of Harvard College are listed Nathaniel Brewster of the class of 1642, probably the son of Francis Brewster of New Haven; Robert Johnson of the class of 1645, son of Robert Johnson of New Haven; Samuel Eaton of the class of 1649, son of Theophilus Eaton of New Haven; Isaac Allerton of the class of 1650, son of Isaac Allerton of New Haven; Michael Wigglesworth of

17 *New Haven Colonial Records, 1653-1665*, pp. 583-584.

18 *Ibid.*, pp. 219-220.

19 *Ibid.*, p. 376.

20 *Plymouth Colony Records*, IX, 20-21.

the class of 1651, son of Edward Wigglesworth of New Haven; John Davis, also of the class of 1651, son of William Davis of New Haven; Recompense Osborn of the class of 1661, son of William Osborn of New Haven; Samuel Street of the class of 1664, son of Nicholas Street, teacher of the church at New Haven; John Harriman of the class of 1667, son of John Harriman, ordinary-keeper at New Haven; Abraham Pierson of the class of 1668, son of Abraham Pierson, pastor of the church at Branford; John Prudden, also of the class of 1668, son of Peter Prudden, pastor of the church at Milford; and Samuel Treat of the class of 1669, son of Robert Treat of Milford. Among the non-graduates are Samuel Malbon, son of Richard Malbon of New Haven; Andrew Goodyear, son of Stephen Goodyear of New Haven; John and Walter Hooke, sons of William Hooke, teacher of the church at New Haven; Jeremiah Peck, son of William Peck of New Haven; and Eleazar Kimberley, son of Thomas Kimberley of New Haven.[21]

In his youth in England John Davenport had departed from Oxford without completing his course, "not from any want of tyme, or of willingnes, or of sufficiency . . . but from want of meanes," and after the lapse of years had returned to take his degree. Subsequently he had shared in the educational activities of the company of feoffees for the purchase of impropriations in England and served as an overseer of the college at Cambridge in Massachusetts Bay. To render higher education more accessible in the colony he had founded, he labored as long as he remained at New Haven to establish an institution of higher learning in the commonwealth on Long Island Sound.

Ten years after the founding of Quinnipiac, the town

[21] John Langdon Sibley, *Biographical Sketches of Graduates of Harvard University* (3 vols., 1873-1885), *passim.*

of New Haven voted to reserve a lot for a college, "wch they dissire maye bee sett vp so soone as their abillitie will reach thervnto."[22] Some years later Stephen Goodyear offered his house at New Haven for the project, but considering a college too great a charge, on June 28, 1652, the town of Guilford refused the house unless Connecticut would join with the New Haven Colony in the undertaking.[23] Unsettled conditions at Harvard College resulted in a renewed effort to found a college at New Haven, and on May 22, 1654, the town voted to bear "a meet proportion of Charge" if a college were established by the jurisdiction.[24] A year later, at a town meeting at which both Davenport and Hooke were present "and spake much To incourag the worke," a committee was appointed "To goe to the seuerall planters in this Towne, and Take from them, what they will freely giue, To this worke."[25] The ensuing canvass resulted in subscriptions to the amount of £300, for which an annual payment of £60 from the town treasury toward the salary of a president and other expenses of the college was later substituted. Milford raised subscriptions to the amount of £100, and the planters of Branford agreed to pay their part of a £60 rate for the maintenance of a college at New Haven "yeare after yeare."[26] On May 30, 1655, a general court for the jurisdiction called a meeting of delegates from the towns of the colony at New Haven on the afternoon of Tuesday, June 19, to receive the pledges of the towns and to decide upon further action.[27] At this meeting about £240 was subscribed in addition to the amount already promised by the town of New Haven. This the delegates considered sufficient to buy and repair a house

22 *New Haven Colonial Records, 1638-1649,* p. 376.

23 *New Haven Town Records, 1662-1684,* p. 84; Guilford Records, A, 128.

24 *New Haven Town Records, 1649-1662,* pp. 213-214.

25 *Ibid.,* pp. 241-242.

26 Branford Records, I, 44.

27 *New Haven Colonial Records, 1653-1665,* pp. 141-142.

for the college,[28] and an institution of higher learning seemed assured. Davenport wrote to Edward Hopkins in London to interest him in the project. John Haynes, Jr., and Fitz John Winthrop made plans to study at the college at New Haven under the presidency of William Leveridge, recently settled at Oyster Bay, during the winter of 1655-1656.[29] Governor Eaton presented Davenport with books to the value of £20 left at New Haven by his brother, Samuel Eaton, to form the nucleus of a college library.[30] Dr. Thomas Browne of Bermuda, who "besides his ministeriall function and his knowledge in the subservient arts, in law and physic, . . . [was] skillfull in the Hebrew, Chaldic, Syriac, Arabic, Grec, Latin, Spanish, Italian and French tongues," offered his services as instructor.[31]

The objections of Leveridge's wife prevented him from undertaking the presidency of the college,[32] but on April 30, 1656, Edward Hopkins replied to Davenport's letter, "That wch the Lord hath given mee in those parts, I euer designed the greatest part of it, for the furtherance of the worke of Christ in those ends of the Earth, And if I vnderstand that a Colledge is begun, and like to be carried on at Newhaven for the good of Posterity, I shall give some encouragm^t^ therevnto." Hopkins died in the following March, and his will, dated March 7, 1657, left

28 *New Haven Town Records, 1649-1662,* pp. 248-249.

29 John Haynes to Fitz John Winthrop, October 1, 1655, Massachusetts Historical Society, Winthrop MSS., XIII, 151, excerpt printed in Massachusetts Historical Society *Proceedings,* 2d series, I, 120.

30 *New Haven Town Records, 1649-1662,* pp. 358-359, 416-417. On the books of Samuel Eaton, see Franklin Bowditch Dexter, "The First Public Library in New Haven," New Haven Colony Historical Society *Papers,* VI, 301-313; "Early Private Libraries in New England," American Antiquarian Society *Proceedings,* new series, XVIII, 138.

31 Thomas Browne to John Winthrop, Jr., March 10, 1657/8, Massachusetts Historical Society *Proceedings,* 2d series, VIII, 287-288.

32 Massachusetts Historical Society *Collections,* X, 14.

his estate in New England, after the payment of debts and certain legacies, and £500 from his estate in England after the death of his wife, to John Davenport and Theophilus Eaton of New Haven and John Cullick and William Goodwin of Hartford, "to give some encouragement in those foreign plantations for the breeding up of hopeful youths in a way of learning, both at the grammar school and college, for the public service of the country in future times."[33]

"Lookeing vpon it as their great Duty to establish some Course (that through the blessing of God) learning may be promoued in the Jurisdiction, as a meanes for the fitting of Instruments for publique service in Church, and com̄onwealth," on May 25, 1659, a general court for the jurisdiction of New Haven attempted to qualify for Hopkins's legacy. The legislature authorized the treasurer of the colony to pay £40 a year "for the furtherance of a gram̄er schoole, for the vse of the Inhabitants of the Jurisdiction," and £8 more to buy such books of Richard Blinman, about to sail for England, as John Davenport and Abraham Pierson should approve as suitable for the school. It appointed the governor, deputy governor, magistrates, and ministers of the colony a committee to decide upon the location of the school and to procure a master.[34]

To John Davenport a colony grammar school was a potential college. To spur on the enterprise, on May 30, 1660, he delivered to the governor and magistrates of the colony a copy of Hopkins's will, an inventory and appraisal of the estate in New England, and other papers

[33] *New Haven Colonial Records, 1653-1665,* p. 370; Somerset House, P. C. C., Ruthen, 141, printed in Henry F. Waters, *Genealogical Gleanings in England* (1901), I, 63-65; *New England Historical and Genealogical Register,* XXXVIII, 315-316; Massachusetts Historical Society *Collections,* 5th series, IX, 17-22.

[34] *New Haven Colonial Records, 1653-1665,* p. 301.

relating to the legacy. On June 4, 1660, he delivered to the general court for the jurisdiction a writing in which he announced the intention of the three surviving trustees—Theophilus Eaton had died in 1658—to give £100 of the legacy to Harvard College and to divide the remainder between John Davenport "for promoueing the Colledg-worke in a graduall way" in the New Haven Colony, and John Cullick and William Goodwin for the promotion of education in the town of Hadley, recently settled by secession from Hartford. Surrendering his interest in the legacy for the furtherance of a college at New Haven to the magistrates and elders of the colony, he requested the town of New Haven to contribute a part of the amount previously spent upon a town school—no longer necessary—toward the expenses of the colony school, to give the use of the Eldred lot if a college and grammar school were established at New Haven, and to pay the income from the oyster shell field toward the necessary disbursements for a college. Pleading "that the Honrd General Court will not suffer this gift to be lost frō. the Colony, but, as it becometh Fathers of the Commonwealth, will vse all good endeavo^{rs} to get it into their hands, and to assert their right in it for the Comō. good, that posterity may reape the good fruit of their Labours, and wisdom, and faithfullnes," he urged the colony to proceed with the grammar school.[35]

To Davenport's plea, the colony responded by adding £100 to outfit a schoolhouse and home for the master to the £40 a year granted in 1659. In the preceding year the town of Guilford had offered the Whitfield house to be used as a colony school, but disregarding the proposal, the colony voted to offer the school first to New Haven, second to Milford, and third to Guilford, and New Haven quickly responded by appointing a committee to provide

[35] *New Haven Colonial Records, 1653-1665,* pp. 356, 369-374.

the necessary buildings. On June 28, 1660, the magistrates and elders of the colony engaged Jeremiah Peck, son of William Peck of New Haven, from 1653 to 1656 a student at Harvard College and, since leaving Harvard, schoolmaster at Guilford, to conduct the colony school, teaching Latin, Greek, and Hebrew, and preparing boys for college at a salary of £40 a year. On the occasion of a visit of Peck to New Haven, on July 11, 1660, the town of New Haven agreed to add £10 to the salary voted by the colony, but refused to grant the income from the oyster shell field to the work until a college was actually under way at New Haven.[36]

In October, 1660, the colony grammar school at New Haven opened its doors. On the recommendation of Jeremiah Peck, in the following year the schoolhouse was enlarged and a more detailed agreement was entered upon between the colony and the schoolmaster.[37] From the start the school was a failure, however, and it never developed into the college of which Davenport had dreamed. Only five or six scholars from the town of New Haven appeared for instruction, and they were hardly of a caliber to justify the expenditures undertaken by colony and town. Loitering away their spare time in the home of Goody Spinage, they caused that estimable lady to be haled before the particular court at New Haven.[38] On September 25, 1661, Peck entered into an agreement with the people of Saybrook to become their minister.[39] Reluctant to admit failure, Davenport urged the town of New Haven to send more pupils to the school, but the colony was entering upon its two-year struggle for survival, and

[36] *Ibid.*, pp. 374-377; *New Haven Town Records, 1649-1662*, pp. 457-459.

[37] *New Haven Colonial Records, 1653-1665*, pp. 407-408; *New Haven Town Records, 1649-1662*, pp. 469-470, 473-474, 485.

[38] *Ibid.*, p. 488; *1662-1684*, p. 5.

[39] Sibley, *Biographical Sketches of Graduates of Harvard University*, I, 569-570.

on November 5, 1662, a general court for the jurisdiction voted to abandon the enterprise. The colony ordered the town of New Haven to repay £40 of the £100 advanced by the colony to outfit a schoolhouse and home for the master, but it was not until after the New Haven Colony had passed out of existence that the town of New Haven surrendered title to two great guns worth £30 to balance accounts with the other towns of the colony.[40]

After the fiasco of the colony school, in December, 1662, the town of New Haven engaged Recompense Osborn, Harvard College, 1661, as an elementary schoolmaster at a salary of £30. In the following spring Osborn gave up the work, and on June 15, 1663, George Pardee undertook "to teach english and to carry them on in lattine soe far as he could alsoe to Learne them to write, [and] something was spoken about teaching arethmaticke as very necessary in these parts," at a salary of £20 from the town and what he could collect from the parents and masters of his pupils. Dissatisfied with the arrangement, John Davenport suggested, on August 31, 1663, that the town employ a grammar schoolmaster at the moment available in the Bay, and on June 27, 1664, Israel Chauncy, a graduate of Harvard College in 1661, was expected at New Haven. Chauncy received a call to assist Adam Blakeman in the ministry at Stratford, however, and funds were low, and Pardee was cheap.[41]

Meanwhile Hopkins's estate had been restrained by Connecticut.[42] But when the trustees agreed to grant £400 of the legacy to Hartford, in the spring of 1664 the River Colony released the property. After the abandonment of the colony school, Davenport suggested that the share of

[40] *New Haven Colonial Records, 1653-1665*, pp. 471-472; *New Haven Town Records, 1662-1684*, pp. 175-176.

[41] *Ibid.*, pp. 15, 19, 48-49, 56, 94.

[42] Massachusetts Historical Society *Collections*, 4th series, VII, 512-514.

the New Haven Colony go to the town of New Haven "to fit youth (by learneing) for the service of god in Church and Comonwealth," and the town responded by voting £30 a year for a grammar school, and appointing a committee of magistrates, elders, deacons, and deputies to receive the bequest.[43] But it was not until 1667, after the New Haven Colony had ceased to exist, and the laws of Connecticut required the town of New Haven to maintain a grammar school, that such a school was again established at New Haven with Samuel Street as master.[44] In February, 1668, this institution boasted only eight in "latting," but that was a beginning, and on April 18, 1668, Davenport assigned £412, New Haven's share in Hopkins's estate in New England, and a half interest in the £500 due after Anne Hopkins's death from his estate in England to a self-perpetuating group of trustees for the maintenance of the grammar school or college already founded at New Haven. At this time he again requested the town to grant the use of the Eldred lot and the income from the oyster shell field to the school.[45]

In 1673 Samuel Street departed to take up the ministry at Wallingford, and the grammar school at New Haven lapsed, but in 1677 it was revived as a Latin and English school. To this school New Haven's share in Hopkins's estate in New England passed. Although often called a college in its early records, it never merited the title. When William Pennoyer, London merchant, member of the Society for propagation of the Gospel in New-England, and kinsman of Robert Pennoyer of Stamford, wished to benefit higher learning within the limits of the quondam New Haven Colony, he bequeathed revenue derived from an estate in Norfolk, England, for the support of two fellows and two scholars at the college at Cambridge in

[43] *New Haven Town Records, 1662-1684*, pp. 83-86.

[44] *Ibid.*, p. 203.

[45] *Ibid.*, pp. 218, 230-235.

Massachusetts Bay, one of the beneficiaries whenever possible to be a descendant of Robert Pennoyer of Stamford, and another to be of "the colony now or late called Newhaven colony."[46]

Not until thirty-five years after the New Haven Colony had ceased to exist did the college of which John Davenport had dreamed come into existence, and not until 1717 was it established at New Haven. So insignificant did this second institution of higher learning in New England long remain that it was not to it but to the college at Cambridge in Massachusetts Bay that the Court of Chancery in England awarded the £500 from Hopkins's English estate.[47] Nor were the efforts of the man who had striven so long and so ceaselessly to establish a college at New Haven recognized. The institution eventually settled at New Haven was called not Davenport but Yale College, in honor of Elihu Yale. A staunch Anglican, Yale had nothing in common with the dissenters at New Haven. His father, David Yale, had been one of the first settlers at Quinnipiac, but had soon departed for Massachusetts Bay, and there joined Robert Child in an attack on the ecclesiastical and civil systems of New England. His grandmother, Anne Eaton, had been excommunicated by the church at New Haven, and after the death of Theophilus Eaton, had lost little time in shaking the dust of the colony on Long Island Sound from her heels. Nevertheless, Yale permitted himself to be persuaded by Jeremy Dummer, colonial agent of Massachusetts Bay and Connecticut in England, to give some books, a portrait

46 Somerset House, P. C. C., Duke, 25, printed in Henry F. Waters, *Genealogical Gleanings in England* (1901), I, 504-506; "Harvard College Records," Colonial Society of Massachusetts *Publications*, XV-XVI, *passim;* Andrew McF. Davis, "Colony of Nox," American Antiquarian Society *Proceedings*, new series, IV, 266-270.

47 "Harvard College Records," Colonial Society of Massachusetts *Publications*, XV-XVI, *passim.*

and the arms of George I, and merchandise to the value of £200 sterling to the infant college at New Haven at the psychological moment to perpetuate his name for all time. Today the stately grandeur of Memorial Quadrangle and the Sterling Memorial Library are reminiscent not of Holy Trinity Church in Coventry, nor of Hilton Castle in the parish of Monk Wearmouth, nor of St. Stephen's in Coleman Street, London, but of the church of St. Giles at Wrexham and of the cathedral at Chester, both associated with the family of Yale! Only as an afterthought has one of a group of residential units been named Davenport College.

CHAPTER VIII

FARMERS, ARTISANS, AND MERCHANTS

LONDON merchants who wished to promote intercolonial and transatlantic commerce as well as Puritans searching for a laboratory in which the "Rules wch the scripture holds forth" might be applied to the government of church and state, the founders of the New Haven Colony located their first plantation and principal town at Quinnipiac or New Haven, the best harbor between the Connecticut River and New Amsterdam. From that point they pushed to the east and to the west, across the Sound to Long Island with its agricultural and dairy products, livestock, fishing, whaling, and wampum, to Delaware Bay, teeming with fish and whales, and up the Delaware and Paugassett rivers, flowing through soil suitable for the cultivation of grain and tobacco and offering access to the trade in beaver and peltry with the Indians of the interior.

The division of the soil was the first step in the economic life of the colony. Like the gathering of churches and the organization of plantation governments, the problem was met by adapting the practices of Massachusetts Bay as they had been outlined in the Cotton code to local needs. The charter of Charles I vested the title to the lands of the Bay Colony in the trading company which had evolved into a commonwealth. After perfecting its title by purchasing the rights of the Indians, the latter regranted the lands to the towns, and the towns in turn divided the soil among their inhabitants. Without charter from the crown, the planters of New Haven, Guilford, and Milford began with the second step and meticulously acquired title to their lands from the Indians. Beginning their settlements at slightly later dates, the planters of Southold, Stamford, and Branford purchased from Quinnipiac lands to which the mother plantation, in advance of settlement, had acquired title from the Indians. Except in the case of Branford, the towns began the division of the soil among their inhabitants before a colonial government came into existence. Probably for this reason the acquisition of title to land and the division of the soil among the inhabitants of the towns were problems which lay within the sphere of activity of the local governments, with which the colony seldom concerned itself.

Adventuring their persons and perhaps investing in a common stock, all heads of families who took part in the settlement of a town became shareholders, although not necessarily equal shareholders, in the lands acquired. Until the end of the seventeenth century ground was plentiful and it was desirable that it be brought under cultivation. With the exception of artisans who came for the specific purpose of plying their trades and certain merchants at New Haven who seem to have waived their rights to outlands, the original planters freely received any man who presented credentials of a good character and a godly life, and granted him a share in all that the town afforded.

Purchased bit by bit as the settlers felt the need of additional territory and the Indians were willing to sell, in time the holdings of the local governments became comparatively vast. The apportionment of these lands in a single division was rendered impossible, first by the piecemeal acquisition of the soil; second by the desire of the Puritan to see the homes of the inhabitants clustered about the meeting-house, an arrangement obviously impossible if each planter received his share in one large piece; and third by his wish to treat all men equitably, and since land varied in quality, to give to each planter a share of each kind of land. The result was that the towns became mosaics of small proprieties of which every planter might own a half dozen or more. Each inhabitant possessed a homelot near the meeting-house, one or more pieces of upland, one or more pieces of meadow, and a share in all undivided lands.

The division of the soil always began with the assignment of homelots. At New Haven[1] and Guilford[2] the residential plots were laid out around a central common and along streets running at right angles from it. At Milford they were laid out along the banks of Mill River and West End Brook,[3] and in Southold along both sides of a long town street.[4] In Oyster Bay they were arranged along streets running parallel to and at right angles from the harbor.[5] In New Haven, Guilford, and Milford the size of the homelots varied with the wealth of the planter and the size of his family, in Guilford between one and ten acres, in Milford between one and seven and one-half acres. In Southold, Stamford and Branford homelots of uniform size were laid out, in Southold lots of about four acres, in Stamford and Branford lots of about half that size. At Oyster Bay a distinction was drawn between the first settlers and those who came later, the former re-

1 For a map of the homelots at New Haven, see Edward E. Atwater, *History of the Colony of New Haven,* frontispiece.

2 For a map of a portion of the homelots at Guilford, see Alvan Talcott, *Chittenden Family* (1882), p. 9.

3 Milford Land Records, I, 78-82. For a map of the homelots at Milford, see Edward E. Atwater, *History of the Colony of New Haven,* p. 155. For an excellent study of the land system of a town which fell within the limits of the New Haven Colony, see Leonard W. Labaree, *Milford, Connecticut: The Early Development of a Town as Shown in Its Land Records* (Tercentenary Commission of the State of Connecticut, 1933).

4 *Southold Records,* I, frontispiece.

5 For a map of the homelots at Oyster Bay, see Howland Delano Perrine, *The Wright Family of Oysterbay, L. I.,* opposite p. 59.

ceiving homelots of six acres, the latter, of only five.[6] Even when the rule of uniformity was followed, planters disposed of their residential plots in whole or in part and the holdings eventually varied in size.

After the clearing of the homelots and the erection of houses and barns, further divisions were in order. Each homelot entitled its owner to a share in the upland and meadow, the common pasture, and the common and undivided lands. Regardless of whether homelots proportionate to the value of each planter's estate and the size of his family or homelots of equal size had been laid out, the upland and meadow were always divided in proportion to persons and estates, with special favor occasionally shown to the minister or magistrate or any person who had rendered unusual service. Some of the towns applied the rule of persons and estate only in a general way. Guilford placed its planters in £500, £250, £100, and £50 groups.[7] Branford seems to have had £500, £200, and £100 groups.[8] Huntington had £200 and £100 groups.[9] If the rule of persons and estate had been followed in the assignment of homelots, the size of the homelot became the basis of calculation in the assignment of upland and meadow.

In all towns planters of small or no estate fared comparatively well. At New Haven they received a small homelot, four acres of planting ground, and for every person in the family an acre beyond the East River.[10] At Guilford they were placed in the £50 group. At Branford the allotment of land to planters with estates of less than £100 was governed by a special rule.

The division of upland and meadow began with the sizing or evaluation of the land to determine the additional

[6] *Ibid.*, p. 34.
[7] Guilford Records, B, 11.
[8] Branford Records, I, 5, 251.
[9] *Huntington Records*, I, 222, 237.
[10] *New Haven Colonial Records, 1638-1649*, p. 43.

quantity of unusually poor land that should be allowed in order to compensate for deficiency in quality. Then the lots were numbered according to the number of planters entitled to share in the division, with an extra lot or two for late comers, the town determining the location of lot No. 1 and controlling the distribution that followed. Finally the planters drew numbers to determine the location of each man's holding, the planter who drew No. 1 taking possession of the corresponding piece of land, the planter who drew No. 2, of the next lot, and so on through the group. In the larger settlements, planters with homelots in a particular quarter were usually assigned upland and meadow in fields as conveniently near as possible. In the smaller settlements, every planter in the town might participate in the division of a single field. A planter who performed unusual service was occasionally permitted to choose the location of his upland and meadow.

In New Haven the first division of outlands was carried through in 1639 and 1640. It consisted of five acres of upland within a radius of two miles from the homelots per £100 of estate and two and one-half acres per person, five acres of meadow within a radius of two miles per £100 of estate and one-half acre per person, and one acre of land in the neck per £100 of estate and one-half acre per person. A second division was authorized almost immediately thereafter. It consisted of twenty acres of upland beyond the radius of two miles per £100 of estate and two and one-half acres per person. Thus each planter owned a homelot, a piece of first division upland, a piece of first division meadow, a piece of land in the neck, and a piece of second division upland, five pieces of land which by a lucky chance might be contiguous but which were probably scattered about the town.

In the other towns grants of land were similarly contrived. In Guilford the first division of upland and meadow took place before 1645, a further division was made in 1646, and the upland and meadow at Hammonassett were divided in 1653. In Milford fields to the southeast and southwest of the homelots were apportioned before 1643, a second division of upland and meadow took place in 1642 and 1643, and further divisions were authorized in 1646 and 1657. Before leaving Wethersfield the planters of Stamford met to determine the number of acres of upland and marsh to be assigned to each, "the man under consideration absenting himself while his case was in hand." The allotments made at this time varied between three and twenty-eight acres. In a town meeting at Stamford in December, 1641, the Wethersfield men ordered a field for the freeholders to be fenced in before the following April.[11]

Subject to the rules and regulations of the towns, common pasture for cows, oxen, sheep, goats, and young cattle, and the woodlands were shared by all inhabitants.

The planters were usually required to erect houses upon their homelots and to bring part of their upland under cultivation within a period of two or three years. The value of the early dwellings varied within wide limits. At New Haven the wealthier inhabitants erected some of the finest houses to be found in seventeenth-century New England. At Branford the houses varied between the £40 dwelling of Robert Rose and the £2 cottage of Mica Tenter. To protect these edifices from fire, the towns required the householders to sweep their chimneys at stated intervals and to keep ladders that would reach to the housetops. Planters were also required to keep the highways before their lands open and free from trees and to take part in the burning of the neighboring woods.

At Guilford the engrossing of land was feared, and without the consent of the plantation court the sale of

[11] Stamford Records, I, 6.

land even to another planter was forbidden.[12] Elsewhere lands passed freely from planter to planter within the settlement. In all towns the sale of land to non-townsmen was forbidden until the purchasers had been passed upon by the towns. Once approved, the newcomers of these early days enjoyed all the rights and privileges of the original settlers.

By 1665 only a beginning had been made in the work of dividing up the lands of the towns. At New Haven the third division of land did not take place until fifteen years after the New Haven Colony had come to an end. Continuing through long years, the process was still going on in some of the towns of the erstwhile New Haven Colony at the time the colonies threw off their dependence upon the mother country and a new nation came into existence.[13]

To some extent all planters of the colony engaged in agriculture, raising peas, beans, wheat, Indian corn, hops, and fruit. Doubtless influenced by the success of the settlers of the neighboring plantation of Saybrook with tobacco, in 1654 both William Leete of Guilford and the town of New Haven gave some thought to that crop. Two years later Milford approved the sale of an island in its harbor to Charles Deal for the cultivation of tobacco. Southold also had its tobacco ground.[14]

A variety of livestock—horses, mares, working oxen, cows, sheep, goats, and hogs—was raised, and to the agricultural products of the colony must be added beef, pork, and dairy products.

[12] Guilford Records, B, 11.

[13] The last recorded meeting of the proprietors of the town of Guilford was held on April 3, 1826.

[14] Papers of General Desborough 1651-1660, Egerton MSS., 2519, fol. 10; *New Haven Town Records, 1649-1662*, p. 207; Milford Land Records, I, 41; Leonard W. Labaree, *Milford, Connecticut: The Early Development of a Town as Shown by Its Land Records*, p. 14; *Southold Records*, I, 84.

The presence of livestock in close proximity to the planting fields made elaborate regulations regarding fencing necessary. The enclosing of homelots was sometimes optional, sometimes required. If the lot adjoined a common field or the land of a neighbor who desired a fence to be erected, it was always required. Planting fields and meadows in which the whole town was interested were fenced by the inhabitants of the town. Lesser areas were fenced by the proprietors of the field. In both cases the fencing was done in proportion to men's holdings in the field. The height of the fence—four feet, four feet two inches, or four and one-half feet—was carefully specified. Lots were drawn to determine the section of fence for which each man was responsible and initialed stakes were driven into the ground at the beginning and end of each man's proportion, a practice probably familiar to those planters who had come from the rural districts of England.[15] In all towns fence-viewers who reported all defects in fencing became important officers.

Regulations regarding livestock were at first made in the town meetings and later by either the town meetings or the townsmen. Swine were yoked and ringed to keep them out of the planting fields and either locked up or driven far into the woods. Common pasture and planting fields thrown open to be used as pasture were stinted, and the number and kind of animals each planter was entitled to put within the field, depending upon the size of his holding and the kind of animal, were carefully stated. By a specified date each spring the fence around the planting fields was repaired and the animals within the field were removed, although sometimes exceptions were made in favor of working cattle and animals too weak to fend for themselves. For about six months of the year the planters

[15] Alfred Ridley Bax, "The Church Registers and Parish Account Books of Ockley, Co. Surrey," *Surrey Archaeological Collections*, X, 24-25.

hired herdsmen to drive out and care for the milch cows, and either themselves took turns in driving the dry cattle to pasture or employed other herdsmen for that purpose. Stray cattle and hogs that broke into the planting fields were picked up by individuals or by the town pounder and placed in the pound until the owner paid a fee and reclaimed them. In every town bulls were maintained for breeding purposes. Horses were branded and cattle earmarked with the insignia of the owner, and both brand and earmark carefully recorded by the secretary of the town. To protect the cattle of the inhabitants, the towns offered bounties for the heads of wolves, bears, and foxes.

Artisans, often woefully inexperienced and their products shoddy and unmarketable, soon appeared in the towns of the colony. Although building was usually a cooperative enterprise, individuals more skilful than their fellows erected or supervised the erection of the crude meeting-houses, schools, and bridges. Among such were William Andrews of New Haven and John and Richard Ogden of Stamford, the Ogdens sufficiently renowned to receive a contract for the construction of a twenty-five-hundred-guilder stone church at New Amsterdam.[16]

In every town a miller appeared. Sometimes he built his own mill, sometimes he operated one erected by a group of undertakers or by the town. At New Haven several individuals who enjoyed a monopoly of the grinding business put up the first mill, and installed John Lovell as miller in 1642, George Larremore in 1648, and William Janes in 1649. The town looked after repairs and regulated the enterprise, leaving the order in which men's corn should be ground to the discretion of the miller and the rule of equity. Complaints of the dilatoriness of the miller in grinding the corn brought to him were numerous. In 1659 the town undertook the construction of a sec-

[16] New York Colonial MSS., II, 18.

ond mill, but before its completion bought and repaired the first one and installed Mathew Rowe as miller. Rowe complained of the mill, and the town voted to build a new edifice on the site of the first. Then Rowe fell ill, and Richard Miles, who "said he was no Milner, (though some thing he had done that way in England when the Milner was out of the way)," was installed. The complaints of his grinding were many, and weary of the enterprise, the town considered selling or letting the mill. In 1662 the destruction of the edifice by fire solved the problem. Until a third mill, like the first built by private enterprise, was completed, the inhabitants of New Haven ground their corn at Milford.[17]

In Guilford in December, 1645, the town completed the construction of a mill. After Henry Whitfield had declined to operate it, the town sold it to Robert Kitchel. The mill was damaged in a storm almost immediately, however, and though the town undertook the necessary repairs, Kitchel sold it back to the plantation for £80. The town installed Thomas Norton as miller in 1646, and Francis Bushnell two years later.[18] Soon after the settlement of Milford, William Fowler undertook the construction of a mill, the town agreeing to take it off his hands at £180 or to permit him to collect satisfactory tolls. In 1645 the planters assisted Fowler in repairing the structure, and in 1647 the town freed the mill lot from rates during Fowler's lifetime and his maintenance and operation of the mill.[19] At Stamford the inhabitants employed Samuel Swayne of Wethersfield to build a mill at the common charge and sold it to Thurston Raynor and Francis Law for £74 10*s*. Destroyed almost immediately,

[17] *New Haven Colonial Records, 1638-1649; New Haven Town Records, 1649-1662; passim.*

[18] Guilford Records, A, 5, 7, 10, 11, 23, 29.

[19] Milford Land Records, I, 2, 9, 15.

probably in a storm, it was soon replaced by a second mill, like the first built at the common charge.[20] The inhabitants of Branford also employed Samuel Swayne, one of the settlers of the town, to erect a mill at the common charge. Upon its completion they let it out, to the builder in 1654, to Nathaniel Gunn in 1660, and to Mica Palmer in 1664.[21] On Long Island John Payne was operating a mill at Toms Creek, Hashamomack, Southold, in 1664.[22] The inhabitants of Oyster Bay granted lands and a stream of water upon which to construct and operate an English mill similar to that at Norwalk on the mainland to Henry Townsend, September 16, 1661, authorizing Townsend to collect tolls of one-tenth of the meal ground. In the neighboring plantation of Huntington William Leveridge seems to have erected the first mill, soon disposing of it to William Ludlam.[23]

At early dates bakers also appeared. In 1640 the plantation of Quinnipiac licensed Peter Brown "to bake to sell so Long as he gives no offence in itt Justly." Upon complaint of the size of loaves of bread in 1649, Governor Eaton read the Massachusetts law regarding bakers to a town meeting at New Haven, and when a code of laws was prepared for the colony in 1655, an assize of bread found a place in it. James Rogers of Milford baked biscuit on a wholesale scale, but not to the entire satisfaction of his customers, and perhaps for this reason, in 1655 the town of New Haven requested Richard Miles to establish a bakehouse for biscuit.[24]

Thomas Naish and his sons John, Joseph, and Timo-

20 Stamford Records, I, 8, 15.

21 Branford Records, I, 19, 40, 177, 227.

22 *Southold Records*, I, 138, 371-372, 429-430.

23 *Oyster Bay Records*, I, 40-41; *Huntington Records*, I, 101-103.

24 *New Haven Colonial Records, 1638-1649*, pp. 29, 466, 495; *New Haven Colonial Records, 1653-1665*, pp. 142-143, 574; *New Haven Town Records, 1649-1662*, p. 260.

thy, and John Potter, Jr., at New Haven, Thomas Smith at Guilford, and William Salmon at Southold followed the calling of smith. In 1648 Branford authorized the erection of a smith's shop and the purchase of a pair of bellows, but depended upon the Naishes and John Potter, Jr., to operate them.

Thomas Osborne and Thomas Jeffrey at New Haven, Benjamin Wright at Guilford, and Miles Merwin at Milford undertook the tanning of hides, and spoiled so many "for want of Skill or Experience in the Tanne of this Country"[25] that leather-sealers became necessary officers in every town. John Meggs, Robert Seely, and Ralph Dayton at New Haven and Philip Grove at Milford made up some of the hides into shoes.

Henry Tomlinson of Milford, John Corey of Southold, and Gabriel Linly of Branford followed the trade of weaving. Sawyers, coopers, wheelwrights, and rope-makers appeared, tailors at New Haven, a dish-turner at Branford, and brick-makers at New Haven and Hashamomack in Southold.

Long interested in the production of bog iron in New England, John Winthrop, Jr., visited the New Haven Colony on a prospecting tour in the spring of 1655.[26] Discovering a convenient place for an ironworks and a furnace between New Haven and Branford, he succeeded in interesting John Davenport, Theophilus Eaton, and Stephen Goodyear of New Haven and Jasper Crane of Branford in the project. On February 13, 1656, John Winthrop, Jr., Stephen Goodyear, undertakers of New Haven with John Cooper as their agent, and undertakers of Branford with Jasper Crane as their agent organized an ironworks company.[27] New Haven and Branford granted

25 *New Haven Colonial Records, 1638-1649*, pp. 86, 215, 345-353, 356; *New Haven Colonial Records, 1653-1665*, pp. 597-598.

26 *New Haven Town Records, 1649-1662*, p. 235.

27 Massachusetts Historical Society, Winthrop MSS., XIII, 115.

the undertakers permission to procure wood, water, ironstone, ore, shells for lime, and other necessaries within their limits, five-eighths from New Haven and three-eighths from Branford.[28] The town of New Haven granted a collier about to come to the ironworks twelve acres of land provided the industry were carried on and the collier remained in the town for a period of three years.[29] The colony freed persons entirely engaged in the ironworks and their estates from rates, and required any one who attached the estate of an undertaker in the enterprise to assume his responsibilities.[30]

Church and town at New Haven and the colonial government had long tried to induce John Winthrop, Jr., to settle at New Haven, the town offering him Richard Malbon's house as a gift if he would make New Haven his permanent abode or rent free if he came but for a time. In order to direct the ironworks from a nearby location, Winthrop at first agreed to rent the Malbon house and later to purchase it outright, paying for it in goats.[31] Elizabeth Davenport oversaw the preparation of the house, the cleaning of the well, the installation of a new pump, the safeguarding of the apples from frost, the warming of the rooms for the reception of the Winthrop family, and the provision of tables and chairs, twenty loads of wood, thirty bushels of wheat, twelve pounds of candles, and a cleanly, thrifty maid-servant.[32] In the fall of 1656 the outstanding metallurgist and physician in

28 *New Haven Town Records, 1649-1662,* pp. 260-261; Branford Records, I, 44; Connecticut State Library, Robert C. Winthrop Collection of Connecticut Manuscripts, I, 84.

29 *New Haven Town Records, 1649-1662,* p. 279.

30 *New Haven Colonial Records, 1653-1665,* pp. 149, 173.

31 *Ibid.,* p. 120; *New Haven Town Records, 1649-1662,* pp. 241, 313-314; Massachusetts Historical Society *Collections,* 3d series, X, 8-12; 4th series, VII, 470-471; Leonard Bacon, *Thirteen Historical Discourses,* pp. 369-371.

32 Massachusetts Historical Society *Collections,* 3d series, X, 12-15; Leonard Bacon, *Thirteen Historical Discourses,* pp. 371-372.

New England took up his residence at New Haven, and in the following spring the ironworks were in operation.[33] On May 21, 1657, the neighboring colony of Connecticut elected Winthrop as governor.[34] This action was taken six days before the general court of elections assembled at New Haven, where, if he had been free, Winthrop would undoubtedly have been chosen to office and eventually to the governorship, for Theophilus Eaton died in the following January. It was a shrewd move on the part of Connecticut, destined to change the history of the two colonies.

After Winthrop's removal to Hartford, interest in the ironworks lagged. In the summer of 1657 Stephen Goodyear bought a vessel capable of carrying twenty or thirty tons of bog ore at New Amsterdam,[35] but he soon decided to dispose of his interest in the works and the town of New Haven protested unless it might pass upon the purchasers.[36] Beyond the jurisdiction of New Haven, Winthrop leased his interest in the undertaking to Thomas Clarke and William Paine of Boston, who took the output of his mines in other parts of New England. Regarding the lease with distrust, New Haven appointed a committee to consider it, but eventually permitted Clarke and Paine to proceed. On April 29, 1658, Branford granted the lessees further concessions.[37] When hearth stones sent from England by Stephen Goodyear proved unsatisfactory, Davenport advocated the importation of stones from Quarry-Hill, near London, as cheaper than the stones a Milford merchant could bring from the Isle of

[33] Massachusetts Historical Society *Collections,* 4th series, VII, 402-405.

[34] *Connecticut Colonial Records,* I, 297.

[35] Massachusetts Historical Society, Winthrop MSS., XIII, 116.

[36] *New Haven Town Records, 1649-1662,* p. 321.

[37] *Ibid.,* pp. 330-331, 349; Branford Records, I, 45; Connecticut State Library, Robert C. Winthrop Collection of Connecticut Manuscripts, I, 84.

Wight.[38] After more than six years of endeavor, the founder of the New Haven Colony was able to inform Winthrop that they had been blowing at the ironworks and produced five sows of iron, and would undertake the manufacture of pots on the morrow.[39] The colony suffered more than it gained from the enterprise, however, for not only were the neighboring lands, highways, and fences injured by the dam at the works, but a group of turbulent, disorderly, non-assimilable workers was introduced into the colony and remained there long after the jurisdiction of New Haven had come to an end.

At about the time the ironworks was established at New Haven, John Tucker announced the intention of making steel at Southold, and desired to be freed from rates. He soon abandoned the enterprise, however, and in 1660 requested liberty to build a sawmill.[40]

More daring than the ironworks was the attempt to build transatlantic vessels on Long Island Sound. As early as 1644 Theophilus Eaton, Stephen Goodyear, Richard Malbon, Thomas Gregson, and perhaps other merchants at New Haven intrusted the construction of an ocean-going vessel to John Wakeman, Joshua Atwater, Jasper Crane, and Richard Miles. Though ill built and very "walt-sided," in due course the ship was completed. Entrusted with a cargo of wheat, peas, hides, beaver, and peltry, and manuscript writings of John Davenport at New Haven and Thomas Hooker at Hartford, about the middle of January, 1646, the vessel ploughed its way through three miles of ice in New Haven harbor and tackled the stormy Atlantic. On board were Thomas Gregson, Nathaniel Turner, George Lamberton, the wife of Stephen Goodyear, and Francis Austin, the last of

38 Massachusetts Historical Society *Collections,* 4th series, VII, 500.

39 *Ibid.,* p. 524.

40 *New Haven Colonial Records, 1653-1665,* pp. 153, 175; *Southold Records,* I, 212.

whom had borrowed £2 10*s*. from Thomas Dunck of Guilford with which to buy a handsome coat to wear when presenting himself to his father in England. After the lapse of many months a mirage of the ship was said to have appeared over the harbor at New Haven, but the vessel itself neither reached its destination nor returned to its port of departure.[41] Despite this initial setback, on October 7, 1646, a second vessel was about to be launched at New Haven; in the summer of 1648 a third vessel was under construction; and in the spring of 1661 Charles Glover laid a fifty-foot keel at Southold.[42]

In addition to the wages which they received, the amount of which was sometimes regulated by the towns,[43] artisans among the original settlers shared in all divisions of land on a parity with the other planters. Craftsmen brought in from without for the specific purpose of plying their trades met with less favorable treatment. They were in great demand and moved frequently, and the towns had no desire to bestow land in perpetuity and a share in future divisions upon an individual who might soon move on to the next town. Itinerant craftsmen consequently received only the use of a small piece of land during their residence in the town.

Every settlement had an ordinary and a shop or two. At New Haven William Andrews, or rather his wife, ran the ordinary, and the Widow Stolyon retailed notions at exorbitant prices.

41 *New Haven Colonial Records, 1638-1649*, pp. 147, 283, 329-333; *Winthrop's Journal*, II, 263, 275-276, 286-287, 346; "Roxbury Land and Church Records," Record Commissioners of the City of Boston, *Sixth Report*, p. 190; William Hubbard, "A General History of New England," Massachusetts Historical Society *Collections*, 2d series, V-VI, 321-322; Cotton Mather, *Magnalia Christi Americana* (1702), Book I, pp. 25-26; Leonard Bacon, *Thirteen Historical Discourses*, pp. 105-107.

42 *New Haven Colonial Records, 1638-1649*, pp. 273, 389-390, 393-396; *New Haven Colonial Records, 1653-1665*, pp. 392-399.

43 *New Haven Colonial Records, 1638-1649*, pp. 44, 52-56, 61.

To the wharves and warehouses of Stephen Goodyear, Thomas Gregson, John Evance, Richard Malbon, Nathaniel Turner, and George Lamberton at New Haven, Alexander Bryan at Milford, and other leading merchants of the colony came the surplus products of the region: peas, flour, biscuit, malt, livestock, dairy products, beef, pork, hides and leather, furs and skins, shingles, clapboards, and pipestaves, fish, the products of the whale, the crude work of the artisans, and wampum.

Within the New Haven Colony the merchants exchanged their goods with merchants from New Netherland[44] and the other English colonies.[45] To further this domestic trade, semiannual markets or fairs for cattle and other goods were held at New Haven on the third Wednesdays of May and September from 1644 to 1655.[46] Money was scarce and trade was carried on by barter or with Indian wampum, a method of exchange which necessitated the regulation of prices and measures.

Beyond the limits of the colony, the merchants found their first, nearest, and best market at New Amsterdam. In New Netherland agriculture was seriously hampered by the imposition of tenths upon the products of the soil. Looking toward New England for food not only for the Dutch possessions on the mainland but for Curaçao, the director general of New Netherland protested when the supply was cut off even in time of war. At New Amsterdam the English merchants traded provisions and wampum for furs and skins, wines and liquors, and ships.[47] By 1656 this trade had reached sufficient proportions to

44 New York Colonial MSS., III, 31, 71; IV, 141, 330, 397.

45 *Aspinwall Notarial Records*, p. 172.

46 *New Haven Colonial Records, 1638-1649*, p. 130; *1653-1665*, p. 147.

47 New York Colonial MSS., III, 19; IV, 268, 301; XI, 6, 25, 41, 70; *New York Colonial Documents*, XIV, 158-159, 184; *Aspinwall Notarial Records*, pp. 239-241; *The Records of New Amsterdam from 1653 to 1674*, III, 272.

justify the appointment of Jan Peecq as broker to the merchants at New Amsterdam, "as he speaks Dutch and English."[48] To encourage the movement of cattle toward New Netherland, in 1658 Director General Stuyvesant established semiannual fairs at New Amsterdam, one for lean cattle throughout the month of May and another for fattened cattle to last from October 20 to November 30, and sent placards in English to advertise the fact to Stamford, Milford, and Southold.[49]

Despite the demand for their products, the English merchants enjoyed the trade of New Netherland only after they had met the impositions of the Dutch West India Company and the director general and council of New Netherland. To equalize burdens borne by Dutch and English merchants, in 1642 Director General Kieft and his council levied an import duty of ten per cent upon all goods upon which an export duty had not been paid in the United Netherlands, and ordered the English to pay the export duties authorized by the "freedoms and exemptions" of 1640.[50] After the Dutch had driven the New Haveners from the junction of the Delaware and Schuylkill rivers, they ordered George Lamberton to pay the export duties authorized by the Dutch West India Company on the beaver skins he continued to carry from the Delaware.[51] This policy of equalizing the burdens of Dutch and English merchants seems to have continued, for upon the arrival of Stuyvesant in 1647, he was greeted by complaints of the English against the high duties on imports and exports collected at New Amsterdam.[52] After

48 New York Colonial MSS., VI, 308.

49 *Laws and Ordinances of New Netherland, 1638-1674*, p. 364; *The Records of New Amsterdam from 1653 to 1674*, VII, 216.

50 *Laws and Ordinances of New Netherland, 1638-1674*, p. 31.

51 New York Colonial MSS., IV, 134; *New York Colonial Documents*, XII, 24; XIV, 41.

52 New York Colonial MSS., XI, 2, 3, 5, 6, 9; *New Haven Colonial Rec-*

pointing out that the English were paying eight per cent less than were the Dutch,[53] in the spring of 1649 Stuyvesant suspended all duties paid by the English.[54] The Dutch merchants promptly complained of the advantage enjoyed by their English rivals, and asked exemption for themselves.[55] To meet the complaint, the directors of the Amsterdam chamber of the Dutch West India Company ordered Stuyvesant to subject the merchants of New England and Virginia to an import duty of sixteen per cent on goods from New England and Virginia, but to permit the free export of goods from New Netherland to New England.[56] Following a reduction from sixteen per cent to ten per cent in the duty on goods from the United Netherlands to New Netherland, provisions and other raw goods from New England were put upon the free list at New Amsterdam, and the duty upon other merchandise from New England was reduced to ten per cent.[57]

The merchants of the New Haven Colony not only struggled themselves against these impositions of the Dutch West India Company and the director general and council of New Netherland, but they aided foreigners to evade them. To escape the payment of customs at New Amsterdam, William Westerhouse and Samuel Goodanhouse, merchants, and Cornelis Claesen Snoy, master, carried to New Haven the *Hercules* or *St. Beninio*, a ves-

ords, 1638-1649, pp. 514-516, 520-522; *Plymouth Colony Records*, IX, 107-108, 113-115.

[53] New York Colonial MSS., XI, 6; *New Haven Colonial Records, 1638-1649*, pp. 520-522.

[54] New York Colonial MSS., XI, 10, 11; *New Haven Colonial Records, 1638-1649*, pp. 532-535; *New York Colonial Documents*, I, 374.

[55] *Ibid.*, I, 259-270, 337; *Laws and Ordinances of New Netherland, 1638-1674*, p. 126.

[56] New York Colonial MSS., XI, 37, 53; *New York Colonial Documents*, I, 344; XIV, 138-139, 169.

[57] *Ibid.*, p. 416; *Laws and Ordinances of New Netherland, 1638-1674*, pp. 343, 348.

sel belonging to an Italian at Amsterdam and sailing from Medemblik. After unloading their cargo at the English port, the Dutch merchants prepared to sail for Virginia to pick up a cargo of tobacco.[58] Director General Stuyvesant and the council of New Netherland had recently sold the "old and decayed" *Swoll* to Stephen Goodyear of New Haven for nine thousand guilders to be paid in provisions and wampum.[59] Learning of the presence of the *St. Beninio* in the English port, they put a Dutch crew aboard the *Swoll,* and gaining entrance to the harbor at New Haven under pretext of delivering the *Swoll* to Goodyear, the crew seized the *St. Beninio* and carried it to New Amsterdam. There the Dutch condemned the vessel for illegal trading and smuggling.[60] To evade the consequences of their act, Westerhouse, Goodanhouse, and a third Dutchman took out citizenship in the New Haven Colony, thus gaining the support of both the colony and the New England Confederation against the authorities of New Netherland.[61]

To enjoy the advantages of dual citizenship, Isaac Allerton, wealthiest of the Pilgrims but at heart more Dutch than English, with mercantile connections in New England and New Netherland, on the Delaware, in Virginia, Barbados, and Curaçao, qualified as an inhabitant of both New Netherland and the New Haven Colony. In New Amsterdam he maintained a house and a quay on the south side of Pearl Street on the East River, between Fulton

[58] New York Colonial MSS., IV, 330, 333, 343, 344, 345, 353; XI, 3, 4, 5, 8, 9; *New York Colonial Documents,* I, 337, 345, 461; *New Haven Colonial Records, 1638-1649,* pp. 508-516, 525-530; *Plymouth Colony Records,* IX, 112-115, 146-148, 182, 189.

[59] New York Colonial MSS., IV, 301, 330.

[60] Against this combination of public and private business, Goodyear continued to protest for some time to come. New York Colonial MSS., XI, 25. Isaac Allerton seems to have purchased the vessel for the account of Thomas Cromwell of Boston. *Aspinwall Notarial Records,* pp. 216-217, 219-220.

[61] *New Haven Colonial Records, 1638-1649,* p. 355.

and Ferry streets, enjoyed burgher privileges, including the right to trade on the North and South rivers, served as a member of the council of eight, contributed toward the expenses of the city, and had sufficient influence with the director general to bring about the removal of Jean Paul Jacquet as commissary on the South River. At New Haven he built a "grand house on the Creek, with Four Porches." When dealing with the Dutch he posed as a resident of New Amsterdam; when dealing with the English he lived at New Haven.[62]

Traveling farther afield, the merchants of the New Haven Colony exchanged their goods for furs and skins, at first at Varkens Kill and the trading-post at the junction of the Delaware and Schuylkill rivers, and after the expulsion of the English from the Delaware at the settlements of the Dutch and Swedes.[63] In Virginia they traded their merchandise for tobacco and perhaps for Negroes and goods brought from England.[64] In the West Indies, especially at Barbados, they exchanged provisions for sugar, a trade which had assumed sufficient proportions by 1651 to justify a group of Barbados merchants in acquiring title to Forrett's or Shelter Island and transforming it into a stopping place in the voyage between England and Barbados.[65] In the Madeiras, the Canaries,

62 New York Colonial MSS., *passim; The Records of New Amsterdam from 1653 to 1674, passim; Aspinwall Notarial Records, passim;* Walter S. Allerton, *A History of the Allerton Family* (1900).

63 *New Haven Colonial Records, 1638-1649,* p. 341; New York Colonial MSS., XI, 34; *Narratives of Early Pennsylvania, West New Jersey, and Delaware, 1630-1707* (1912), p. 158.

64 *New Haven Colonial Records, 1638-1649,* pp. 35, 335; New York State Library, General Entries, I, 1664-1665, 151, calendared in University of the State of New York, *State Library Bulletin, History No. 2,* May 1899, p. 61; Maverick's Description of New England, Egerton MSS., 2395, fols. 397-411, printed in *New England Historical and Genealogical Register,* XXXIX, 33-48.

65 *Ibid.; An Account of Some of the Labours, Exercises, Travels and Perils, by Sea and Land, of John Taylor* (London, 1710).

Spain, Portugal, and Italy, the merchants of the New Haven Colony exchanged their goods for wines and the products of the semi-tropics; at Boston, Plymouth, Hartford, and Saybrook, for the manufactures of New England and Old;[66] in Newfoundland, for fish;[67] and in England, for manufactures of all kinds.[68]

With the exception of the prohibition of the sale of arms and ammunition to the Indians by all the colonies of New England, the duties on the commerce of the Connecticut River imposed by Connecticut to pay for the fort at Saybrook,[69] and the retaliatory duties levied by Massachusetts Bay,[70] the trade of New England was free. The single-staple colonies of Virginia and Barbados welcomed the provisions of New England. Within the English world, only the mother country, endeavoring to add to its revenue from the customs, to encourage English shipping, and to make England the staple for goods coming from and going to the colonies, imposed restrictions. The early Stuarts required the shipment of the tobacco of Virginia to England. The Commonwealth subjected tobacco shipped to the mother country by way of New England to duties. In 1650 it forbade traffic with foreigners, and in 1651 it required the importation of colonial products into England and its colonies in vessels owned by Englishmen and manned by a crew the majority of which was English.

66 *New Haven Colonial Records, 1638-1649*, pp. 35, 281; *Winthrop's Journal*, II, 126; *Aspinwall Notarial Records*, pp. 22, 85, 106, 241.

67 Maverick's Description of New England, Egerton MSS., 2395, fols. 397-411, printed in *New England Historical and Genealogical Register*, XXXIX, 33-48.

68 *New Haven Colonial Records, 1638-1649*, pp. 298-299; *New Haven Colonial Records, 1653-1665*, pp. 176, 186. For an account of the trade of New England by John Scott, who knew Long Island, see Sloane MSS., 3662.

69 *Connecticut Colonial Records*, I, 119-122, 189-190; *Plymouth Colony Records*, IX, 80, 89-93, 120-136.

70 *Massachusetts Colony Records*, II, 268-270; *Plymouth Colony Records*, IX, 153-158.

In 1660 the restored Stuart monarchy reënacted the law of 1651 with the added provisions that three-fourths of the crew of every English ship must be English, and that sugar, tobacco, cotton-wool, indigo, ginger, fustic, and other dyewoods must be carried from the English colonies directly to England. In 1662 it excluded foreign-built but English-owned ships from the category of English ships. In 1663 it made England the staple for all goods shipped to the English colonies, salt for the fisheries, horses and provisions from Scotland and Ireland, and wines from the Madeiras and Azores only excepted.[71]

To the restrictions imposed by the mother country the merchants of the English colonies paid little heed. The tobacco of Virginia continued to be carried to the Dutch colony.[72] Englishmen and English ships frequented the ports of New Netherland and Dutchmen and Dutch ships the ports of the English colonies.[73] Only the provision in the law of 1660 that the master of a vessel trading in enumerated commodities in an English colony must give bond to carry those commodities to England, Ireland, or another English colony for a moment non-plussed them. Soon recovering their equanimity, however, they gave the bond, carried the tobacco of Virginia to a port in New England or to Oyster Bay or Huntington on Long Island, and having thus conformed to the letter of the law, from those points transshipped it to New Amsterdam, a voyage which rather mystified their Dutch customers.[74] Blissfully ignorant of any prohibition of Anglo-Dutch com-

[71] George Louis Beer, *The Origins of the British Colonial System, 1578-1660* (1908); *The Old Colonial System, 1660-1754* (2 vols., 1912).

[72] *Laws and Ordinances of New Netherland, 1638-1674*, pp. 139-140, 189, 307-308; *New York Colonial Documents*, XIV, 371, 400.

[73] *Ibid.*, p. 225; *New Haven Colonial Records, 1653-1665*, pp. 25, 112; *The Records of New Amsterdam from 1653 to 1674*, II, 364.

[74] *Ibid.*, IV, 298, 303; *New York Colonial Documents*, XIV, 566-567.

merce in 1660,[75] merchants of the New Haven Colony were probably not without a share in the traffic.

As a commercial enterprise, at the end of a quarter of a century the New Haven Colony had not met with the expectations of the founders. The harbor at Quinnipiac proved incommodious. The merchants of the colony died or removed. The remaining inhabitants resorted to the cultivation of the barren soil. The glories of the chief town on Long Island Sound departed.[76] But a commercial colony does not spring full-fledged from the brow of Jove, and in a quarter of a century not much more than a beginning can be made. Had the New Haven Colony acquired the territory between the Hammonassett and the Delaware rivers, and continued to exist, in time it would undoubtedly have developed into all that its founders envisaged.

[75] *New Haven Colonial Records, 1653-1665*, p. 344.

[76] Maverick's Description of New England, Egerton MSS., 2395, fols. 397-411, printed in *New England Historical and Genealogical Register*, XXXIX, 33-48.

CHAPTER IX

NEW ENGLAND CONFEDERATES

TO settle differences among the Puritan colonies of New England and to offer a united front to the Indians, New France, New Netherland, and New Sweden, the New England Confederation was called into existence. The commissioners of the kingdom of Christ on the shores of Long Island Sound usually traveled to meetings of the United Colonies at Boston, at Hartford, or at Plymouth at the expense of the colony,[1] but in 1646, 1651, 1655, and 1660 the confederates convened at New Haven. Over the first three meetings on the Sound, Governor Eaton presided, and over the last, Governor Newman.

In 1643 the New Haven Colony received the permission of its Puritan neighbors to extend its jurisdiction over Milford and Southampton, and in 1657, over Oyster Bay and Huntington.[2] On October 23, 1643, Milford took its place in the New Haven Colony,[3] but probably dismayed by the narrow franchise and the illiberal terms of union offered by New Haven, Southampton voted to join Connecticut on March 7, 1645,[4] and Huntington on April 10, 1660.[5] East Hampton and Setauket or Ashford on Long

[1] In 1659 at a cost of £5 in good merchantable beaver. *New Haven Colonial Records, 1653-1665,* p. 300.

[2] *Plymouth Colony Records,* IX, 10; X, 195.

[3] *New Haven Colonial Records, 1638-1649,* pp. 110-111.

[4] Connecticut State Library, Connecticut Archives, Town and Lands, I, 7; *Southampton Records,* I, 31.

[5] *Huntington Records,* I, 23.

Island also chose union with the River Colony,[6] and Oyster Bay retained its independence.

At their meetings the commissioners of the four colonies recommended to one another legislation to promote the spiritual, political, economic, and intellectual welfare of New England. These recommendations the New Haven Colony usually accepted, but loss of the colony's records for the period from 1644 to 1653 often renders it impossible to say just when this was done.

Although the New Haven Colony had sprung from Massachusetts Bay, and in its ecclesiastical and civil organizations followed the practices of the Bay Colony, its political and economic interests were more akin to those of Connecticut. Equally menaced by the Indians of southern New England and the Dutch of New Netherland, until 1660 the colony on the Sound and the colony on the River saw eye to eye. The New Haven Colony supported Connecticut in the latter's efforts to extend its jurisdiction over the Pequot territory,[7] and to collect customs at Saybrook,[8] and Connecticut sympathized with the aspirations of the New Haven Colony to establish plantations on the Delaware. The greatest tragedy in the history of Christ's kingdom on Long Island Sound is that its death blow came from the hand of its closest ally.

The Indians were ever before the attention of the four confederates. Toward the friendly savages from whom they had acquired title to their lands in return for a few pots and kettles and the promise of protection, and to whom lands had been assigned in the unsettled areas within the limits of the colonies, the settlers of New England adopted an attitude of paternalism. The New Haven Colony prohibited the sale of cider and liquor to the na-

[6] Connecticut Archives, Town and Lands, I, 8, 9.

[7] *Plymouth Colony Records,* IX, 19, 79, 96-97.

[8] *Ibid.,* pp. 80, 89-93, 120-136, 153-158.

tives, and in time of danger loaned them powder with which to protect themselves.[9]

Soon aroused to the spiritual as well as to the physical needs of their protégés, John Eliot, teacher of the church at Roxbury in Massachusetts Bay, and Thomas Mayhew, Jr., of Martha's Vineyard, undertook the education and conversion of the children of the forest. In an effort to awaken interest in England in the missionary endeavors of the first settlers of New England, *New Englands First Fruits*[10] was published in London in 1643. In it the anonymous author devoted more space to the growing grace of the red men than to the recently founded college at Cambridge in Massachusetts Bay. *The Day-Breaking, if not The Sun-Rising of the Gospell With the Indians in New-England,* also anonymous but variously ascribed to John Eliot, John Wilson, pastor of the church at Boston, and Thomas Shepard, pastor of the church at Cambridge, appeared in 1647. Thomas Shepard issued *The Clear Sunshine of the Gospel breaking forth upon the Indians in New-England* in the following year. Edward Winslow returned to England as the agent of Massachusetts Bay in December, 1646, and published *The Glorious Progress of the Gospel, amongst the Indians in New England* in 1649.

Through the efforts of Winslow, on July 27, 1649, the Long Parliament incorporated the President and Society for propagation of the Gospel in New-England, and authorized it to collect and invest funds, the revenues to be disposed of through the commissioners of the United Colonies of New England for the furtherance of the work among the Indians of New England.[11] Establishing itself

9 *New Haven Colonial Records, 1653-1665,* pp. 195, 219, 299, 597.

10 The first of the so-called Eliot tracts, eleven pamphlets published in London from 1643 to 1671 to stimulate interest in the conversion of the Indians in New England, nine of which have been reprinted in Massachusetts Historical Society *Collections,* 3d series, IV, and as *Sabin's Reprints,* nos. iii, v-vii, ix-x.

11 C. H. Firth and R. S. Rait, editors, *Acts and Ordinances of the Inter-*

at Coopers' Hall in Basinghall Street, London, the society proceeded to collect funds through England and Wales. To encourage subscriptions and to meet criticism of its work, it published *Strength out of Weakness. Or a Glorious Manifestation of the Further Progresse of the Gospel amongst the Indians in New-England* in 1652; *Tears of Repentance: Or, A further Narrative of the Progress of the Gospel Amongst the Indians in New-England* in 1653; *A Late and Further Manifestation of the Progress of the Gospel amongst the Indians in New-England* in 1655; *A further Accompt of the Progresse of the Gospel amongst the Indians in New-England* in 1659; *A further Account of the progress of the Gospel Amongst the Indians In New-England* in 1660; and *A Brief Narrative of the Progress of the Gospel amongst the Indians in New-England* in 1671.

After the formation of the Society for propagation of the Gospel in New-England, the commissioners of the United Colonies of New England devoted much of their time to the consideration of letters from the president and society, to drafting replies to these letters, and to directing the work among the Indians of New England. They took John Eliot and Thomas Mayhew, Jr., into their employ, and soon added William Leveridge of Sandwich in the colony of New Plymouth, Richard Blinman of Pequot, and others to their staff of workers. They placed Indian boys, and girls too, in the homes of ministers to be taught to read and to write, and boys in grammar schools to be taught Latin and thus prepared for Harvard, erected a building at the college in which to house

regnum, II, 197-200. With the Restoration the act of parliament establishing the society lapsed, but Charles II chartered it as "The Company for Propagation of the Gospel in New England and the parts adjacent in America," February 7, 1662, and it continues to function to this day. See *History of the New England Company* (1871); *The New England Company of 1649 and John Eliot* (Prince Society, 1920).

them, and filled it with English students until the natives were ready for a higher education in the classics and Puritan theology. They undertook the education of the sons of Thomas Stanton, the Indian interpreter, whom they hoped to use in their Indian work, and disciplined one of them when he failed to take advantage of his opportunities in New England's first center of learning.[12] They sponsored the publication of *A Primer or Catechism* in 1654 and again in 1662, *The Book of Genesis* and *The Gospel of Matthew* in 1655, *A Few Psalms in Metre* in 1658, *A Christian Covenanting Confession* in 1660 and 1670, *The New Testament* in 1661 and 1680, both *Old and New Testaments* in 1663 and 1685, *The Psalms* in 1663, Richard Baxter's *Call to the Unconverted* in 1664 and 1688, an abridgement of Lewis Bayly's *Practice of Piety* in 1665 and again in 1685, *The Indian Grammar Begun* in 1666, *The Indian Primer* in 1669 and again in 1687, *Indian Dialogues* in 1671, *The Logick Primer* in 1672, and Thomas Shepard's *The Sincere Convert* in 1689. These works the indefatigable John Eliot translated into the language of the Indians of Massachusetts Bay, and Samuel Green and Marmaduke Johnson in partnership or as individuals printed on the first press in the English colonies at Cambridge in Massachusetts Bay.[13]

Although the New Haven Colony was remote from the scenes of activity of the first missionaries among the Indians, the elders of the colony on the Sound were not without a share in the Indian work. John Davenport wrote the appendix signed "An unworthy Labourer in Christs work here, and an ardent desirer of further progresse thereof in New-England. J. D." to Winslow's *The*

12 *Plymouth Colony Records,* IX-X, *passim;* Daniel Gookin, "Historical Collections of the Indians in New England," Massachusetts Historical Society *Collections,* 1st series, I, 141-232.

13 Wilberforce Eames, *Bibliographic Notes on Eliot's Indian Bible* (1890); *Plymouth Colony Records,* X, 314, 316, 447-449.

Glorious Progress of the Gospel, amongst the Indians in New England (1649). In 1656 he was one of seven ministers whom the President and Society for propagation of the Gospel in New-England considered recommending to the commissioners of the United Colonies of New England to be joined with the commissioners in the direction of the work in New England.[14] On his way to England in 1650, Henry Whitfield, pastor of the church at Guilford, observed the work of Thomas Mayhew, Jr., at Martha's Vineyard and of John Eliot near Roxbury. After his arrival in the mother country he became a member of the Society for propagation of the Gospel in New-England. In 1651 he published *The Light Appearing More and More towards the Perfect Day.* In 1652 and 1655 he recommended for publication the pamphlets issued by the society. In 1651 Abraham Pierson, pastor of the church at Branford, and John Higginson, pastor of the church at Guilford, undertook the study of the language of the Quiripis of southern New England. When Thomas Mayhew, Jr., was lost at sea in the winter of 1657-1658, Thomas Mayhew, Sr., recommended that Pierson and Higginson be asked to carry on the work among the Indians of Martha's Vineyard.[15] Although the two ministers did not assume this responsibility, in 1653 Pierson had begun the preparation of a catechism for the Quiripis, and some years later he published it as *Some Helps for the Indians* (Cambridge, 1658). Translation into the language of the Quiripis probably did not render more lucid his dogmatic avowal that "there is but one true God . . . Because the reason why singular things of the same kind are multiplied is not to be found in the nature of God; for the reason why such like things are multiplied is from the fruitfulnesse of their causes: but God hath no cause

[14] *The New England Company of 1649 and John Eliot,* pp. 17-18.
[15] *Plymouth Colony Records,* IX, 204; X, 210.

of his being, but is of himself therefore he is one,'"[16] and the statement undoubtedly served to convince the Indian that the religion of his white brother was one of mystery. The value of the work for other purposes is questionable. In 1659 Pierson visited the natives of Wethersfield. In the following year he attended a public meeting of Indians in Massachusetts Bay. When John Stanton proved to be too great a problem for Harvard College, he undertook the education of that youthful hope of the commissioners of the United Colonies. In 1662 the commissioners urged him to settle among the Pequots at Souther Toune, now Stonington. In 1664 he reported that he traveled a distance of a hundred miles eight times a month to visit the Indians.[17] For his endeavors, in 1652 he received the commendation of the commissioners. In the following year he was granted £12 out of the funds sent from England. In 1654 and the two years thereafter he received £15; from 1657 to 1660, £20 annually; from 1661 to 1664, £30 annually; and in the year of his removal to New Jersey, £15. After the settlement of William Leveridge at Oyster Bay and of Richard Blinman at New Haven, they continued their work among the Indians. In addition to the amounts paid to Pierson, Leveridge, and Blinman, in 1654 and in most years thereafter the commissioners of the United Colonies appropriated £5 to be distributed among the deserving Indians of the New Haven Colony.[18]

The wisdom of the efforts in New England and Old to convert the red men to seventeenth-century Puritanism and, by a wise distribution of clothing and tools, to induce them to listen to sermons, to pray in their families morning and evening, to ask grace before meals, to wear English clothes, to lay out towns in the New England manner, to build English houses, churches, and schools,

[16] Connecticut Historical Society *Collections,* III, 1-67.
[17] *Ibid.,* XXI, 158-160.
[18] *Plymouth Colony Records,* X, 227, 262, 288, *passim.*

to enter into plantation covenants to establish town governments based upon the word of God,[19] and by mastering the Indian catechism and Bible and frequent public confessions of their sins and professions of their faith to prepare themselves for a church estate—an ideal achieved only in 1660—is doubtful. Abraham Pierson found the natives "very slow, and sleight-spirited." The commissioners of the United Colonies of New England could see little evidence of conversion in some of their protégés. The commissioners sent by Charles II to investigate conditions in New England in 1664 believed that the red men listened to sermons because they were paid to do so, and if the sermons were no more inspiring than was the catechism of Abraham Pierson, they were probably correct.[20] But the sincerity of the workers cannot be questioned.

Quite different was the treatment meted out to the hostile Indians who lived beyond the settled areas of New England, who made necessary the continual carrying of arms, the ever-vigilant watches, and the trained bands, and who with French, Dutch, and Swedes shared responsibility for the formation of the New England Confederation.

More sheltered from red warriors than its confederates, the colony on the Sound nevertheless coöperated with its neighbors in their dealings with the savages. In the summer of 1639 Theophilus Eaton considered inadvisable an expedition proposed by Connecticut against Sowheag and his followers suspected of harboring Pe-

[19] John Eliot, *The Christian Commonwealth* (London, 1659), reprinted in Massachusetts Historical Society *Collections*, 3d series, IX, 127-164, a work which after the Restoration Massachusetts Bay thought it advisable to suppress.

[20] *Plymouth Colony Records*, IX, 203-205; Egerton MSS., 2395, fols. 426-435; Thomas Hutchinson, *A Collection of Original Papers* (1769), pp. 420-421.

quots at Mattabezeck,[21] but in the following fall the general court at Quinnipiac passed sentence of death on Nepaupuck, a Pequot who had killed Abraham Finch of Wethersfield in the course of the war fought before Quinnipiac was founded.[22]

At the first meeting of the commissioners of the United Colonies of New England at Boston in September, 1643, the representatives of the New Haven Colony were equally guilty with those of Massachusetts Bay, Connecticut, and New Plymouth in voting to deliver Miantonomo the Narragansett, at the moment a prisoner at Hartford, to his rival, Uncas the Mohegan, to be dealt with as Uncas saw fit after the commissioners of Connecticut and New Haven had safely arrived at their homes.[23] In the war against the Pequots Miantonomo had been the ally of Massachusetts Bay and Connecticut but at this time he was also the friend of the outcasts of the Bay Colony at Providence, Aquidneck, and Shawomet. The inevitable outcome of the cruel murder of Miantonomo was war between Mohegans and Narragansetts, and on October 14, 1643, a general court at New Haven voted to send six men to join eight from Connecticut to assist Uncas.[24]

On October 27, 1643, a general court for the jurisdiction of New Haven refused to furnish men to march under Captain John Underhill against the Indians, at the time on the warpath against the Dutch of New Netherland, but the towns of the colony took steps to protect themselves, and the colony offered to furnish corn for men and food for cattle and to lend Captain Underhill £20 to encourage him to settle at Stamford if Stamford would agree to repay the amount out of Underhill's sal-

21 *Connecticut Colonial Records,* I, 19-20, 31-32; Benjamin Trumbull, *A Complete History of Connecticut,* I (1797), 107-108.

22 *New Haven Colonial Records, 1638-1649,* pp. 22-24.

23 *Plymouth Colony Records,* IX, 10-12, 14-15.

24 *New Haven Colonial Records, 1638-1649,* p. 110.

ary.[25] Failing to distinguish between Dutch and English, in the course of the war the natives not only murdered Englishmen in New Netherland, among them the indomitable Anne Hutchinson and her household on or near Anne's Hoeck, but killed an Englishman between Stamford and Uncoway or Fairfield within the jurisdiction of Connecticut, and attacked a woman at Stamford within the jurisdiction of the New Haven Colony. Thus aggrieved, Connecticut and New Haven did not wait for the commissioners of the United Colonies of New England to assemble, but sent an expedition against the red men. New Haven furnished twenty men and took captive and executed Busheage, the Indian guilty of the murderous attempt on the woman at Stamford. Although Massachusetts Bay and New Plymouth approved of the expedition against the red men, the two northerly confederates refused to bear any part of its cost.[26]

In the summer of 1645 the smoldering hostility between Mohegans and Narragansetts flared up. On June 21 a general court for the town of New Haven appointed Governor Eaton, the members of the particular court at New Haven, and Captain Richard Malbon and Lieutenant Robert Seely of the recently organized artillery company a council of war to take what action seemed necessary to strengthen Uncas against the Narragansett Indians. In the following month the commissioners of the United Colonies met in special session at Boston to deal with trouble between Massachusetts Bay and the French in Acadia. At this time they agreed to send Major Edward Gibbons and an expedition of three hundred men against the Narragansetts, Massachusetts Bay to furnish one hundred and ninety men; New Plymouth and Con-

[25] *Ibid.*, pp. 116-117.

[26] *Ibid.*, pp. 134, 135, 146; *Plymouth Colony Records*, IX, 26-27, 68; *Winthrop's Journal*, II, 196.

necticut, forty each; and the New Haven Colony, thirty men under Lieutenant Robert Seely. In the ensuing preparations for war the New Haven Colony expended more than its proportionate share, but before hostilities actually broke out, the Narragansetts came to terms. They agreed to pay two thousand fathom of good white wampum or a third part of good black wampum peage in four installments, and to deliver four Indian children to the commissioners of Massachusetts Bay as security for the payment; to pay the tribute due on the Pequots in their charge by a treaty between Uncas the Mohegan and Miantonomo the Narragansett and Connecticut, September 21, 1638; to maintain peace with the Mohegans; and to lay their grievances before the commissioners of the United Colonies at a meeting to be held at New Haven in September, 1646. Of five hundred fathom of wampum to be paid within twenty days, the commissioners allotted four hundred fathom to Connecticut and the New Haven Colony and one hundred fathom to Uncas.[27]

When the commissioners of the United Colonies assembled for the first time at New Haven in September, 1646, there were negotiations with the savages in full measure. Englishmen complained of Indians, and the natives of one another. Inhabitants of Windsor said that the Indians had burned their pitch, tar, cart, tools, and bedding to the value of £100. The magistrates of Connecticut complained that Sequasson, sachem on the Connecticut River above the river towns and the friend of Miantonomo, had plotted to take their lives, and Sequasson was sent for, and brought to New Haven by his friends, but on the outskirts of the town escaped, and refused to come before the commissioners "because he had brought no present."

[27] *New Haven Colonial Records, 1638-1649,* pp. 167-169; *Plymouth Colony Records,* IX, 32-49; British Museum, Lansdowne MSS., 1052, fol. 7, printed in *New England Historical and Genealogical Register,* XLVI, 355-356.

The Indians of Pequot complained of the tyrannies of Uncas, and Uncas himself was present to press charges against his rivals. Summoned to this meeting in the preceding year, the Narragansetts had forgotten all about it, however, and of the two thousand fathom of wampum they had paid only one lot of one hundred and seventy fathom and another of fifteen or twenty fathom and "a few old kettles." "Beinge a contemptible some," the commissioners had spurned the latter payment, which probably surprised the Indians, for they were bartering away the lands of New England for similar sums and wares. At this time and at meetings at Boston in the summer of 1647, at Plymouth in September, 1648, at Boston in July, 1649, and at Hartford in September, 1650, the commissioners had to exert pressure to collect the balance due from the Narragansetts by the agreement of 1645.[28]

In the fall of 1648 Indians at Stamford murdered John Whitmore, deputy of Stamford to the general court for the jurisdiction of New Haven. In the following July the commissioners of the United Colonies, in session at Boston, authorized Thomas Stanton to demand the murderers. Stanton received no satisfaction from the Indians, and on September 10, 1649, a general court for the town of New Haven ordered the guard to be doubled on the Lord's days and on lecture days and all men not of the guard to carry their swords to meetings. On September 24 a general court of the colony authorized a rate of £200 and appointed governor and magistrates a council of war. Connecticut raised forty-five men for an expedition against the Indians. But there is no evidence that the forces of the New Haven Colony and Connecticut marched against the natives at this time, although at a later date

[28] *Plymouth Colony Records*, IX, 66-76, 82, 85-89, 106-107, 116-118, 144-145, 168-169.

the two allies asked the New England Confederation to reimburse them for their preparations.[29]

Upon complaint of Uncas that the Long Island Indians were bewitching and killing his men, the commissioners in session at Hartford in 1650 authorized Connecticut to commission John Mason of Saybrook, Edward Howell and John Gosmer of Southampton, and Thomas Benedict of Southold to inquire into the matter, but again there is no evidence that action was taken.[30]

Meanwhile, tribute due on the Pequots by the treaty signed by Uncas the Mohegan, Miantonomo the Narragansett, and Connecticut, September 21, 1638, remained unpaid. In 1650 the commissioners appointed Thomas Stanton official interpreter and collector of tribute at an annual salary of £30, and a year later agreed to remit all tribute due before 1650 and to demand the payment of tribute only until 1660.[31] Of the tribute collected after 1650, the New Haven Colony received a share.

At the time of the first Anglo-Dutch War, Uncas the Mohegan was responsible for the rumor that the Dutch of New Netherland were engaging his adversaries to attack the English. Although both Dutch and Narragansetts denied the report, the attack of Ninnegrett, chieftain of the Niantics, a division of the Narragansetts, on the Indians at the eastern end of Long Island tributary to the English seemed to verify it. At their meeting at Boston in September, 1653, seven of the eight commissioners of the United Colonies voted to send an expedition of two hundred and fifty men against the Niantics, Massachusetts Bay to furnish one hundred and sixty-six men; New Plymouth, thirty; Connecticut, thirty-three; and the New Haven Colony, twenty-one. Simon Brad-

[29] *Plymouth Colony Records*, IX, 141-142; X, 108; *New Haven Colonial Records, 1638-1649*, pp. 481, 482, 484; *Connecticut Colonial Records*, I, 197.

[30] *Plymouth Colony Records*, IX, 167.

[31] *Ibid.*, pp. 190-191, 207.

street, commissioner of Massachusetts Bay and president of the New England Confederation, and the council of the Bay Colony felt no obligation to protect the Indians of Long Island, however, and opposed the expedition. Without the coöperation of the largest of the confederates, action was futile.[32]

As Ninnegrett's attacks on the Indians of Long Island continued, Connecticut and the New Haven Colony determined to intervene. On August 23, 1654, a general court for the jurisdiction of New Haven voted to send Lieutenant Robert Seely and five others equipped with twelve pounds of powder and thirty pounds of lead in Seely's boat to coöperate with Major John Mason and men from Connecticut in protecting their friends on Long Island.[33] Ninnegrett refused to pay tribute for the Pequots in his charge, or to appear before the commissioners of the United Colonies and asked that "the English would lett him alone." In session at Hartford in September, 1654, the commissioners authorized an expedition of forty horsemen and two hundred and seventy foot soldiers to go against him. Of the total, the New Haven Colony was asked to furnish thirty-one foot soldiers, sixteen of them to meet a commander-in-chief to be appointed by Massachusetts Bay at Thomas Stanton's at Pequot on October 13. On October 9 Samuel Willard led the Massachusetts contingent out of Boston. A week later he was joined by men, boats, and provisions from the New Haven Colony and Connecticut at Thomas Stanton's. The frightened Pequots promptly agreed to settle where the English should appoint. Ninnegrett at first betook himself to a swamp, but on October 18 agreed to surrender the Pequots in his charge to the English but refused to pay past-due tribute on them or the cost of the expedition.

[32] *Ibid.*, X, 4-12, 22-25, 43-50, 88-90, 96-99, 101, 427.
[33] *New Haven Colonial Records, 1653-1665*, pp. 117-118.

Well satisfied with these achievements, on October 24 Willard and the Massachusetts forces were back in Boston.[34]

Long Island continued to suffer at the hands of the Niantics. Feeling that Willard had permitted Ninnegrett to slip through his fingers, the commissioners of the United Colonies in session at New Haven on September 20, 1655, commissioned John Youngs, Jr., of Southold to ply up and down between Pawcatuck and Pequot in a vessel with six, ten, or twelve men to watch the movements of Ninnegrett. Through the winter and spring of 1655-1656 Youngs did this at a cost of £153 1*s.* 2*d.*, of which the New Haven Colony paid its share.[35]

Friction between Uncas and his rivals continued, and complaints came before every meeting of the commissioners of the United Colonies. But in 1658 Francis Newman succeeded Theophilus Eaton as governor of the colony on the Sound, and he refused to become imbroiled in Indian quarrels,[36] and avoided open warfare with the savages.

In September, 1644, and during the summer of 1645 the representatives of Massachusetts Bay brought negotiations between the Bay Colony and the French in Acadia to the attention of the commissioners of the United Colonies in session at Hartford and Boston. Seeking an alliance of French and English against the Mohawks or Iroquois, in September, 1651, Father Gabriel Druillettes of the Society of Jesus, and John Paul Godefroy, agents of Governor Louis d'Ailleboust and the council of New France, attended the meeting of the commissioners at New Haven. Although the New Haven Colony was far

[34] *New Haven Colonial Records, 1653-1665*, pp. 119-120; *Plymouth Colony Records*, X, 114-117, 125-127, 130-133, 145-148, 434-437; Connecticut State Library, Robert C. Winthrop Collection of Connecticut Manuscripts, II, 149.

[35] *Plymouth Colony Records*, X, 148-152, 154-155.

[36] Massachusetts Historical Society, Winthrop MSS., XV, 113-114.

distant from all settlements of the French in America, at these times the commissioners of the colony on the Sound voted with Massachusetts Bay and New Plymouth in an effort to win the support of the two northern confederates against Dutch and Swedes to the southwest.[37]

With New Netherland and New Sweden the New Haven Colony was always at swords' points. Despite the protests of the Dutch, the English had taken possession of territory on the Connecticut River, along the shores of Long Island Sound, and finally on Long Island and along the Delaware River. In the years which followed, trade between Dutch and English was uninterrupted, intermarriage of the two nationalities was common, and Director General Kieft congratulated the English on the formation of the New England Confederation, but beneath this seeming friendliness, territorial rivalry smoldered. In 1639 and again in 1640 the Dutch repulsed Englishmen planted by James Forrett, agent of William Alexander, Earl of Stirling, in the vicinity of Schout's Bay, and forced them to remove to the eastern end of Long Island. In the spring of 1641 the Dutch permitted the settlers sent out by George Lamberton and Nathaniel Turner to proceed past Manhattan Island toward the Delaware only on condition that they would settle beyond the limits of New Netherland, and when Lamberton disregarded the promise and began a settlement at the junction of the Delaware and Schuylkill rivers, the Dutch lost little time in driving him out, and encouraged the Swedes to take a similar stand against the English at Varkens Kill. In 1642 and 1644 the Dutch forced the English settlers at Greenwich on the mainland and at Hemp-

[37] *Plymouth Colony Records*, IX, 24-25, 56, 60, 199-203; John Gilmary Shea, trans., "Journal of an Embassy from Canada to the United Colonies of New England in 1650, by Father Gabriel Druillettes of the Society of Jesus," New York Historical Society *Collections*, 2d series, III, Part I, 303-328.

stead on Long Island to submit to the government of New Netherland.[38]

At the first meeting of the commissioners of the United Colonies of New England at Boston in September, 1643, Theophilus Eaton and Thomas Gregson, representatives of New Haven, complained of the affronts to which their colony had been subjected by both Dutch and Swedes. On the order of the commissioners, John Winthrop, governor of Massachusetts Bay and president of the New England Confederation, wrote to Director General Kieft of New Netherland and Director General Printz of New Sweden, and George Lamberton entered into negotiations with Printz.[39]

Of what the director general of New Netherland replied to Winthrop, there is no record. In January, 1644, Printz caused some of the English who were still on the Delaware to be examined in the presence of a mixed group of Swedes, Dutch, and English. The hearing exonerated the Swedish director general of the charges of wronging the English, of driving them from their plantation, of forcing them to swear allegiance to the crown of Sweden, of reproaching them, of speaking evil against the English nation, and of plotting against the life of Lamberton. In the following spring Printz sent a copy of the findings to Winthrop, to be laid before the next meeting of the commissioners of the United Colonies of New England.[40]

In his negotiations with Printz, Lamberton seems to

[38] New York Colonial MSS., IV, 62-69, 123-124; X, Part III, 93; *New York Colonial Documents,* II, 144-150; XII, 23-24; XIV, 28-31; *Plymouth Colony Records,* IX, 181; X, 13-14; see my article, "The Earl of Stirling and the Colonization of Long Island," *Essays in Colonial History,* pp. 74-95.

[39] *Plymouth Colony Records,* IX, 13; *Winthrop's Journal,* II, 141-142.

[40] Frederic Kidder, "The Swedes on the Delaware and Their Intercourse with New England," *New England Historical and Genealogical Register,* XXVIII, 42-50.

have justified the right of the English to the Delaware by the charter issued by Charles I to the Governor and Company of the Massachusetts Bay in New England, which recited the grant by James I to the Council for New England of the territory between the fortieth and forty-eighth degrees of north latitude. Printz seems to have told Lamberton that upon presentation of a copy of the charter and a commission from the New England Confederation, he would permit the New Haveners to proceed with their plantation on the Delaware. At any rate, in the spring of 1644 Governor Eaton asked Winthrop for these documents, and in response to the request, the general court of Massachusetts Bay issued a copy of the charter and several blank commissions signed by John Winthrop as governor of Massachusetts Bay and president of the New England Confederation. In the controversy regarding possession of the Delaware, both charter and commissions were without legal value, but in the absence of a more authentic document, they served very well to overawe the director general of New Sweden.[41]

During the ensuing five years the New Haven Colony was engaged in inaugurating a colonial government and in settling the towns of Southold on Long Island and Stamford and Branford on the mainland, and for the moment abandoned its efforts to take possession of the Delaware.

Despite these domestic interests, friction between the New Haven Colony and New Netherland continued. The merchants of New England objected to the duties they were forced to pay in New Netherland. The Dutch objected to the meeting of the commissioners of the United Colonies of New England "at the Red Mounte . . . within the limits of New Netherlande," and to the trad-

[41] *Winthrop's Journal*, II, 160-161; Massachusetts Archives, II, 167-168.

ing post erected by merchants of the New Haven Colony at Paugassett. Both Dutch and English believed that their opponents were selling guns and ammunition to the Indians, and encouraging the natives to rise against them. In July, 1649, the commissioners of the United Colonies of New England, in session at Boston, forbade both French and Dutch to trade with the Indians within the limits of New England. Ordinarily both Dutch and English favored rendition of fugitives from one colony to another, but in the heat of the controversy regarding the *St. Beninio,* the New Haven Colony refused to deliver William Westerhouse and Samuel Goodanhouse and three servants of the Dutch West India Company to New Netherland. The director general and council of the Dutch colony retaliated with a proclamation that all runaways from the New Haven Colony, prisoners, bondsmen, freemen, debtors, creditors, servants, and masters, upon taking an oath of allegiance to the United Netherlands would be welcomed in New Netherland, carefully explaining, however, that neighborly correspondence would be observed with all other colonies, even Connecticut, which, like the New Haven Colony, was settled within the limits of New Netherland.[42]

By 1649 the government of the New Haven Colony was functioning smoothly. The towns constituting the colony at its widest extent were settled, and pressure of population was beginning to be felt. Under these circumstances the colony revived its claim to the territory on the Delaware which merchants from New Haven had bought from the Indians in 1641 and 1642. On June 7, 1649, Governor Eaton informed Director General Stuyvesant of the in-

[42] New York Colonial MSS., IV, 353; XI, 1, 2, 3, 5, 6, 8, 9, 11; *New York Colonial Documents,* XII, 52; XIII, 21, 23; XIV, 77; *New Haven Colonial Records, 1638-1649,* pp. 265-266, 333, 355, appendix; Massachusetts Archives, II, 365; *Plymouth Colony Records,* IX, 107-108, 113-115, 149.

tention of his colony to maintain its rights, and in New Netherland the report spread that many families of English would soon migrate to the south.[43]

Claiming all territory between the Connecticut and Delaware rivers for the Dutch West India Company, Stuyvesant met Eaton's notice of intended aggression by warning not only the governor of the New Haven Colony but Governor John Endecott and Major General Edward Gibbons of Massachusetts Bay and Governor William Bradford of New Plymouth that he intended to maintain the title of the Dutch to the South River and would resist any attempt of the English to settle there.[44]

In July, 1649, the New Haven Colony laid its claim to the Delaware before a special session of the commissioners of the United Colonies at Boston. At this time the colony on the Sound found its confederates reluctant actively to sponsor its expansion. The representatives of Massachusetts Bay, Connecticut, and New Plymouth left the New Haven merchants "to theire Just libbertie to dispose Improve or plant the land thay haue purchased in those parts or any part therof as thay shall see Cause," but would commit themselves no further.[45]

Stuyvesant had long desired to meet with the commissioners of the United Colonies of New England to arbitrate the differences between New Netherland and New England and to perfect an offensive and defensive alliance against the Indians. John Winthrop, governor of Massachusetts Bay, also desired that the disputes between New Netherland and Connecticut and the New Haven Colony might be settled "least if a warre or brojles

[43] New York Colonial MSS., XI, 11; *New York Colonial Documents,* XII, 52; *New Haven Colonial Records, 1638-1649,* pp. 534-535; Adriaen van der Donck, *Remonstrance of New Netherland* (1856), p. 24.

[44] New York Colonial MSS., XI, 2, 11; *New York Colonial Documents,* XII, 39-40, 50-53; *New Haven Colonial Records, 1638-1649,* pp. 535-536.

[45] *Plymouth Colony Records,* IX, 140-141.

Arise betweene them wee be chardged and enwrapped in it,'' and met the advances of the director general of New Netherland with courtesy. In 1648 and 1649 the commissioners of the United Colonies did not find it convenient to meet at Hartford, however, and in 1649 Stuyvesant felt that a journey to Boston was too great an undertaking. Proposing a consultation with Governor Eaton at New Haven, the Dutch director general was promptly told to remain at home. Finally, after more than three years of delay, in September, 1650, the director general of New Netherland, George Baxter, his English secretary, and Thomas Willett, merchant of Plymouth and New Amsterdam, traveled to the meeting of the commissioners of the United Colonies of New England at Hartford.[46]

At this time the principal issues between New England and New Netherland were the boundary between English and Dutch on the mainland and on Long Island, the conflicting claims to the land on the Connecticut River upon which the Dutch had erected Fort Good Hope, the reception of fugitives from New Netherland by the New Haven Colony, the prohibition of trade between Dutch and Indians within the limits of New England, and the conflicting claims of New Netherland and the New Haven Colony to territory on the Delaware. After much bickering, the commissioners of Connecticut and the New Haven Colony named Simon Bradstreet of Massachusetts Bay and Thomas Prence of New Plymouth, and the director general of New Netherland named George Baxter and Thomas Willett as arbitrators to settle the differences between English and Dutch and to arrange an offensive and defensive alliance against the Indians.[47]

[46] New York Colonial MSS., XI, 2, 7, 8, 9, 10; *New York Colonial Documents,* XII, 39-41; *New Haven Colonial Records, 1638-1649,* pp. 525-527, 530-533; Massachusetts Archives, II, 327; Thomas Hutchinson, *A Collection of Original Papers* (1769), pp. 225-226.

[47] *Plymouth Colony Records,* IX, 171-188.

By the ensuing award, the boundary between New England and New Netherland was placed at the west side of Greenwich Bay on the mainland and at the west side of Oyster Bay on Long Island. For the time being New Netherland was to retain jurisdiction over Greenwich but the arbitrators and the director general of New Netherland seem to have agreed that upon the ratification of the award by the states general of the United Netherlands, the Dutch would hand that settlement over to the English. The Dutch were to retain Fort Good Hope. Provision was made for the mutual exchange of fugitives. Both the New Haven Colony and New Netherland were left "in Status quo privs to plead and Improve theire Just enterests at Delaware for planting or Trading as they shall see Cause; . . . tell the Right may bee further Considered and Justly Issued either in Europe or heere by the two States of England and Holland." An alliance of New England and New Netherland against the Indians was referred to the four confederates.[48]

In the New Haven Colony the award was interpreted as *carte blanche* to proceed with plans for a plantation on the southern border of New Netherland. In the town of New Haven a settlement on the Delaware became a topic of common conversation. At a special town meeting, December 17, 1650, at which every one present expressed an opinion regarding the project, it was voted that part of the town should remove to the Delaware. Three months later the town appointed a committee composed partly of those who intended to migrate and partly of those who intended to remain in New Haven to settle a government for the new plantation. Finally, about April 1, 1651, fifty men, among them Jasper Crane and Robert Seely, carrying the commission that had been issued to the New Haven Colony on the order of the general court of Massa-

[48] *Ibid.*, pp. 188-190.

chusetts Bay in 1644, sailed from New Haven for the Delaware.[49]

Quite different was Peter Stuyvesant's interpretation of the award. Learning of the proposed expedition from New Haven, the director general of New Netherland threatened to use force of arms against those of the English who should invade Dutch territory. When the vessel carrying Crane and Seely touched at New Amsterdam, he seized the commission of the English, imprisoned the leaders in the home of Martin Cregier, and released them only after they promised to abandon the undertaking. In a letter dispatched to Governor Thomas Dudley of Massachusetts Bay, he asked that the support of the United Colonies of New England be withheld from his aggressive neighbors on Long Island Sound.[50]

Proceeding to rally its forces, the New Haven Colony endeavored to interest Captain John Mason of Saybrook in the Delaware project. In September, 1651, Jasper Crane, William Tuttle, and other inhabitants of the towns of New Haven and Branford appealed to the commissioners of the United Colonies of New England in session at New Haven for support against the Dutch. Governor Eaton appealed to the confederates of the New Haven Colony for assistance on the Delaware, and asked Edward Winslow, agent of Massachusetts Bay in England, to procure a patent from parliament for the region.[51]

The confederates met the proposals of the New Haven Colony with coolness. Connecticut granted Mason permission to serve on the Delaware for a period of three months, but refused to permit him to depart permanently from the River Colony. With one of the commissioners of

[49] *New Haven Town Records, 1649-1662,* pp. 54, 66, 86.

[50] New York Colonial MSS., XI, 36; *New York Colonial Documents,* XII, 69-70; *Plymouth Colony Records,* IX, 214.

[51] *Connecticut Colonial Records,* I, 227; *Plymouth Colony Records,* IX, 199, 210-212.

New Plymouth dissenting, the commissioners of the United Colonies supported the New Haven Colony to the extent of writing to the director general of New Netherland "to protest against his jniurius proceedinges to assert the English Right and to Require satisfaction for the Damage donn to our frinds and confeaderats of Newhauen." They also wrote to Winslow in behalf of the colony on the Sound. But to the petitioners of New Haven and Branford they replied, "wee think it not meete to enter into a present Ingagement against the Duch Chusing Rather to suffer Iniuries and affronts (at least for a time) then in any Respects to seem to bee to quicke." But perhaps to shift responsibility for the refusal to render more active assistance, they offered a suggestion. With the approval of the New Haven Colony the petitioners might send a hundred or a hundred and fifty men outfitted with a suitable vessel or vessels, arms, and ammunition to the Delaware within a period of twelve months, to be subject to the government of the New Haven Colony until the New England Confederation should order otherwise. If while these immigrants remained peaceful and inoffensive they met with opposition from Dutch and Swedes, then the four colonies would furnish soldiers to be paid for by the planters on the Delaware. In that case, the unpurchased lands on the Delaware and the trade with the natives were to be mortgaged until the charges were paid.[52]

To the letter of the commissioners Stuyvesant replied that he had shown the New Haveners civil, respectful, neighborly usage, but that he could not and would not permit them to settle within the limits of New Netherland.[53]

[52] *Connecticut Colonial Records,* I, 227; *Plymouth Colony Records,* IX, 199, 213-215, 222.

[53] *Ibid.,* X, 21.

To the New Haven Colony, news of the outbreak of the first Anglo-Dutch War and the report that the Dutch of New Netherland were arousing the Narragansetts against the English seemed to offer an opportunity not only to push its claim to the Delaware but to conquer New Netherland. The smallest of the Puritan commonwealths would then sweep along the coast from the Hammonassett River to the Delaware. The colony met the situation by prohibiting commerce with New Netherland and the export of provisions, and levying heavy rates upon the towns. When four members of the council of Massachusetts Bay asked the commissioners of the United Colonies to convene at Boston, May 11, 1653, the colony on the Sound responded so quickly, and so stressed the urgency of the situation, that the commissioners met three weeks sooner than had at first been planned.[54]

From April 19 to June 2, 1653, the commissioners of the United Colonies of New England sat in special session at Boston. Although the Hartford award had attempted to settle all disputes between English and Dutch antedating 1650, at this time the commissioners reviewed relations between New England and New Netherland from 1640 up to and including the rumored incitement of the Indians in 1652 and 1653. When they were unable to agree upon a course of action, the council and the neighboring elders of Massachusetts Bay suggested that it behooved "a people professing to walke in the [spirit of the] Gospell of peace haueing to doe with a people [howsoeuer] pretending to the same profession," to give their adversaries an opportunity to reply to the charges made against them. Thus advised, the commissioners authorized Francis Newman of the New Haven Colony and John Leverett and William Davis of Massachusetts Bay and

[54] *New Haven Colonial Records, 1653-1665,* pp. 15, 45, 46; Massachusetts Archives, III, 7.

Thomas Stanton of Connecticut, interpreter to the Indians, to proceed to New Netherland to investigate the situation. The inclusion of Thomas Stanton indicated where the agents of the New England Confederation were expected to look for evidence of Dutch perfidy. Meanwhile the commissioners considered the possibility of war between New England and New Netherland and voted that in the event of the outbreak of hostilities, John Leverett, at the moment spying out the land in New Netherland, would lead an army of five hundred men against the Dutch colony. Of this force Massachusetts Bay would furnish three hundred and thirty-three men; New Plymouth, sixty; Connecticut, sixty-five; and the New Haven Colony, forty-two. During the campaign the commissioners would sit at New Haven as a council of war. Chosen at general courts of election in May, 1652, for terms of one year, the commissions of the representatives of Massachusetts Bay, Connecticut, and the New Haven Colony expired during the absence of the agents of the confederation to New Netherland, but at the request of the general court of Massachusetts Bay, the commissioners tarried for the return of their emissaries.[55]

Disregarding all efforts of the director general and council of New Netherland to convince them that the Dutch were not in league with the natives, the agents of the New England Confederation contented themselves with a mass of hearsay evidence picked up among the English and Indians at the western end of Long Island and at Stamford.

With a written report of the activities of the agents, on May 21, 1653, Leverett and Davis returned to Boston. At the request of the general court of Massachusetts Bay,

[55] *Plymouth Colony Records*, X, 3-77; *Massachusetts Colony Records*, III, 311.

the commissioners named William Hauthorne, William Bradford, Roger Ludlow, and Theophilus Eaton to join with Samuel Symonds, Daniel Dennison, John Leverett, and Humphrey Atherton, appointed by the general court of Massachusetts Bay, to state the case between New England and New Netherland. The group failed to agree, and Eaton stated the case for the pro-war party, Dennison, for the anti-war party, and the imbroglio was presented to the general court of Massachusetts Bay and the neighboring elders. Not yet awakened to the possibility of extending their own colony across the territory claimed by New Netherland, deputies and elders of the colony upon which the brunt of war with New Netherland would fall advised "itt to bee most agreeable to the Gosspell of peace which wee professe and safest for these collonies to forbeare the vse of the sword, till the Lord by his prouidence and by the wisedome of his seruants sett over vs shall further cleare of his mind either for our settled peace or most manifest grounds of warr." The general court of the Bay Colony added that a war with New Netherland would be a war of aggression and beyond the power of the commissioners of the United Colonies to declare. With this impasse, the special session of the New England Confederation came to an end.[56]

On June 20, 1653, the refusal of Massachusetts Bay to take part in a war against New Netherland and its interpretation of the articles of confederation were laid before a general court for the jurisdiction of New Haven. The general court appointed William Leete and Thomas Jordan to join Thomas Welles and David Wilton of Connecticut in a journey to Massachusetts Bay to point out the Bay Colony's errors of interpretation and to demand that Massachusetts Bay either furnish its proportion of

[56] *Plymouth Colony Records,* X, 35-77; *Massachusetts Colony Records,* III, 311-313, IV, Part I, 141-144.

five hundred men or permit the enrollment of volunteers within its limits for the conquest of New Netherland, and send commissioners to a meeting of the New England Confederation to convene at New Haven August 4 or 11.[57]

On August 3, 1653, replies of Governor John Endecott dated July 14 and of the council dated July 21 and 22 were before a general court of the New Haven Colony. Governor and council of Massachusetts Bay pointed out that six commissioners of the United Colonies of New England had never determined upon war, that the general court of the Bay Colony would not meet until August 30, that meanwhile the council was without power to raise troops, and that a special session of the New England Confederation at New Haven in the summer of 1653 hardly seemed necessary. Unable to proceed without the support of the largest of the confederates, the colony on the Sound released the provisions and disposed of the beer for soldiers held in the colony in the expectation of war with New Netherland, but continued the prohibition of commerce with the Dutch.[58]

When the commissioners of the United Colonies of New England met in regular session at Boston in September, 1653, Massachusetts Bay held to its strange and unexpected interpretation of the articles of confederation. Maintaining that the Bay Colony had broken its covenant with its confederates, the New Haven Colony turned to England for assistance in ousting the Dutch from New Netherland.[59]

On June 21, 1653, after the aspirations of the New Haven Colony had been frustrated by Massachusetts Bay,

[57] *New Haven Colonial Records, 1653-1665,* pp. 4-14; *Connecticut Colonial Records,* I, 244; Massachusetts Archives, II, 171-173.

[58] *New Haven Colonial Records, 1653-1665,* pp. 18-25; Massachusetts Archives, II, 351-352; III, 10.

[59] *New Haven Colonial Records, 1653-1665,* pp. 37-38; *Plymouth Colony Records,* X, 78-112.

some of those present at a general court for the town of New Haven "desired that the Parliament in England may be informed how things haue bine Caried heare."[60] William Hooke of New Haven and, at the request of William Leete of Guilford, Samuel Desborough, at this time in England, appealed to Oliver Cromwell.[61] On October 12, 1653, the general court of the New Haven Colony appointed John Astwood of Milford, representative of the New Haven Colony at meetings of the New England Confederation in 1648, 1649, 1652, and 1653, to invoke the help of the lord general in the removal of the Dutch from New Netherland.[62]

On October 6, 1653, one of the letters of William Hooke was before the Council of State in England.[63] Coincident with his elevation to the protectorate the appeal of the general court of the New Haven Colony reached Cromwell. Probably because the request of the colony on the Sound coincided with his own plans, on February 8, 1654, Cromwell commissioned Major Robert Sedgwick of Charlestown in Massachusetts Bay and Captain John Leverett, Sedgwick's son-in-law, both at the moment in England, to go with the ships *Black Raven, Hope, Church,* and *Augustine* to Massachusetts Bay in New England, Pequot harbor, New Haven, or other good port within the limits of the United Colonies of New England, "as providence shall order the wind, and other occurrences," to coöperate with the New England Confederation in the extirpation of the Dutch and the vindication of the right

60 *New Haven Town Records, 1649-1662,* p. 181.

61 John Thurloe, *State Papers,* I, 564-565; Papers of General Desborough 1651-1660, Egerton MSS., 2519, fols. 10-11, printed in *New England Historical and Genealogical Register,* XLI, 356-359; Henry F. Waters, *Genealogical Gleanings in England* (1901), I, 246-249.

62 *New Haven Colonial Records, 1653-1665,* pp. 37-38.

63 State Papers, Domestic, Interregnum, Council of State, Fair Order Book, September 28, 1653—November 1, 1653, p. 50.

of the English nation to the soil of North America.[64] Had the emissaries succeeded in carrying out their instructions, the English conquest of New Netherland would have taken place under the lord protector in 1654 instead of under Charles II ten years later.

Furnished with general merchandise to be exchanged in New England for masts for the navy, and £200 to defray contingent expenses, on March 9, 1654, Sedgwick and Leverett set sail from Portsmouth in the *Black Raven.* On March 15 they left the Isle of Wight. Three days later they seized the *St. John Baptist,* illegally condemned it as a Dutch vessel, and carried it with them. On April 20 they arrived at the Azores. Here they decided to send the *Black Raven,* which had proved itself unseaworthy, back to England. On May 2 the leaders continued their voyage in the *Augustine.* On June 5 they arrived at Boston and found the *Hope* and *Church* awaiting them.[65]

Sedgwick and Leverett immediately dispatched the letters of the lord protector to the governors of Massachusetts Bay, New Plymouth, Connecticut, and the New Haven Colony. On June 9, 1654, the general court of Massachusetts Bay granted Sedgwick and Leverett permission to raise five hundred volunteers "not under any legal engagements" within the limits of the colony, but declined to take any official part in the expedition against New Netherland. New Plymouth sent Miles Standish and Thomas Willett, as usual without authority to act, to Sedgwick and Leverett, who promptly sent them home to understand more fully the mind of their general court. On June 9 the general court of the New Haven Colony

[64] John Thurloe, *State Papers,* I, 721; II, 419, where the date is erroneously given as February 17, 1654; Massachusetts Historical Society *Collections,* 4th series, II, 230-232.

[65] State Papers, Domestic, Interregnum, LXXI, nos. 5, 120; LXXII, no. 16; LXXVII, nos. 67, 79; LXXIX, nos. 76, 231-235; LXXX, nos. 23, 52; XCI, no. 81; John Thurloe, *State Papers,* II, 418-419.

commissioned William Leete and Thomas Jordan to go to Boston to consult with Sedgwick and Leverett regarding the campaign against New Netherland, the colony borrowing £5 in silver from the Widow Wigglesworth to pay the expenses of its commissioners. On June 13 the general court of Connecticut commissioned John Mason and John Cullick for the same purpose.[66]

On June 17 Sedgwick and Leverett, Leete and Jordan, Mason and Cullick met as a council of war at Charlestown to plan an expedition against New Netherland. In addition to two hundred men from the ships and three hundred volunteers hoped for from Massachusetts Bay—it had soon become evident that five hundred men could not be raised—the commissioners agreed that Connecticut should impress two hundred men and the New Haven Colony one hundred and thirty-three, all to be outfitted with arms and ammunition and provisions by Sedgwick and Leverett and the colonies of Connecticut and New Haven. It was planned that the men from the ships and the volunteers from the Bay Colony would set out from Boston on June 27. As the expedition passed Connecticut and New Haven, the men from those colonies would fall in. At a meeting of Sedgwick and Leverett and the commissioners of Connecticut and the New Haven Colony on June 20 it seemed probable that an expedition of nine hundred foot and a troop of horse would move against New Netherland within a week. On the same day a council of war at Plymouth took steps to impress fifty men within the limits of New Plymouth to serve under Captain Miles Standish and Lieutenant Mathew Fuller in the expedition against the Dutch, impressed the bark of Samuel Mayo and the boat of James Cole to carry the troops

[66] John Thurloe, *State Papers,* I, 721-722; II, 418-420, 425-426; *Massachusetts Colony Records,* IV, Part I, 195; *New Haven Colonial Records, 1653-1665,* pp. 100-102; *Connecticut Colonial Records,* I, 259-260; Thomas Hutchinson, *A Collection of Original Papers* (1769), pp. 252-254.

to New Amsterdam, and authorized Thomas Willett to accompany Sedgwick and Leverett to Manhattan and to assist them with advice and counsel. On June 23, 1654, the general court for the jurisdiction of New Haven took steps to raise and outfit the contingent of the colony on the Sound. It authorized Nicholas Augur and John Brockett to accompany the expedition as surgeons and Abraham Pierson, pastor of the church at Branford, as chaplain.[67]

Meanwhile, Director General Stuyvesant of New Netherland had continued to advocate a league of English and Dutch against the Indians and to oppose war between New England and New Netherland. In the spring of 1653 he offered to meet with the commissioners of the United Colonies at Boston. When the agents of the New England Confederation left New Amsterdam without waiting for his reply to the charges made against New Netherland, he sent Augustine Herrman to Boston to make peace with his English neighbors. In the spring of 1654 he had been forced to arrest John Youngs, Jr., of Southold and John Scott of Southampton nearby when those turbulent spirits invaded the waters of New Netherland, "to trade peacefully at New Amsterdam," according to the commissioners of the United Colonies of New England, to wage war on New Netherland, according to the commission from Rhode Island which they carried. But he sent Martin Cregier and Cornelis van Tienhoven to New Haven to explain that the yachts commissioned by the Dutch at that time were intended only for the suppression of piracy.[68]

[67] John Thurloe, *State Papers*, II, 419-420; *Plymouth Colony Records*, III, 53-57; *New Haven Colonial Records, 1653-1665*, pp. 107-110.

[68] New York Colonial MSS., V, 233, 242, 246; VIII, 1016-1018; XI, 61, 62; *New York Colonial Documents*, XIV, 254-256; *Plymouth Colony Records*, X, 59-70, 175, 425-426; *The Records of New Amsterdam from 1653 to 1674*, I, 174, 188; *New Haven Colonial Records, 1653-1665*, pp. 51, 66.

The efforts of Stuyvesant to maintain peace came to an end, however, when almost three weeks before the arrival of Sedgwick and Leverett at Boston Isaac Allerton proved his loyalty to New Netherland despite his grand house at New Haven by warning the director general of the Dutch Colony of the impending attack of the English. Thus cautioned, director general and council of New Netherland set about enlisting men, consulting with the Dutch but not with the English towns on Long Island, raising money, and engaging workers to repair the fort at New Amsterdam.[69]

At this crucial moment printed proclamations of peace between England and the United Netherlands issued by the council in England, April 22, 1654, and by the lord protector, four days later, arrived in Massachusetts Bay. Although Sedgwick and Leverett were willing to proceed with the enterprise against New Netherland, the commissioners of Connecticut and the New Haven Colony voted to abandon it.[70]

Despite this setback, the New Haven Colony held to its plan to establish a settlement on the Delaware. To further its purpose, it hoped to take advantage of the feeling between Dutch and Swedes. In Europe relations between the United Netherlands and Sweden were strained. In America the nationals of the two countries had long been at one another's throats. In 1648 Stuyvesant ordered the erection of Fort Beversreed at the junction of the Delaware and Schuylkill rivers. Printz retaliated by ordering the building of a blockhouse in front of Fort Beversreed. In 1651 Stuyvesant ordered the erection of Fort Casimir, a league below Fort Christina and controlling the Delaware River. On May 20, 1654, Johan Ris-

[69] New York Colonial MSS., V, 254-365, *passim; New York Colonial Documents,* XIV, 267-283.

[70] John Thurloe, *State Papers,* II, 418-419.

ing arrived in New Sweden as the successor of Director General Printz. Immediately adopting an attitude of aggression toward New Netherland, the new director general of New Sweden seized Fort Casimir and renamed it Fort Trinity. Soon after the arrival of Rising, news reached America that on April 11, 1654, England and Sweden had signed a treaty of alliance, and on May 8, 1654, a second agreement providing for the observance of friendship and goodwill between the colonies of the two nations. To the New Haven Colony it seemed that the government of Cromwell had entered into an alliance with a power able and willing to help it to withstand New Netherland.[71]

At the request of the general court of the New Haven Colony, on July 6, 1654, Governor Eaton dispatched a letter to Rising. Informing the director general of New Sweden of the rights which individuals of the New Haven Colony held in large tracts of land on both sides of Delaware Bay and River, he requested a neighborly correspondence in trade and planting between the two colonies.[72]

The new director general of New Sweden had come with no intention of aiding a third power to establish itself within the limits of New Sweden. On July 22, 1654, he and his council produced the Indian deeds to New Sweden, and on August 1, 1654, they sent copies attested by the oldest inhabitants of New Sweden to Eaton.[73] Thus rebuffed, in the following September Eaton laid the claim of the New Haven Colony and the letter of Rising before

71 New York Colonial MSS., XVIII, 1-8; *New York Colonial Documents,* I, 601; XII, 38-39, 43-47; George Chalmers, *A Collection of Treaties between Great Britain and Other Powers* (1790), I, 20-29; Amandus Johnson, *The Swedish Settlements on the Delaware, 1638-1664,* II, 621, 753-755.

72 *New Haven Colonial Records, 1653-1665,* p. 112; *New Haven Town Records, 1649-1662,* p. 223; *Plymouth Colony Records,* X, 127.

73 Amandus Johnson, *The Swedish Settlements on the Delaware, 1638-1664,* II, 574.

the commissioners of the United Colonies of New England in session at Hartford, and the commissioners wrote to the Swedish director general.[74]

Despite the hostility of Rising, a group of fifty or sixty "bretheren and Neighbours" at New Haven and individuals from other plantations expressed a desire to further the work on the Delaware in person or estate if it "might be Caried on, and foundations laide, According to God." Agreeing to buy the rights of the original proprietors for £300 to be paid in installments over a period of four years, they asked the protection of the New Haven Colony for the plantation they proposed to found, "till by the blessing of God, they may be able of themselues to set vp a Com̄on Wealth According to the fundamentalls for Gouermt laid at Newhauen." Failing to interest John Davenport and Theophilus Eaton in removal, they asked that Samuel Eaton and Francis Newman might accompany them as magistrates, if need be at the expense of the colony.[75]

To the proposed migration of Samuel Eaton and Francis Newman, the general court of the New Haven Colony assented, but it made clear to the prospective settlers that the Delaware was and must remain part of the New Haven Colony. Looking into the future, however, the general court agreed that if the plantations on the Delaware became more important than the territory on Long Island Sound, the governor and general court of the colony might alternate yearly between New Haven and the Delaware, and even that eventually the seat of government might be transferred to Delaware.[76]

Planning to set out for the Delaware after the harvest of 1655, the New Haveners were again doomed to frustra-

[74] *Plymouth Colony Records*, X, 127-128.
[75] *New Haven Town Records, 1649-1662*, pp. 226-227.
[76] *New Haven Colonial Records, 1653-1665*, pp. 128-131.

tion. On orders of the directors of the Dutch West India Company to avenge the conquest of Fort Casimir, through the summer of 1655 the Dutch at New Amsterdam fitted out an expedition for the conquest of New Sweden. On Sunday, August 26/September 5, 1655, Director General Stuyvesant and a fleet of seven vessels and six or seven hundred men sailed from the Dutch metropolis. On September 1/11 they retook Fort Casimir, and on September 15/25 they seized Fort Christina and the entire South River. Stuyvesant loaned Rising eight hundred guilders secured by the property of the crown of Sweden with which to betake himself in the *Bear* or *Brindled Cow* to England or France, and forced the Swedes on the Delaware to take an oath of allegiance to the United Netherlands or to return to Sweden.[77]

After 1655 the New Haven Colony saw its strongest opponent in complete control of Delaware Bay and River. In the expansion of the colony on the Sound Massachusetts Bay and New Plymouth were uninterested. The lord protector of England watched New Netherland and corresponded with the English on Long Island under the jurisdiction of the Dutch,[78] but was not yet ready to act. Through long experience the New Haven Colony had learned that with the assistance of Connecticut only, it could not cope with New Netherland. Awaiting a combination of circumstances that would make the conquest of the Dutch colony possible, the kingdom of Christ on the shores of Long Island Sound watched its neighbors to the southwest. In 1664 the moment came, but with it, not only the conquest of New Netherland, but the downfall of the New Haven Colony.

[77] *New Haven Town Records, 1649-1662,* pp. 235-237; New York Colonial MSS., VI, 74-87, 121, 124, 129, 143, 144, 348; XII, 13-18, 27, 28; XVIII, 14-20; *New York Colonial Documents,* XII, 85-97, 101-111.

[78] New York Colonial MSS., XII, 80; *New York Colonial Documents,* XIV, 417.

CHAPTER X

PURITAN ENGLAND

AT a time when the imposition of high-church ceremonies in the church, summary procedure in the Court of Star Chamber, and arbitrary taxation by writs of ship-money made conditions in England seem intolerable to many, the Davenport company migrated to Massachusetts Bay. To escape a governor general expected from England and an extension of the abuses of the mother country to America, the immigrants moved beyond the limits of the Bay Colony and settled on the outskirts of New England. They drew toward them kindred souls from New England and Old, and the first plantation at Quinnipiac soon expanded into the New Haven Colony.

A delay of a few years would have made the migration of the group first to Massachusetts Bay and later to Quinnipiac unnecessary. They had hardly arrived in Boston when rioting at St. Giles's, July 23, 1637, at the Tolbooth, September 25, and throughout the city of Edinburgh, October 18, foreshadowed the Puritan revolution.[1] The plantation of Quinnipiac had existed less than three years when the Long Parliament assembled.

During the Puritan administration, friends of the New Haven Colony rose rapidly to positions of influence in the mother country. Isaac Penington of the parish of St. Stephen, Coleman Street, was a member of both Short and Long Parliaments, the high court of justice for the trial

[1] Samuel R. Gardiner, *History of England from the Accession of James I. to the Outbreak of the Civil War, 1603-1642*, VIII (1884), 304-324.

of Charles I, and the first, second, and fourth Councils of State. Owen Rowe, also of the parish of St. Stephen, Coleman Street, sent his young son Nathaniel with the Davenport company to New England and planned to follow, and lands were laid out for him in both Massachusetts Bay and New Haven. With the gathering of the Long Parliament he remained in England, however, and served as a member of the high court of justice and signed the death warrant of the king. In 1641 Hugh Peter, the friend of John Davenport, returned to England as one of three agents of Massachusetts Bay. After exerting great influence as chaplain in the parliamentary army, he met with Oliver Cromwell, Nathaniel Fiennes, and others at the Star in Coleman Street and plotted the death of Charles Stuart. Under the régime which followed he served as one of the preachers before the Council of State with lodgings in Whitehall and a salary of £200 a year. Attaining great influence in affairs of state, he was facetiously addressed as Archbishop of Canterbury, which "passed very well."[2] The younger Henry Vane served as a member of both Short and Long Parliaments and of the Councils of State. Late in 1645 George Fenwick, representative of the grantees of the Earl of Warwick at Saybrook and near neighbor of the settlers of the New Haven Colony, returned to England. There he immediately took his place in the Long Parliament. He was appointed to the high court of justice but did not attend the trial of the king. In 1654 and 1656 he sat in parliaments called by the protector. Oliver Cromwell, whose sister Jane had married John Desborough, brother of Samuel Desborough of Guilford, and whose cousin Jane Whalley was the wife of William Hooke, the colleague of John Davenport in the church at New Haven, was a member of both Short and

[2] C. H. Firth on Hugh Peters or Peter in the *Dictionary of National Biography.*

Long Parliaments. He rose from the rank of captain of a troop of horse to the office of lord general of the army. From 1649 to 1653 he was a member of all Councils of State. From December 16, 1653, until his death, September 3, 1658, he served as lord protector of England, and had he desired it, might have had the title of king.

With the ascendancy of the Puritan party in England, the prestige of New Haven greatly increased, for the colony approached the Puritan ideal more than did Massachusetts Bay and far more than did Connecticut. In 1648 it received the recognition of a committee of both houses of parliament. During the ascendancy of Oliver Cromwell it lay near to the heart of the lord protector of England.

But with the coming of the millennium in the mother country, the colony lost its *raison d'être*. Not only was it no longer necessary for non-separating Congregationalists to seek a refuge in the wilderness across the sea, but on the contrary a movement from the New World toward the Old set in, and the colony lost some of its outstanding inhabitants. Owen Rowe, Mrs. Eldred, and one Lucas of the parish of St. Stephen, Coleman Street, and one Dearmer, for all of whom lands had been laid out at New Haven, remained in England. The company of colonists to gather which Samuel Eaton returned to Cheshire failed to materialize. In 1648 Thomas James of New Haven left the colony. About 1650 Robert Newman and Richard Malbon of New Haven, Henry Whitfield of Guilford, and George Alsop of Milford went home. In the following year Samuel Caffinch of New Haven and Samuel Desborough of Guilford removed, the latter to serve as the commissioner of parliament in the army, one of the commissioners of customs at Leith, one of nine councillors of the kingdom of Scotland, keeper of the great seal of Scotland, and representative of Midlothian in the parliament of 1656 and of Edinburgh in the parliament of 1659.[3] In 1653 Mark Pierce of New Haven and John Hoadley of Guilford departed. About 1655 John Evance of New Haven and Thomas Jordan of Guilford returned to England. In 1656 William Hooke, teacher of the church at New Haven, left, and was subsequently engaged to gather a church in the family of the lord protector.[4] Soon after the death of Theophilus Eaton in 1658 Anne Eaton departed. And in 1659 Robert Seely went to England.

Even John Davenport thought of abandoning the colony he had founded. As early as 1642 "divers Lords of the upper house, and some 30 of the house of commons," among them Isaac Penington and William Spurstowe of the parish of St. Stephen, Coleman Street, and a minority of ministers who stood for the independency of churches, invited John Cotton, Thomas Hooker, and the founder of the New Haven Colony to return to England in order to take part in the Westminster assembly of divines. Had not the church at New Haven opposed his departure, and letters from Hugh Peter advised delay, Davenport would probably have gone at this time.[5] In 1651 it was rumored through New England that both John Davenport and Theophilus Eaton were returning to England.[6] Never enjoying good health, the pastor of the church at New Haven was extremely ill in 1654 and for that reason thought of his native land. John Winthrop, Jr., assured him that delay would not render his case less curable, however, and he tarried until the following year.[7] In 1655 the impending departure of William Hooke, the death of Sam-

[3] Papers of General Desborough 1651-1660, Egerton MSS., 2519.

[4] Massachusetts Historical Society *Collections,* 3d series, I, 181-184.

[5] *Winthrop's Journal,* II, 71-72; Thomas Hutchinson, *The History of the Colony of Massachusets-Bay,* I (1760), 115-116.

[6] Massachusetts Historical Society *Collections,* 4th series, VI, 76.

[7] *Ibid.,* VII, 469-470; Connecticut Historical Society *Collections,* III, 318-320; Massachusetts Historical Society, Winthrop MSS., XII, 93, 97.

uel Eaton, and the difficulty of supplying the church at New Haven with satisfactory officers made departure increasingly difficult. Three years later friends in England were still urging Davenport's return home,[8] but he remained at New Haven ten years longer.

With the accession to power of their friends, the elders and magistrates at New Haven hoped to legalize the position of the colony and to add to its territory. On November 11, 1644, a general court for the jurisdiction voted "to putt forth their best Endeuo^rs^ to procure a Pattent frō the Parliament as Judging itt a fitt season now for thatt end."[9] It was indeed a fit season. Before 1640 the authorization of colonies had not fallen within the sphere of the legislature, but a commission of the Long Parliament headed by Robert Rich, Earl of Warwick, recently appointed governor-in-chief and lord high admiral of the English plantations in America, had just granted a free and absolute charter of incorporation with powers of government to the outcasts at Providence, Portsmouth, and Newport.[10] In 1644 the intention of the general court of the New Haven Colony seems to have been to join with Connecticut in procuring one patent under which two separate and distinct colonial governments would function.[11] The colony appointed Thomas Gregson to undertake the voyage to England and furnished him with £200 in good, merchantable beaver to defray expenses, but in 1646 Gregson perished in the "walt-sided" vessel constructed at New Haven, and with him the colony's application to parliament for a patent. Connecticut bought Saybrook and secured George Fenwick's promise of the territory between Narragansett Bay and the Connecticut

8 Massachusetts Historical Society *Collections*, 4th series, VII, 495.

9 *New Haven Colonial Records, 1638-1649*, pp. 149-150.

10 Ebenezer Hazard, *Historical Collections*, I, 538-540.

11 *New Haven Colonial Records, 1638-1649*, p. 211; *New Haven Colonial Records, 1653-1665*, pp. 519-520.

River, and authorized Fenwick to procure a patent for the colony, a mission which remained unexecuted,[12] but for the time being the New Haven Colony took no further steps to legalize its position. In 1651, at a moment of dispute with New Netherland, Governor Eaton authorized Edward Winslow, the agent of Massachusetts Bay in England, to procure a patent covering the Delaware region for the New Haven Colony.[13] Winslow's petition in behalf of Theophilus Eaton and the colony came to the attention of the Council of State, and was referred first to the committee for plantations and later to the committee for foreign affairs,[14] but it was without result, probably because at the moment England and the United Netherlands were at peace. With friends in high office in England, and its right to exist unchallenged, the New Haven Colony made no further efforts to secure a charter before 1660.

The kingdom of Christ on the shores of Long Island Sound always enjoyed the favor of Oliver Cromwell. Probably as early as 1650, as lord general of the army, he suggested the removal of the colony to the city of Galway, Ireland.[15] In 1654, as lord protector of England, he met the supplication of the New Haven Colony for assistance against New Netherland by dispatching Major Robert Sedgwick and Captain John Leverett with four ships to New England to seize the Dutch colony. Fearful

[12] *Connecticut Colonial Records*, I, 266-270, 585-586; Connecticut Archives, Town and Lands, I, 3; Connecticut State Library, Robert C. Winthrop Collection of Connecticut Manuscripts, III, 328-329.

[13] *Plymouth Colony Records*, IX, 199.

[14] State Papers, Domestic, Interregnum, Council of State, Fair Order Book, December 1, 1651—April 30, 1652, p. 290.

[15] John Thurloe, *State Papers*, I, 565; Massachusetts Historical Society *Collections*, 4th series, II, 115-118; William Hubbard, "A General History of New England," Massachusetts Historical Society *Collections*, 2d series, V-VI, 525-526; Cotton Mather, *Magnalia Christi Americana* (1702), Book I, p. 26; Frank Strong, "A Forgotten Danger to the New England Colonies," *Annual Report* of the American Historical Association for 1898, pp. 77-94.

that the expedition would arrive in America too late to accomplish its purpose, he suggested to friends of the colony removal "to a place where they should have towns, habitations, lands, staple commodities etc.," which John Higginson, pastor of the church at Guilford, interpreted to mean Hispaniola or Mexico.[16] When John Astwood of Milford arrived in England as the agent of the New Haven Colony in the spring of 1654 Cromwell repeated his suggestion of removal to a place "where they might haue Cittyes ready builded and land ready tilled and where staple Comodityes might be raised," as more satisfactory "than either to remoue the dutch or plant in Delawar." Astwood replied that he thought the New Haveners "would rather chuse the nearer and probably more peaceable though the poorer, Than be remoued farther wth more hazard to loose peace, and gaine riches," but he was asked to consider the proposal and to return to the protector at a later date,[17] and probably only his last illness and death in the summer of 1654 prevented his compliance.[18]

On December 26, 1654, an English fleet under Generals William Penn and Robert Venables sailed from Portsmouth. It failed miserably in its attack on Hispaniola, but in May, 1655, took Jamaica. Upon receipt of this information, Cromwell undertook to people the conquered island from Old England and New. Out of his great love, care, and tender regard for New England in general and the New Haven Colony in particular, he furnished Daniel Gookin of Cambridge in Massachusetts Bay, who in 1654

16 Connecticut Historical Society *Collections*, III, 318-320.

17 William Leete to Samuel Desborough, October 10, 1654, Papers of General Desborough 1651-1660, Egerton MSS., 2519, fols. 10-11; printed in *New England Historical and Genealogical Register*, XLI, 356-359; Henry F. Waters, *Genealogical Gleanings in England* (1901), I, 246-249.

18 John Astwood's will, dated June 27, 1654, was proved August 31, 1654. See Henry F. Waters, *Genealogical Gleanings in England* (1901), I, 81.

had returned to England, with £300, and dispatched him in the *Fraternity,* Peter Cole owner, to lay before the inhabitants of New England the feasibility of removal to Jamaica. On September 21 instructions for Gookin were considered by the council, and on September 26 they were approved. By them Gookin was authorized to offer to the inhabitants of New England twenty acres of land with all improvements adjoining a good harbor for every male over the age of twelve transported, and ten acres for all others, the land to be held in free and common socage and to pay a quit-rent of a penny per acre after the expiration of seven years, the inhabitants to enjoy freedom of customs on goods sent to England for a space of three years from September 29, 1656, and as wide powers of self-government as were possessed by any incorporated city or town in England, subject, however, to a governor and commander-in-chief to be appointed by Cromwell. The offer indicates that neither Cromwell nor the council grasped the extent of the territories and powers of government already seized by the settlers of New England.[19]

On January 20, 1656, Daniel Gookin arrived at Boston, and communicated his mission to Governor Endecott and some of the principal inhabitants of the Bay Colony. On March 7 the council granted him liberty to proceed with his mission, and under date of March 25 a proclamation was printed and sent through New England. In April the

19 John Thurloe, *State Papers,* III, 753; IV, 28-30, 440, 449; V, 6-7, 509-510; VI, 362; State Papers, Domestic, Interregnum, CII, nos. 46-49; CXL, no. 41; Council of State, Fair Order Book, April 3, 1655—March 21, 1656, pp. 297-298, 303-306, 426; Warrant Book, December 19, 1653—March 4, 1656, p. 177; *Massachusetts Colony Records,* IV, Part I, 273; *New Haven Colony Records, 1653-1665,* p. 180; *New Haven Town Records, 1649-1662,* pp. 278, 279; Cotton Mather, *Magnalia Christi Americana* (1702), Book I, p. 26; Thomas Hutchinson, *The History of the Colony of Massachusets-Bay,* I (1760), 190-192; Frederic William Gookin, *Daniel Gookin, 1621-1687,* pp. 85-103; Frank Strong, "A Forgotten Danger to the New England Colonies," *Annual Report* of the American Historical Association for 1898, pp. 77-94.

emissary of the lord protector visited Connecticut and New Haven. At the latter place he delivered to Governor Eaton a letter from Cromwell, a copy of his instructions and a supply of the printed proclamations intended for the towns of the colony.

On May 14, 1656, letters from Cromwell and the instructions of Gookin were considered by the general court of Massachusetts Bay and on May 19, by a town meeting at New Haven. On May 28 these documents and a letter from Major Robert Sedgwick, who had been sent from England to reinforce Generals Penn and Venables at Jamaica, were before a general court of the New Haven Colony. The general court of Massachusetts Bay dispatched several individuals with Captain Martin of the *Hope* to Jamaica to report on the island. The town of New Haven sent Richard Miles to interview Captain Martin, apparently already familiar with Jamaica, before he sailed. In New England three hundred individuals, young persons, of the poorer sort, many of them women, held themselves in readiness to migrate.

Reports from Jamaica to New England were not encouraging. In the tropical island men were dying by hundreds and God seemed to disown the enterprise of the English. Under these circumstances, not even the tardy permission to choose their own governor could induce the New Englanders to exchange the wilderness which they held free from all quit-rent and governed as they pleased for a limited area on a West Indian island to be held subject to quit-rent and supervision from England. On November 13, 1657, Gookin sailed for England feeling that his mission had been a failure.

After two decades of salutary neglect and unusual benevolence from those in power in the mother country, the leaders of the New Haven Colony received rumors of the restoration of Charles II to the throne of England with disbelief followed by dismay. "Here is a report brought from Virginia, by a ship lately arrived there from England, in 5 weekes, that the King of Scots is in London," wrote John Davenport to John Winthrop, Jr., April 20, 1660, "which I doe no more credit then that report of the Quakers, concerning General Munkes being in London, and sole General, by Lamberts and Fleetewoodes Laying downe theyre co̅missions, or the establishm^t of the presbyterian way. All which, I hope, with many other rumours, will be found not true, in sundry particulars, when we shall receive our Letters from England."[20] But Charles II had indeed been restored to the throne of England. In July the news reached Boston, and from that place it was quickly relayed to New Haven. "Our comfort is, that the Lord raigneth," wrote John Davenport to Winthrop, August 1, "and his counsels shall stand. In rightly obeying this King we shall become faithful to whatsoever powers he settes over us."[21]

20 Massachusetts Historical Society, Winthrop MSS., III, 145, printed in Massachusetts Historical Society *Collections,* 4th series, VII, 511-513.

21 Massachusetts Historical Society, Winthrop MSS., III, 146, printed in Massachusetts Historical Society *Collections,* 4th series, VII, 515-517.

CHAPTER XI

THE END OF CHRIST'S KINGDOM

THE restoration of Charles II to the throne of England filled the leaders at New Haven with dread of what the future might hold in store for the New Haven Colony. Without legal status under Charles I, it had cowered on the outskirts of New England. Although high in favor with all enemies of the monarchy, in the two decades between the coming together of the Long Parliament and 1660 it had not succeeded in legalizing its status. With the Restoration it made no effort to enter into relations with the Stuart régime and cringed from the sight of the crown.

News from England further dismayed the leaders of the colony. The liberal declaration of general pardon issued by Charles II at Breda, April 4, 1660,[1] was followed by an act of parliament, August 29, 1660, which excluded more than one of the friends of the colony from the benefits of the declaration.[2] Death had rescued George Fenwick and Oliver Cromwell, but on October 16, 1660, Hugh Peter went to a bloody execution at Charing Cross and was subsequently vilified with Cromwell.[3] In the following year Isaac Penington and Owen Rowe died in the Tower. On June 14, 1662, Sir Henry Vane was executed on Tower Hill. William Hooke lived in and about London in concealment, sometimes lodging in Swanne Alley in the parish of St. Stephen, Coleman Street, sometimes living

1 State Papers, Domestic, Interregnum, CCI, no. 4.

2 12 Chas. II, c. xi.

3 Massachusetts Historical Society *Collections*, 4th series, VIII, 166.

in the home of William Sydenham, sometimes in the family of one Gold, a wealthy merchant and justice of the peace at Clapham.[4] Of the colony's erstwhile patrons, only Samuel Desborough received the pardon of the crown.[5]

In their first moment of terror the leaders of the colony thought of betaking themselves, their church, their civil government, and their laws beyond the limits of the territory controlled by England. They had long experienced the ability of the Dutch to withstand the English, and they thought of seeking refuge under the jurisdiction of the colony which in 1654 they had moved heaven and earth to conquer. Through John Stickland of Huntington and Brian Newton of New Netherland, on February 15, 1661, and April 29, 1661, they approached Director General Stuyvesant.[6] At this time the Delaware was out of the question, for after the conquest of New Sweden the directors of the Dutch West India Company had granted Fort Casimir, to be henceforth known as Fort Amstel, and the surrounding country to the city of Amsterdam, and at this moment they were negotiating the transfer of the entire South River to the city. Turning from the region of which they had long dreamed, the New Haveners asked whether the territory known as Achter Col, on the mainland to the west of Staten Island, was open for settlement, and whether the Dutch would grant it to a company of honest men of the English nation who might desire to settle under the jurisdiction of New Netherland.[7]

Anxious to establish an outpost against the Raritan

[4] *Ibid.*, pp. 174, 177, 179, 194.

[5] Papers of General Desborough 1651-1660, Egerton MSS., 2519, fol. 34.

[6] Brian Newton was an Englishman faithful to the Dutch, yet reluctant to act against the English. New York Colonial MSS., XII, 22; *New York Colonial Documents*, XIV, 322.

[7] New York Colonial MSS., IX, 639, 641, 643, 897, 899, 907; X, Part I, 73, 77, 145, 147; *New York Colonial Documents*, XIII, 193-195, 208-211, 216-218, 221-222.

and Nevesink Indians, the director general and council of New Netherland welcomed the advances of the English. On May 23/June 2, 1661, they granted the group permission to send some of their number to examine the site, and Stuyvesant received the viewers with courtesy and encouragement.

Then followed months of negotiation between individuals of the New Haven Colony and New Netherland. Carrying with them a letter in which Deputy Governor Mathew Gilbert assured Stuyvesant that the Englishmen were "true men and noe spies," in November, 1661, Benjamin Fenn and Robert Treat, magistrates, Richard Law, deputy to the general court of the jurisdiction from Stamford, and Jasper Gunn, deacon of the church at Milford, visited New Amsterdam. In March, 1662, John Gregory, formerly of the town of New Haven but at this time of Norwalk, journeyed to the Dutch metropolis. In May, 1662, John Gregory, Philip Grove, formerly of Milford but at this time of Stratford, and Robert Treat visited New Amsterdam. The English proposed to carry their church, their government, their laws, and their customs into Dutch territory, and naïvely demanded complete autonomy under the protection of the colony they had formerly tried to conquer. They asked that their church or churches might enjoy all the powers, privileges, and liberties of the Congregational way. They desired to order all judicature and civil affairs within themselves, to choose their own magistrates and officers, to constitute and keep courts, to make laws and orders, and to proceed according to the New Haven code of 1656. They asked that the Indian title to the land upon which they proposed to settle might be extinguished and that they might dispose of land to approved inhabitants. They desired to trade freely with both Dutch and English. Most important of all, they asked that the grant might be confirmed by an authentic instrument signed and sealed by the proper authorities in the United Netherlands, for the English, especially those who had never possessed a charter, worshipped a great seal as an idol.

On November 18/28, 1661, March 1/11, 1662, and May 10/20, 1662, Director General Stuyvesant and the council of New Netherland considered the proposals of the English. They were willing to grant the New Haveners liberty to enjoy their churches and consociation, to obtain title to their lands from the Indians, and to enjoy freedom of trade, but felt that "in Strainge places, we may finde, but must make noe Lawes," and replied that they desired to reserve to themselves the right to confirm magistrates and officers to be nominated in double number by the English—the practice in all other English plantations within the limits of New Netherland—to ratify laws and ordinances, and to hear appeals in civil and criminal cases involving more than £50.

At this point negotiations were suspended, partly because Stuyvesant wished to consult his superiors in the United Netherlands; partly because the New Haveners had recovered from their first fright and hesitated to take a step that would sever them from New England; and partly because William Leete, deputy governor and at this time chief magistrate of the New Haven Colony, had bethought himself of another solution for the difficulties of the colony.

On March 14, 1661, a general court of the neighboring colony of Connecticut authorized an address to Charles II and the expenditure of £500 to secure a confirmation of the privileges and liberties of the lords and gentlemen upon whom Robert Rich, Earl of Warwick, reputed grantee of the Council for New England, had bestowed forty leagues of territory along the coast to the west of Narragansett Bay, to part of which Connecticut had subsequently acquired title from George Fenwick. Two months later a court of elections considered an address to the crown drafted by John Winthrop, Jr., governor of the colony, and appointed a committee to complete the address and to draft a petition for a patent.[8]

Learning of Connecticut's proposed effort to secure a charter from the crown, William Leete visited John Winthrop, Jr., and revived the idea of 1644 of one patent under which two separate and distinct colonial governments might function. This time the colony of Connecticut, as less offensive to Charles II, was to take the initiative in securing the grant. Leete seems naïvely to have expected that, having secured a charter, Connecticut would stand between the New Haven Colony and the crown, and permit the colony on the Sound to go on much as it had in the past.[9]

With the proposal of Leete, John Davenport was not in sympathy. Connecticut had always been less orthodox than the New Haven Colony. Queries issuing from the general court at Hartford had resulted in the assembly of elders at Boston in 1657 at which the Half-Way Covenant was first promulgated, and at this time the principle of a wider baptism was receiving some acceptance in the churches to the north. Although the privilege of voting for officers of the jurisdiction may have been bestowed no more liberally in the River Colony than in Massachusetts Bay and the New Haven Colony, in Connecticut the requirement of church-membership was unexpressed. Far more important to the rank and file, in Connecticut the right to participate in the affairs of their respective towns was granted to all admitted inhabitants. The founder of the colony on the Sound feared that a charter procured by Connecticut to cover the territory of both

8 *Connecticut Colonial Records,* I, 361-362, 367-368.

9 State Papers, Domestic, Charles II, LXIX, no. 5; Massachusetts Historical Society *Collections,* 4th series, VII, 548-550, 552-553.

Connecticut and the New Haven Colony would result in the prevalence of the laws and practices of the less orthodox colony.[10]

In Connecticut Leete's proposal met with approbation. On June 7, 1661, a general court at Hartford approved of the address to the king, a petition for a patent, and instructions authorizing Winthrop, about to carry both documents to England, to ask for a grant of territory bounded by the southern line of Massachusetts Bay, the western line of New Plymouth, and Delaware Bay or as far as may be that way, and adjacent islands not already disposed of.[11]

Coincident with the negotiations with New Netherland and Connecticut, the position of the New Haven Colony was further jeopardized by the arrival of Edward Whalley and William Goffe at New Haven. These men had sat in the high court of justice for the trial of Charles I and signed the death warrant of the king. In company with William Jones, late of St. Martin's in the Fields, Middlesex, and his wife Hannah, the daughter of Theophilus and Anne Eaton, on their way to New Haven to take possession of the Eaton estate, and Daniel Gookin of Cambridge in Massachusetts Bay, quondam agent of the lord protector to New England, on May 14, 1660, they sailed from Gravesend in the vessel of Captain Pierce. Arriving at Boston July 27, they brought to New England confirmation of the news of the restoration of the Stuarts. They were well received by Governor Endecott of Massachusetts Bay, and after spending some time in Boston, took up their abode with Daniel Gookin in Cambridge.[12]

[10] *New Haven Colonial Records, 1653-1665,* p. 521; *New Haven Town Records, 1662-1684,* p. 13.

[11] *Connecticut Colonial Records,* I, 369-370, 579-585; Massachusetts Historical Society, Winthrop MSS., XII, 23.

[12] C. O. 1: 15, no. 82; Lemuel A. Welles, *The History of the Regicides in New England* (1927).

Meanwhile, on May 18, 1660, the House of Lords ordered the seizure of Whalley and Goffe. On June 6, 1660, the king ordered the two regicides to surrender within fourteen days. On August 29, 1660, an act of parliament exempted them from pardon. Upon a report that they had been seen in Kent, on September 19, 1660, a Privy Council at Whitehall authorized the attorney general to prepare a proclamation offering a reward for their apprehension, and on September 22, 1660, a royal proclamation to that effect was issued.[13] Following a report that the two regicides had fled to New England, the king, on March 5, 1661, issued a special order to the governor or magistrates of New England for their arrest.

When news of the act of parliament excepting Whalley and Goffe from pardon reached Massachusetts Bay in a weekly intelligence sent by way of Barbados, the two regicides decided to remove from the colony. They had crossed the ocean with William and Hannah (Eaton) Jones of New Haven. Whalley was the brother, and Goffe, the nephew by marriage of Jane Hooke, wife of the former teacher of the church at that place. As soon as Davenport learned of the presence of the two men in New England, he expressed the intention of inviting them to New Haven, but delayed doing so until after the meeting of the commissioners of the United Colonies of New England at New Haven in September, 1660, in order that he might entertain John Winthrop, Jr., at that time.[14] Probably at Davenport's suggestion, on February 26, 1661, Whalley and Goffe set out from Boston. Guided by Simon Lobdell, formerly of Milford and at this time of Hartford, they passed through Hartford without stopping, and on March 7, 1661, arrived at the home of John Davenport in New Haven.

[13] For the order to the attorney general to prepare, see P. C. 2: 54, p. 168. Copies of the three proclamations are in Yale University Library.

[14] Massachusetts Historical Society *Collections,* 3rd series, X, 37-39.

For almost eight weeks Whalley and Goffe lived in the home of Davenport. On April 30 they crossed the road to the home of William Jones, with whom they had sailed from England. On May 11 they moved to a mill two miles from town. From May 13 to 15 they camped at Hatchet Harbor, and through the summer of 1661 in a cave, supposedly on top of West Rock. On June 24 they appeared in the town of New Haven. On August 19 they moved to the home of Micah Tomkins in Milford. There they lived in seclusion for more than three years.[15]

Upon receipt of news of the royal proclamation of September 22, 1660, on March 8, 1661, Governor Endecott and the assistants of Massachusetts Bay ordered the secretary of the colony to issue a warrant for the arrest of Whalley and Goffe.[16] After the arrival of the royal order of March 5, 1661, Endecott sent Thomas Kellond and Thomas Kirke, two young merchants recently arrived from England and zealous in the royal cause, with John Chapin to guide them, to Governor Winthrop of Connecticut, Deputy Governor Leete of the New Haven Colony, and Director General Stuyvesant of New Netherland, with letters from himself and copies of the king's order.[17] On May 7 Kellond and Kirke set out from Boston. Three days later Governor Winthrop received them at Hartford, and on May 11 Samuel Martin guided them from Wethersfield to the home of Deputy Governor Leete at Guilford.

William Leete and his fellow magistrates knew that Whalley and Goffe were within the limits of the colony on

[15] Fearful of the impending visit of the royal commissioners, in the fall of 1664 Whalley and Goffe spent a week or more in the cave on the outskirts of New Haven in which they had passed the spring of 1661, and on October 13, 1664, set out for Hadley in Massachusetts Bay.

[16] C. O. 1: 15, no. 51.

[17] *Ibid.*, nos. 48, 49, 50; New York Colonial MSS., IX, 627-631; *New York Colonial Documents*, III, 41-42.

the Sound, but they gave Kellond and Kirke no assistance in their efforts to take them. After informing the inhabitants of the town of New Haven that "for theire respect to two Traitors they would doe themselves injury and possibly ruine themselves and the whole Colony of New-Haven," on May 14 the two emissaries left for New Amsterdam. From that place they returned to Boston by sea.[18]

Shortly after the unsuccessful search for the regicides, Massachusetts Bay received a letter from John Leverett in which the former agent of the Bay Colony in England pointed out the dissatisfaction felt with the colony in the mother country, and the necessity of proclaiming the king, appointing an agent to represent the colony in England, and apprehending the regicides. In the name and by order of the council of Massachusetts Bay, on July 4, 1661, Secretary Edward Rawson wrote to Governor Leete, reporting the contents of Leverett's letter and pleading with Leete to sacrifice Whalley and Goffe.[19]

On August 1, 1661, Governor Leete laid Rawson's letter before a general court at New Haven, and the colony took a few wavering steps toward obedience. The general court sent something which Leete had prepared petitionwise for the king to the council of Massachusetts Bay, apparently to be forwarded by the council of the Bay Colony to Charles II, asked Massachusetts to inform the king that the New Haven Colony adhered to the address that had been made to him by Massachusetts in the previous December, and agreed to share with Massachusetts the expense of maintaining an agent in England.[20] The

[18] C. O. 1: 15, no. 59; Thomas Hutchinson, *A Collection of Original Papers* (1769), pp. 334-338.

[19] C. O. 1: 15, no. 83; Thomas Hutchinson, *A Collection of Original Papers* (1769), pp. 338-341; *New Haven Colonial Records, 1653-1665,* pp. 419-420.

[20] Massachusetts Historical Society *Collections,* 4th series, VII, 548-550; *New Haven Colonial Records, 1653-1665,* pp. 420-422.

colony would not surrender its friends to certain death, however, and although at the moment the regicides lurked on the outskirts of the town of New Haven, the general court of the jurisdiction denied that they were within its limits. William Leete visited Boston and persuaded John Norton, teacher of the First Church, to plead his cause with Richard Baxter, a Presbyterian divine in the confidence of those who had brought about the restoration,[21] and he himself sent "a pittifull letter" to England.[22] John Davenport dispatched an apology to the general court of Massachusetts Bay and a letter to Thomas Temple, governor of the forts in Nova Scotia, about to depart from Boston for England, in the latter resorting to obvious falsehood to whitewash himself and his colony. "This is my great Intendment in this lines," he wrote, "humbly to Craue yor mindfullnesse of me and helpefullnesse Toward mee in this Exigent, And not for my Selfe alone doe I make this humble Request, But allso on the Behalfe of this Poore Colloney and of our Goueno^r^ and majestrates, who wanted neither will nor Industery to haue Serued his Matie in apprehending the 2 Collonells, but were Preuented and Hindered by gods ouerruilling Prouidence, which with held them that they Could not Exiqute their true Purpose therein; And the same Prouidence Could haue done the same, in the same Curcumstances, if they had bine in London, or in the Tower."[23] Following the proclamation of Charles II by Massachusetts Bay, August 8, 1661, a general court at New Haven, August 21, voted to proclaim the king in the presence of the artillery company on the following day.[24]

But when the royal order to the governor or magistrate

21 Richard Baxter, *Reliquiae Baxterianae* (1696), Part II, p. 292.

22 Massachusetts Historical Society *Collections*, 4th series, VIII, 182.

23 C. O. 1: 15, no. 81, printed in Massachusetts Historical Society *Collections*, 3d series, VIII, 327-330.

24 *New Haven Colonial Records, 1653-1665*, pp. 422-423.

of New England for the arrest of Whalley and Goffe was laid before the commissioners of the United Colonies of New England, in session at Plymouth, September 5, 1661, and they issued an order for the apprehension of the regicides, Benjamin Fenn of Milford, the town in which Whalley and Goffe were at the moment concealed, one of the representatives of the New Haven Colony, refused to sign it.[25] "I am almost amazed sometimes to see what crosse cape[rs] some of you do make," wrote William Hooke from London. "I should breake my shinnes should I doe the like."[26]

Meanwhile, on June 21, 1661, John Winthrop, Jr., had informed Director General Stuyvesant of his intended departure for England, and perhaps of the plan to procure one charter to cover Connecticut and the New Haven Colony, but certainly not of his instructions to ask for a grant of the territory held by the Dutch, and had inquired about vessels at New Amsterdam.[27] With all friendliness the Dutch governor replied that the master of the *Trowe*, the largest of three ships then in the harbor, would await Winthrop until the following week.[28] Armed with the address and petition of Connecticut to the crown, Winthrop sailed from New Amsterdam.[29] He also carried instructions, a letter of credit, and letters of introduction from his colony, and the proposal of William Leete,[30] but he was without a copy of the grant of the Earl of Warwick,

[25] *Plymouth Colony Records*, X, 269-270; Thomas Hutchinson, *A Collection of Original Papers* (1769), pp. 344-345.

[26] Massachusetts Historical Society *Collections*, 4th series, VIII, 178-179.

[27] *Ibid.*, 5th series, VIII, 73.

[28] *Ibid.*, I, 391.

[29] New York Colonial MSS., XIV, 64; *New York Colonial Documents*, XIV, 515.

[30] *Connecticut Colonial Records*, I, 370, 579-585; Connecticut Archives, Foreign Correspondence, II, 1-3; Connecticut State Library, Robert C. Winthrop Collection of Connecticut Manuscripts, III, 330; Connecticut Historical Society *Collections*, XXIV, 7.

for one could not be found. From September 6 to 12 he visited the city of Amsterdam in the United Netherlands. On September 15 he arrived at the port of Harwich, England, and on Wednesday, September 18, at London.[31] There he took up his abode with Mrs. Whiting in Coleman Street, next door to the church of which John Davenport had at one time served as vicar.[32] In the mother country, friends and acquaintances understood that he had come as the representative of both Connecticut and the New Haven Colony.[33]

The newly arrived agent of New England Puritanism undoubtedly commanded more respect than any other man who could have been sent to the mother country at this time.[34] Educated at Trinity College, Dublin, a member of the Inner Temple, widely traveled, he had made his second voyage to America in 1635 as the governor appointed by the grantees of the Earl of Warwick. In 1661 he carried to England instructions to act with the advice and counsel of the surviving grantees, some of them in positions of influence in the restored Stuart régime. He had long dabbled in science and medicine, and corresponded with such men as Robert Boyle, Kenelm Digby, Samuel Hartlib, and William Brereton. Almost as soon as he arrived in England Brereton proposed his name for membership in the society for promoting experimental philosophy which Charles II had recently taken under his

31 Massachusetts Historical Society, Winthrop MSS., V, 29.

32 Massachusetts Historical Society *Collections*, 5th series, I, 394; Massachusetts Historical Society *Proceedings*, 2d series, I, 126; Massachusetts Historical Society, Winthrop MSS., VI, 3, 5.

33 Massachusetts Historical Society *Collections*, 4th series, VIII, 187.

34 Frederick John Kingsbury, "John Winthrop, Junior," American Antiquarian Society *Proceedings*, new series, XII, 295-306; Thomas Franklin Waters, *A Sketch of the Life of John Winthrop the Younger* (1899); Robert H. Murray, *Dublin University and the New World* (1921), pp. 63-88; W. H. Cooke, editor, *Students Admitted to the Inner Temple, 1547-1660* (1877), pp. 241, 252. There is no adequate biography of John Winthrop, Jr.

patronage and which the king incorporated as the Royal Society in the following year. On January 1, 1662, Winthrop was admitted to the organization, and during his sojourn in England took an active part in its proceedings.

In his efforts to procure a charter for Connecticut, Winthrop was aided by both the grantees of the Earl of Warwick and his friends in the society for promoting experimental philosophy. Lord Saye and Sele, lord privy seal, too ill to be of much assistance himself, gave Winthrop a letter to the Earl of Manchester, lord chamberlain of the king's household, "a noble and a worthy L^{d} and one that loues those that are godly," in which he asked Manchester to assist the governor of Connecticut in every possible way.[35] He also referred the governor to William Jessop, at one time clerk of the grantees, and Colonel Crowne for information about the earlier patent. Samuel Hartlib introduced Winthrop to Benjamin Worsley, who "hath much the eare of the Ld Chauncellour, and I believe in reference to the Plantations Hee is Privy to most Transactions."[36]

In the name and behalf of the colony of Connecticut, Winthrop presented several petitions to the crown, asking for "all and singular like powres Jurisdic̃cons rights liberties and priuiledges for your Petic̃oners Plantac̃on bounded on the East by Narogansett Riuer com̃only called Narogansett Bay, where the bounds of New Plimouth plantacon end, and on the North by the line of the Massachusett plantacon, and on the South by the Ocean Sea and in longitude as the line of the Massachusetts Colony ruñeth from east to west, with the Ilands adioyning possessed by your Petic̃oners as were formerly granted to the other Plantac̃ons of new England by your Ma:^{ties} Royall predecessors to be held and enioyed im̃edi-

[35] Massachusetts Historical Society *Collections*, 5th series, I, 394.

[36] Massachusetts Historical Society *Proceedings*, XVI, 215.

ately from and under your most excellent Ma^ty^ by vertue of a Charter to bee granted to your Peticōners.'"[37]

Despite the efforts of Samuel Maverick, at the moment painting dark pictures of New England to Clarendon,[38] at first Winthrop met with no opposition. On February 12, 1662, the Privy Council referred his petition to the attorney general, asking advice regarding the powers, privileges, estates, and interests to be granted. Attorney General Palmer advised granting the powers asked for, but referred the question of exemption from customs to the lord treasurer.[39] On February 28 the warrant to prepare a bill was issued.[40] Probably in connection with other matters, the Privy Council summoned Thomas Temple and John Winthrop, Jr., to wait upon it on Thursday, March 6, at three o'clock in the afternoon.[41] On April 23 the charter passed the privy seal,[42] and on the afternoon of May 10 it passed the great seal,[43] and was ready for enrollment at the hanaper office and the rolls.[44]

By the charter of 1662 Charles II bestowed upon the colony of Connecticut "All that parte of our Dominions in Newe England in America bounded on the East by Norrogancett River, comonly called Norrogancett Bay, where the said River falleth into the Sea, and on the North by the lyne of the Massachusetts Plantation, and

[37] C. O. 1: 16, no. 17; Massachusetts Historical Society, Winthrop MSS., XII, 23; Connecticut Archives, Foreign Correspondence, I, Part I, no. 1; Bodleian Library, Rawlinson MSS., A, CLXXV, 109; CLXXVI, 113; *Annual Report* of the Connecticut Historical Society for 1904, p. 23.

[38] New York Historical Society *Collections*, 1869, pp. 19-22.

[39] C. O. 1: 16, no. 17.

[40] *Ibid.*, no. 27.

[41] P. C. 2: 55, p. 558; C. O. 5: 903, pp. 5, 6.

[42] Patent Roll, 14 Charles II, Part 11, no. 10; C. O. 1: 16, no. 46.

[43] "This day, May 10th, in the afternoon, the Patent for Connecticut was sealed," Winthrop wrote in an almanac for 1662, Connecticut Historical Society *Collections*, I, 52.

[44] John Winthrop, Jr., to Samuel Wyllys, May 12, 1662, Massachusetts Historical Society, Belknap Papers, 1637-1788, p. 6.

on the south by the Sea, and in longitude as the lyne of the Massachusetts Colony, runinge from East to West, (that is to say,) from the said Narrogancett Bay on the East to the South Sea on the West parte, with the Islands therevnto adioyneinge.''[45] Probably unwittingly, the Stuart king had granted Connecticut half of the colony of Rhode Island and Providence Plantations and all of the New Haven Colony,[46] and intentionally had disregarded the rights of New Netherland, for by the charter Connecticut swept indefinitely westward.

During the winter of 1661-1662 Winthrop had longed for spring that he might sail for home with the first ships.[47] As negotiations for the charter drew to a close, he gave Edward Cowes, Giles Sylvester, and William Maskeline, merchants who supplied him with £500 to meet expenses, a draft on John Talcott, treasurer of Connecticut, for two thousand bushels of wheat at three shillings sixpence the bushel, and twelve hundred bushels of peas at two shillings sixpence, to be delivered to them or to their assigns at New London before November 30, 1662,[48]

45 *Connecticut Colonial Records,* II, 3-11.

46 A memorandum of Sir Edward Nicholas, Secretary of State, February 6, 1662, indicates that at that time he thought that New Haven was an independent colony. C. O. 1: 16, no. 13. Although the proprietors of the Narragansett country asked for the king's letters only to Massachusetts Bay and Connecticut, C. O. 1: 17, no. 51, Charles II addressed letters to the governors and assistants of Massachusetts Bay, New Plymouth, the New Haven Colony, and Connecticut, June 21, 1663 (State Papers, Domestic, Entry Books, X, 1662-1663, pp. 90-91; C. O. 1: 17, nos. 52, 53, 54; C. O. 5: 903, pp. 22-23; *Plymouth Colony Records,* X, 320; *New Haven Colonial Records, 1653-1665,* pp. 499-500), as though unaware that, by the grant to Connecticut more than a year before, the New Haven Colony had been extinguished. The grant to Connecticut was probably made without thought of the consequences to the New Haven Colony. There is not a scrap of evidence that the king intended to abolish the colony on the Sound to punish it for sheltering Edward Whalley and William Goffe, the regicides.

47 Massachusetts Historical Society *Collections,* 4th series, VII, 520-521; VIII, 179.

48 Massachusetts Historical Society, Winthrop MSS., X, 17-18; Connecti-

and prepared to return to New England. His departure was delayed for more than a year, however, by the claims of John Clarke, one of the founders of Newport, Rhode Island, since 1652 resident in England as the agent of the colony of Rhode Island and Providence Plantations.[49]

Meanwhile, in June, 1662, news of the grant to Connecticut reached New England, and soon after that one copy of the charter arrived at Hartford. When the commissioners of the United Colonies of New England as-

cut State Library, Robert C. Winthrop Collection of Connecticut Manuscripts, III, 332, 334; *Connecticut Colonial Records,* I, 385-386; Connecticut Historical Society *Collections,* I, 52-55.

49 In January, 1662, and again in February, Clarke petitioned the crown that Rhode Island and Providence Plantations might be taken under the royal wing. On March 25 the king referred the first of these petitions to the next sitting of the council. After the charter to Connecticut had passed the great seal, on May 14 and May 16 Clarke presented additional petitions. In the first he requested that the recent grant to Connecticut might be reviewed, and the grant of the commission of parliament in 1644 to the plantations of Providence, Portsmouth, and Newport might be confirmed by a royal charter. In the second he asked that the boundary between Connecticut and Rhode Island might be determined either by Winthrop and Clarke or by a committee of the Privy Council. These facts Winthrop learned with amazement. C. O. 1: 15, nos. 4, 6-9, 34; Bodleian Library, Clarendon MSS., LXXVI, fols. 255, 272; *Rhode Island Colonial Records,* I, 485-491; New York Historical Society *Collections,* 1869, pp. 44-45. Robert Boyle and Thomas Temple attempted to reconcile the conflicting claims of the two agents without results, and Winthrop turned the problem over to William Thursby of the Middle Temple and one Laurence and left London to attend to personal matters. Massachusetts Historical Society *Collections,* 5th series, VIII, 75-76. After a hearing before Robert Boyle, Thomas Temple, Samuel Maverick, and John Scott, and a debate before the lord chancellor, William Brereton, Robert Thompson, Benjamin Worsley, Richard Deane, and John Brookhaven, arbitrators, fixed the boundary between Connecticut and Rhode Island at the Pawcatuck River, and to harmonize the award with the charter already issued to Connecticut, changed the name of the Pawcatuck to the Narragansett River. Winthrop and Clarke agreed to accept the award, and on July 8, 1663, the colony of Rhode Island and Providence Plantations received a charter from the crown over the territory to the east of the Pawcatuck. Egerton MSS., 2395, p. 393; C. O. 1: 17, nos. 18, 19; Patent Roll, 15 Charles II, Part 15, no. 3; Massachusetts Historical Society, Winthrop MSS., XII, 24, 26; XIII, 30; Massachusetts Historical Society *Collections,* 5th series, VIII, 82-83; IX, 50-52.

sembled at Boston, September 4, 1662, the first *bona fide* grant to a Puritan colony of New England was read. Somewhat doubtful of the portent of the charter, William Leete and Benjamin Fenn of the New Haven Colony wrote in the margin of the records of the confederation, "Wee cannot as yett say that the procurement of this Pattent wilbe acceptable to vs or our Collonie." Thomas Danforth of Massachusetts Bay added to his signature of the records of the meeting, "vnderstanding th^{t} of Kenectecott Pattent, so as not to violate the articles of confederation otherwise I consent not to it," and Leete and Fenn added to their signatures, "Subscribed in Mr Danforthes sence."[50]

Whatever may have been the original intention of the magistrates of the River Colony, royal authorization whetted their ambition. Refusing to surrender a moiety of the legal right of the colony to the territory of the New Haven Colony and New Netherland, they notified the towns within the limits of the colony on the Sound that they fell within the grant to Connecticut and invited them to send deputies to the general court scheduled to meet at Hartford, October 9, 1662. They authorized John Youngs, Jr., of Southold to take possession of Long Island, part of which belonged to the New Haven Colony, part, to New Netherland.[51]

Long irked by the narrow franchise enforced in the strictest of the Puritan commonwealths in New England, a majority of the inhabitants of Southold on Long Island and a faction of malcontents in Guilford and Stamford on the mainland saw in the grant to Connecticut an op-

[50] *Plymouth Colony Records,* X, 286-287, 289.

[51] Connecticut Archives, Town and Lands, I, 12; Colonial Boundaries, II, 1; Robert C. Winthrop Collection of Connecticut Manuscripts, I, 1; Connecticut Historical Society *Collections,* XXIV, 8-9; New York Colonial MSS., X, Part I, 263; *New York Colonial Documents,* XIV, 518. The correct date of the letter of Peter Stuyvesant is October 3/13, 1662.

portunity to throw off the jurisdiction of the New Haven Colony and responded with alacrity to the invitation of the River Colony to send representatives to Hartford. After receiving the town of Southold and inhabitants of Guilford and Stamford under its jurisdiction, appointing John Youngs, Jr., as commissioner on Long Island, appointing constables to function at Guilford, Stamford, and Greenwich, and notifying the inhabitants of Westchester that they too fell within the jurisdiction of Connecticut, the general court of the River Colony appointed Mathew Allyn, Samuel Wyllys, Samuel Stone, and Samuel Hooker a committee to treat with the New Haven Colony regarding union.[52]

Accompanied by Joseph Fitch, on October 15, 1662, the committee appointed by the general court at Hartford appeared before a court of magistrates at New Haven and presented a copy of the charter of Connecticut and a statement that the New Haven Colony was included in the grant and asked that the union of the two colonies might forthwith take place.[53]

With prophetic vision, on May 28, 1662, a general court of the New Haven Colony had authorized Governor Leete and the magistrates and elders of New Haven and Branford to function in emergencies but to make no change in the government of the colony without its consent. Neither the court of magistrates nor the emergency committee possessed authority, therefore, to act on the proposals of Connecticut. The former designated October 29 as a day of extraordinary seeking of God by fasting and prayer for guidance regarding the proposed union with Con-

[52] *Connecticut Colonial Records,* I, 386-390, 405.

[53] Connecticut State Library, Robert C. Winthrop Collection of Connecticut Manuscripts, I, 3, 4; Connecticut Archives, Miscellaneous Papers, I, 67; *New Haven Colonial Records, 1653-1665,* pp. 465-468; New York Colonial MSS., X, Part II, 93-103; XV, 17; *New York Colonial Documents,* XIV, 526-527.

necticut. The magistrates and ministers of New Haven, Branford, and Milford agreed to lay the charter of Connecticut and the demands of the committee of the River Colony before the freemen of the colony, but requested Connecticut to take no action until the New Haven Colony had communicated with John Winthrop, Jr.[54]

Probably to prepare the freemen of the central town for the forthcoming meeting of the freemen of the colony, on October 31 the charter, the proposals of Connecticut, and the reply of the magistrates and ministers of New Haven, Branford, and Milford were read to a general court for the town of New Haven. After John Davenport and Nicholas Street had spoken in opposition to union, the freemen of the town of New Haven voted disapproval of the action of Connecticut.[55]

On the morning of November 4 the freemen of the colony assembled at New Haven and the three documents were read to this larger gathering. Following a recess of an hour and a half to consider whether or not the charter had brought into existence one body politic where formerly there had been two, and whether or not they desired the union of Connecticut and the New Haven Colony to take place, the freemen reassembled. John Davenport read a paper that he had prepared in opposition to union and the freemen of the colony voted to defer action until John Winthrop, Jr., had returned to New England and the New England Confederation had been consulted. They appointed the magistrates and elders of the colony and Richard Law of Stamford a committee to so inform the general assembly of Connecticut, and if this were without avail, to consider an address to Charles II, for the colony on the Sound had gone unpersecuted for two

[54] Connecticut Archives, Miscellaneous Papers, I, 68; *New Haven Colonial Records, 1653-1665,* pp. 453, 465, 469.

[55] *New Haven Town Records, 1662-1684,* pp. 12-14.

years and a half and was recovering from its first fears of the Stuart king.[56]

Undiscouraged by its original rebuff, on March 11, 1663, a general assembly at Hartford appointed Deputy Governor John Mason, Mathew Allyn, John Talcott, John Allyn, and Samuel Wyllys if Deputy Governor Mason were unable to serve, a committee to continue negotiations with the New Haven Colony. On March 20 the two Allyns and Wyllys were in New Haven. In behalf of Connecticut, they offered that if the union of the two colonies were consummated, the churches of the New Haven Colony should be undisturbed, for after all the Half-Way Covenant had not yet received universal acceptance even in Connecticut. They were willing that the magistrates of the New Haven Colony should continue to exercise their office until the following May. They promised that a proportionate number of the assistants of Connecticut would henceforth be chosen from within the limits of the New Haven Colony, and that freemen of the New Haven Colony would be received as freemen in Connecticut. They said that New Haven, Milford, Branford, and Guilford would be erected into a county within which powers of judicature would be exercised, and that a court of assistants would sit annually or oftener at New Haven to hear appeals from the county court. They promised that the towns of the New Haven Colony might each send two representatives to the general assembly at Hartford. To these proposals the New Haven committee through Governor Leete replied that the colony was under appeal to Charles II![57]

The appeal of the New Haven Colony to the crown proved to be only "a dreame of rich reuenues to an

[56] *New Haven Colonial Records, 1653-1665,* pp. 467-471, 473-475.

[57] Connecticut Archives, Miscellaneous Papers, I, 69, 70; *Connecticut Colonial Records,* I, 396; *New Haven Colonial Records, 1653-1665,* pp. 475-477.

awakeing poore man.''[58] In 1643 Emmanuel Downing had carried one John Scott to New England. Five years later Scott was the apprentice of Lawrence Southwick of Salem in Massachusetts Bay. In company with John Youngs, Jr., he invaded the waters of New Netherland in 1654 and was taken prisoner by the Dutch. In 1658 he was an inhabitant of Southampton on Long Island, and somewhat later of the neighboring settlement of Setauket or Ashford. He was also one of the proprietors of the Narragansett country. Learning of the restoration of Charles II to the throne of England, he remembered that his father had advanced £14,300 to Charles I and lost his life in the royal cause, and that he himself had cut the girths of the parliamentary forces at Turnham Green. To discover what favors might be reaped from past services to the house of Stuart, toward the end of 1660 he sailed from New Amsterdam in the *Eyckenboom* for England. Upon his arrival he seems to have asked for a grant of Long Island and to have been refused. Wearing a miniature of Charles II in a gold frame on a gold chain about his neck, in England claiming it to be the gift of James, Duke of York, in New England, of the king himself,[59] he returned to New England. From knowledge gained abroad he assured the committee appointed by the freemen of the New Haven Colony that their territory was not included in the grant to Connecticut, and accepted the commission of the colony on the Sound to return to England either to secure satisfaction from John Winthrop, Jr., or to present the cause of the colony at court.[60] On the morning of March 2 or 3, 1663, he was again in Lon-

[58] Connecticut Archives, Miscellaneous Papers, I, 81; *New Haven Colonial Records, 1653-1665*, p. 531.

[59] Thomas Hutchinson, *A Collection of Original Papers* (1769), pp. 380-381; New York Colonial MSS., XIV, 32, 64; *New York Colonial Documents*, XIV, 506, 515; New York Historical Society *Collections*, 1869, p. 47.

[60] Massachusetts Historical Society, Winthrop MSS., X, 18.

don and met with Nathaniel Whitfield, son of Henry Whitfield, founder of Guilford, Robert Thompson, a London merchant, member of the Society for propagation of the Gospel in New-England, friend of Edward Hopkins, and recent purchaser of the Whitfield holdings in Guilford, and William Hooke, former teacher of the church at New Haven, and presented the case of the New Haven Colony to John Winthrop, Jr.[61] Already embroiled with John Clarke of Rhode Island and Providence Plantations, the governor of Connecticut was anxious to settle the dispute between Connecticut and the New Haven Colony without attracting the attention of the authorities. Mentioning Leete's request that one patent to cover the territory of Connecticut and the New Haven Colony be procured, he denied that he intended to infringe the rights of the colony on the Sound. At the request of the friends of the New Haven Colony he sent off a letter, the preliminary draft of which had been prepared by Thompson but which Winthrop modified, to Deputy Governor John Mason and the general assembly of Connecticut, in which he expressed regret that inhabitants of the New Haven Colony had been received as freemen of Connecticut, and the hope that union by unanimous consent would be arrived at.[62] After the dispatch of the letter to Mason and the assembly Winthrop hastily sent off a second epistle in which he apologized for the tone of the one drafted by Thompson and urged the deputy governor not to force the union of Connecticut and the New Haven Colony, but to let the initiative come from New Haven.[63] Ignorant of this second letter and not overzealous for the independ-

[61] State Papers, Domestic, Charles II, LXIX, no. 5.

[62] Massachusetts Historical Society *Collections,* 5th series, VIII, 80-81; *New Haven Colonial Records, 1653-1665,* pp. 498-499, 522-523, 534; Connecticut State Library, Robert C. Winthrop Collection of Connecticut Manuscripts, II, 250.

[63] Massachusetts Historical Society *Collections,* 5th series, VIII, 77-80.

ence of the colony on the Sound, the agents of New Haven were appeased, and the cause of the New Haven Colony never reached the crown.

As soon as a settlement of the dispute between John Winthrop, Jr., and John Clarke had been arrived at, Winthrop sailed for home, carrying with him a duplicate of the charter to Connecticut.[64] He was met at Boston by Richard Olmstead and Jeremiah Adams, sent by the River Colony, June 6, 1663, to fetch him, and proceeded post-haste to Hartford.[65] News of his arrival precipitated letters of protest from all sides. Leete explained that he had had in mind a charter that would cover but not control the New Haven Colony. John Davenport expressed the belief that Winthrop came with an olive branch in his mouth, for neither Charles II nor Connecticut could intend to destroy the kingdom of Christ on the shores of Long Island Sound.[66] Director General Stuyvesant of New Netherland expressed joy that the governor of Connecticut had arrived and the hope that the misunderstandings regarding boundaries between the Dutch and the English would soon be cleared up.[67]

Although John Winthrop, Jr., opposed the coercion of his neighbors to the south, he favored the union of Connecticut and the New Haven Colony and the conquest of New Netherland, and his arrival was followed by no change in the policy of the aggressive little colony on the River. On August 19, 1663, the general assembly at Hartford appointed Deputy Governor John Mason, Samuel Wyllys, Daniel Clarke, and John Allyn, or any two or three of them, a committee to treat with the New Haven Colony. A week later this committee was in New Haven

64 *Connecticut Colonial Records,* I, 407.

65 Massachusetts Historical Society, Winthrop MSS., X, 18.

66 Massachusetts Historical Society *Collections,* 4th series, VII, 521-524, 550-553.

67 *Ibid.,* 5th series, I, 395-396.

and renewed the overtures of the previous March. By this time the New Haven Colony knew that its appeal to Charles II had come to nothing, and to postpone the inevitable, it made the return of its seceded inhabitants a *sine qua non* to further negotiation. At the same time it asked whether, in the event of the ultimate union of the two colonies, "the fundamentall lawes for Governm^{t} especially th^{t} touching the Qualificacons of ffreemen shalbe the same wth Boston or our (i e) members of some one or oth^{r} of o^{r} Churches." This last was a condition which Connecticut could not and would not meet. To the query the committee of the River Colony replied, "we are ready to grant That they shalbe men of a religious carriage visibly soe haueing and possessing Some competency of Estate, And shal bring a Certificate affirmatiue that they are thus Quallified from the Deacons of the Church and Two of the Select men of the Towne where they liue And if there be noe deacons then some other knowne and approued persons w^{t}h the Select men as before: . . . That the ffreemen of these Plantat^{s} shall haue power to chuse all Publ country officers exept Assistants To weet. Comission^{r}s Deputies and Constables, As for Select men who are to ord^{r} the civil prudentiall affaires of the Respectiue Townes they to be yearly chosen by a maior Vote of the approued Inhabitants wth other necessary Towne officers in th^{r} respect: Pl: in this County." On October 22, 1663, a general court at New Haven voted to seek a letter of exemption from the crown, and to ask its agents, probably the same individuals who had represented the colony in negotiations with Winthrop in the preceding spring, to consider the advisability of securing a patent covering the territory of the New Haven Colony. To cover the cost of procuring a patent if that were decided upon, the general court authorized a rate of £300. On December 30, 1663, an effort to collect arrears in rates from the secessionists at Guilford led to a riot, to quell which the troops at New Haven and Branford were called out. As a result of this fracas, on January 7, 1664, a general court at New Haven appointed John Davenport and Nicholas Street to put the grievances of the New Haven Colony into writing, and "Newhavens Case Stated" appeared.[68]

Throughout the struggle with Connecticut the opponents of union in the New Haven Colony clung to the idea of removing beyond the limits of the territory controlled by England. When it became evident that Connecticut would not respect the sovereignty of its confederate, Robert Treat of Milford reopened negotiations with Director General Stuyvesant of New Netherland, June 29, 1663.[69]

To the Dutch West India Company and the states general of the United Netherlands, the restoration of Charles II to the throne of England represented an opportunity to people New Netherland with Englishmen out of sympathy with the restored Stuart régime. In reply to Stuyvesant's inquiry of 1662, the directors of the company ordered him to make every effort to encourage the migration of the New Haveners to New Netherland, even to the extent of permitting them to bring with them their printed code of laws of 1656, and under certain circumstances, waiving appeals in criminal cases.[70]

With this authorization, the director general of New Netherland proceeded to sound Oratam, sachem of the Hackensack Indians, regarding the willingness of the natives to sell the hook of land behind the Kil van Kol to the Dutch. With a settlement at this point in mind, on July

[68] Connecticut Archives, Miscellaneous Papers, I, 71-81; *Connecticut Colonial Records,* I, 407-408; *New Haven Colonial Records, 1653-1665,* pp. 476, 491-495, 501-503, 512-537.

[69] New York Colonial MSS., X, Part II, 231; *New York Colonial Documents,* XIII, 266-267.

[70] New York Colonial MSS., XIII, 143; XV, 7; *New York Colonial Documents,* III, 37-39; XIII, 239-240; State Papers, Holland, CLXIV, 23-24.

10/20, 1663, director general and council agreed to grant to the New Haveners almost complete autonomy within the limits of the Dutch colony, reserving only the right to confirm officers and laws and to hear appeals "in darke and dubious matters, especially in Wich Craft," and in civil suits in which more than £100 Flemish was involved. These concessions they agreed to confirm in a public instrument, charter, or patent, properly subscribed and sealed, not by the authorities of the United Netherlands, but by themselves.[71]

The migration of the opponents of union from the New Haven Colony to Achter Col within the limits of New Netherland seemed so likely to reach consummation that in 1663 John Davenport sent John Cotton's *Discourse About Civil Government in a New Plantation Whose Design is Religion,* written twenty-five years before this time to guide the planters of Quinnipiac in establishing a government based upon "Moses his judicials," to Samuel Green and Marmaduke Johnson in Cambridge in Massachusetts Bay to be printed for the guidance of those about to set out for Achter Col. At this crucial moment New Netherland fell before the aggressions of Connecticut.[72]

Like John Davenport, Director General Stuyvesant of New Netherland had believed that the return of John Winthrop, Jr., to New England would result in the amicable settlement of all misunderstandings between his colony and Connecticut. With the intention of securing a confirmation of the boundaries between the territories of the Dutch and the English which had been agreed upon at Hartford in 1650 or some other satisfactory settlement,

[71] New York Colonial MSS., X, Part II, 228, 233-237; *New York Colonial Documents,* XIII, 280-282.

[72] See my article, "The Authorship of a Discourse About Civil Government in a New Plantation Whose Design is Religion," *American Historical Review,* XXXVII, 267-269.

he journeyed to the meeting of the commissioners of the United Colonies of New England at Boston in September, 1663. When his trip proved without avail, he sent Cornelis van Ruyven, Oloff Stevenson van Cortlandt, and John Lawrence as commissioners of New Netherland to the general assembly which met at Hartford, October 8, 1663, only to be met again with evasions. At the desire of the schout, burgomasters, and schepens of New Amsterdam, the director general called a meeting of delegates from the Dutch towns in the vicinity of New Amsterdam to meet October 21/November 1, 1663, to consider the state of the country. Driven to desperation, on November 5/15, 1663, he agreed to surrender title to Westchester to Connecticut on condition that both Connecticut and New Netherland would forbear to exercise coercive jurisdiction over the English towns at the western end of Long Island until the boundary between New Netherland and New England should be determined.[73]

The conduct of John Scott added to the difficulties of the Dutch colony. On his second visit to England Scott had presented the case of the New Haven Colony to John Winthrop, Jr., taken part in the negotiations between John Winthrop, Jr., and John Clarke, and laid the case of the proprietors of the Narragansett country before the crown. Asking for a grant of the government of Long Island for himself, he had discovered that the Earl of Stirling had sold his rights to James, Duke of York, and that Charles II intended to add to the lands of the Earl of Stirling the province of New Netherland and to confirm the whole by a royal charter. Scott learned of these developments about a year before the information reached

[73] New York Colonial MSS., X, Part II, 287-387 *passim;* XV, 59, 68-69; *New York Colonial Documents,* II, 224-226, 385-393, 477-479; *Plymouth Colony Records,* X, 299-304; *Connecticut Colonial Records,* I, 415-416; Connecticut Archives, Town and Lands, I, 15; Connecticut Historical Society *Collections,* XXI, 145-146.

Connecticut. Adding his complaints of the Dutch to those of John Winthrop, Jr., he had joined Samuel Maverick and Richard Baxter in drafting plans for the conquest of New Netherland.[74]

With a letter of Charles II in favor of the Narragansett proprietors, Scott returned to New England. On Long Island he ordered the arrest of John Cooper of Southampton as a traitor to the king and undertook to prosecute him at Hartford. Assuring the towns at the eastern end of Long Island that they lay within the grant to the Duke of York and need no longer pay rates to Connecticut, he undertook to negotiate with the River Colony in behalf of the town of Southampton. Dissatisfied with the contents of a letter from Southampton to the government of Connecticut, on the way to Hartford he heaved it overboard. From the chief town on the river, he dispatched a rather meaningless epistle to his friend, Undersecretary Joseph Williamson, December 14, 1663, probably to impress John Winthrop, Jr., by whom the letter was perused and copied. Forgetting that he himself had assured the people of Long Island that they no longer fell within the limits of Connecticut, he entered agreements and contracts between himself and the people of Setauket or Ashford in the colonial records of Connecticut, accepted from the River Colony the office of commissioner at Setauket with magisterial power throughout Long Island, and promised to assist the colony in the seizure of Long Island from the Dutch. Returning to Long Island, he sat with John Talcott, John Youngs, Jr., and Richard Woodhull as the commissioner of Connecticut at a court held at his own house at Setauket.[75]

[74] *New York Colonial Documents*, III, 46; Thomas Hutchinson, *A Collection of Original Papers* (1769), pp. 380-381; Massachusetts Historical Society, Winthrop MSS., XII, 27; Connecticut Archives, Foreign Correspondence, I, Part I, 2; *Rhode Island Colonial Records*, I, 466-467.

[75] Connecticut Archives, Town and Lands, I, 10, 11, 13, 24, 29, 30; Massa-

Meanwhile, after the agreement of November 5/15, 1663, between Connecticut and Director General Stuyvesant, the inhabitants of the English towns at the western end of Long Island were puzzled by the River Colony's apparent abandonment of its claim to jurisdiction over them. Learning of Scott's activities at the eastern end of the island, they appealed to that representative of many interests. Again remembering the impending grant to James, Duke of York, Scott entered upon what at the moment he considered the most advantageous design of his career. In company with John Youngs, Jr., who apparently believed that he was acting for Connecticut, about the end of December, 1663, he visited Oyster Bay, Hempstead, Flushing, Rustdorp or Jamaica, Middelburgh or Newtown, and Gravesend. Replacing the original town names with others of good English origin, he informed the inhabitants that they fell within the limits of a grant to James, Duke of York, organized the towns under his presidency, and summoned the director general of New Netherland to a conference. With a hundred and fifty recruits, horse and foot, colors flying, trumpets sounding, and drums beating, he visited Breuckelen, Midwout, Amersfoort, New Utrecht, and Bushwick, and proclaimed the Duke of York. On January 1/11, 1664, and January 4/14, 1664, Director General Stuyvesant sent commissioners to negotiate with Scott at Midwout and at Rustdorp or Jamaica. On February 24/March 5 the director general and council of New Netherland went to meet Scott at Hempstead. To prevent the plundering of the Dutch towns on Long Island, the Dutch agreed at this third meeting that the English might control the English towns on Long Island until the boundary between New Netherland and New England should be determined by

chusetts Historical Society, Winthrop MSS., XVIII, 28; C. O. 1: 17, no. 102; *New York Colonial Documents*, III, 47-48.

the governments of the United Netherlands and England.[76]

Reports of the activities of Connecticut's recently appointed magistrate soon reached Hartford. By the agreement between Connecticut and New Netherland, November 5/15, 1663, Connecticut had for the moment abandoned its claim to the western end of Long Island, but since on February 24/March 5, 1664, Stuyvesant had surrendered the English towns to Scott, the River Colony revived its claim and sent Samuel Wyllys and Mathew Allyn to settle the towns under the jurisdiction of Connecticut. In June Governor Winthrop himself visited the English towns, deposed the magistrates set up by Scott, and in the presence of Director General Stuyvesant and commissioners of New Netherland swore in others to succeed them.[77]

Meanwhile, on March 3, 1664, a court at Hartford ordered its secretary to authorize Richard Woodhull of Setauket to issue a warrant for the arrest of Scott and his abettors if some one would undertake to prosecute them for abusing the corporation and its members. A week later a general court ordered the seizure of Scott as a traitor to the colony. On the morning of March 21 Jonathan Gilbert, marshal of Connecticut, and five or six others attempted to take Scott at New Haven. Claiming to have the authorization of the crown under the sign manual for his acts, Scott offered to stand trial before the combined magistrates of Connecticut and the New Haven Colony, or at Boston, or in New Plymouth, or in

[76] Connecticut Archives, Town and Lands, I, 18-21, 23, 25-27, 30; Robert C. Winthrop Collection of Connecticut Manuscripts, I, 6, 10; Connecticut Historical Society *Collections,* XXI, 146-147; Massachusetts Historical Society, Winthrop MSS., XVIII, 29; New York Colonial MSS., XV, 112, 121; *New York Colonial Documents,* II, 393-406; XIV, 544-548.

[77] *Connecticut Colonial Records,* I, 423; New York Colonial MSS., XV, 131, 138; *New York Colonial Documents,* II, 407-409; XIV, 549-555.

Virginia, or before the king and council, and with a bodyguard of between ten and fifteen New Haveners, crossed the Sound to Setauket. On March 26 Nathan Gold of Fairfield sent Nathaniel Seely and fifteen or sixteen others in a vessel to Setauket with a special warrant for Scott's arrest. Despite his bodyguard, Scott was seized and carried prisoner first to Stratford and later to Hartford, where he was placed in "hold and chains." On May 12 his estate was sequestered. Six days later William Pitkin, attorney of the colony, undertook to prosecute him before the particular court at Hartford for usurping the authority of the king and defaming the king's majesty. Waiving jury trial, Scott was found guilty on May 24, sentenced to pay a fine of £250, to suffer imprisonment at the court's pleasure, degradation from his office of commissioner on Long Island, disfranchisement, and disqualification as a witness before all civil courts in the colony, and ordered to give bond of £500 for good behavior toward the colony and all persons of the corporation before his not too imminent departure. In July he escaped from his gaoler and made his way back to his home at Setauket.[78]

The unwillingness of Connecticut to fix a boundary between New Netherland and New England probably became more intelligible to Director General Stuyvesant when Ensign Nyssen informed him, April 11/21, 1664, of a report that the English would take New Netherland within the next six or eight weeks, and Thomas Willett of Plymouth added, June 28/July 8, 1664, that an expedition was actually *en route* to seize the Dutch colony.[79]

[78] Office of the Secretary of State, Hartford, Probate Records, III, 14, 16-17; Connecticut State Library, Robert C. Winthrop Collection of Connecticut Manuscripts, I, 9, 10; Connecticut Archives, Town and Lands, I, 28, 31-35; Massachusetts Archives, II, 183, 184, 387; *Connecticut Colonial Records,* I, 418, 420-424, 430, 436, 441; Connecticut Historical Society *Collections,* XXI, 152-158.

[79] New York Colonial MSS., X, Part III, 251; XV, 119, 134.

John Winthrop, Jr., and John Scott had suggested the conquest of New Netherland, but it benefited neither. On March 12, 1664, before the expedition to take the Dutch colony left England, Charles II granted the territory between the Connecticut and Delaware rivers to his brother, James, Duke of York, and on June 24, 1664, while the expedition was in mid-ocean, the Duke of York regranted that half of his province between the Hudson and Delaware rivers to John, Lord Berkeley, and Sir George Carteret.[80]

On April 23, 1664, Richard Nicolls, Robert Carr, George Cartwright, and Samuel Maverick were appointed a royal commission to reduce "the Dutch in and neare Long Island, or any where within the Limits of our owne Dominion," apprehend the regicides, inquire into the enforcement of the navigation acts, and investigate the state of New England. Furnished with the *Guinea,* the *Elias,* and two other vessels, four hundred and fifty men, and the king's letter to John Winthrop, Jr., the commissioners set sail for Gardiner's Island at the eastern end of Long Island.[81]

On July 23, 1664, Nicolls and Carr arrived at Boston in the *Guinea* and learned that three days earlier Cartwright and Maverick and the other vessels had reached Piscataqua. The leaders promptly dispatched a letter to John Winthrop, Jr., announcing their intention to do the crown some service near his colony, and a week later

[80] Patent Roll, 16 Charles II, Part 8, no. 6; Aaron Leaming and Jacob Spicer, *The Grants, Concessions, and Original Constitutions of the Province of New-Jersey* (1752), pp. 3-11; Francis N. Thorpe, *The Federal and State Constitutions, Colonial Charters, and Other Organic Laws of the States, Territories, and Colonies* (1909), V, 2533-2535.

[81] C. O. 1: 18, nos. 48-52; C. O. 324: 1, fols. 205-249; Egerton MSS., 2395, fols. 387-395; Connecticut State Library, Robert C. Winthrop Collection of Connecticut Manuscripts, III, 308; Connecticut Archives, Foreign Correspondence, I, Part I, 3; Massachusetts Historical Society, Winthrop MSS., XII, 27.

asked him to meet them at the western end of Long Island. They found Massachusetts Bay no more willing to take part in an expedition against New Netherland than it had been in 1654, but this time the expedition was less dependent upon colonial support.[82]

Warned of the impending attack by Ensign Nyssen and Thomas Willett, Director General Stuyvesant acquired provisions from the New Haven Colony, like New Netherland a sufferer from the aggressions of Connecticut, and sent spies into New England to watch for the arrival of the English fleet. His fears were somewhat allayed, however, by the assurance of the directors of the Dutch West India Company that the expedition from England had as its object the reduction of New England to one form of government in things temporal and spiritual, and the assertion of Thomas Willett that all danger had passed.

Reinforced by John Winthrop, Jr., whose coöperation must have been half-hearted indeed when he learned that the statements of John Scott had been quite correct, and that two-thirds of Connecticut had been handed over to James, Duke of York, and supported also by John Scott and his hastily regathered troop of horse and foot,[83] the

82 New York State Library, General Entries, I, 1664-1665, 2, 7, 8, printed in University of the State of New York, *State Library Bulletin, History No. 2*, May 1899, pp. 55, 72-78; Massachusetts Historical Society, Winthrop MSS., V, 51.

83 John Scott failed to profit from the conquest of New Netherland. On September 11, 1664, Nicolls granted him a safe return to Setauket or Ashford, but through the machinations of Connecticut he lost the lands on Long Island that he had purchased from the Indians. When Nicolls ordered him to produce the deed or writing under which he had been acting at a court of assizes, he fled to Barbados. Although he was an adventurer of the first order, he enjoyed the friendship of Joseph Williamson in England and of John Leverett in New England, and his arrest by Connecticut brought protests from Massachusetts Bay, New Plymouth, and the New Haven Colony, and it hardly seems possible that he could have been the deep-dyed villain that he has been depicted by the colony with whose plans for aggression he interfered. C. O. 1: 19, no. 14; C. O. 1: 20, no. 151; New York State Library, General Entries, I, 1664-1665, 46, printed in University of the State

English frigates assembled before New Amsterdam, August 16-18, 1664. At this time there were only three thousand pounds of powder and lead or two pounds per man capable of bearing arms in the whole of New Netherland, and the Dutch were in no position to withstand an attack. On August 29/September 8, 1664, Director General Stuyvesant surrendered to the English. On September 3 Carr left to take possession of the Delaware, and a week later Cartwright, to take Fort Orange.[84] The government of the Dutch colony within the limits of which the New Haveners had hoped to find refuge gave way to the government of the brother of Charles II.

Upon the arrival of the royal commissioners with instructions to inquire into conditions in New England, Massachusetts Bay advised Connecticut and the New Haven Colony to compose their differences that the charters of New England might not be endangered. Connecticut sent John Whiting, associate pastor of the church at Hartford, and Thomas Bull to New Haven with news of the presence of the commissioners, the advice of the Bay Colony, and the request that the New Haven Colony accept the union of Connecticut and New Haven.[85]

It was becoming increasingly difficult for the New Haven Colony to carry on. The secessionists refused to pay rates and the treasury was so nearly empty that the salary of the governor had been reduced from £50 to £40 and that of the deputy governor from £20 first to £15 and

of New York, *State Library Bulletin, History No. 2,* May 1899, pp. 59, 115; New York State Library, Miscellaneous Records, II, Orders, Warrants, Records, Permits, etc., 1662-1669, 117; *New York Colonial Documents,* III, 86, 136; XIV, 557, 590.

84 New York Colonial MSS., XV, 138, 140; XX, 1; *New York Colonial Documents,* II, 250-253, 367, 372, 432; III, 70; XIV, 551-555; New York State Library, General Entries, I, 1664-1665, 23, 30, 31, 32, 34, 35, 58, printed in University of the State of New York, *State Library Bulletin, History No. 2,* May 1899, pp. 57-58, 95-98, 101-105, 125-127; Massachusetts Historical Society, Winthrop MSS., V, 187.

85 *New Haven Colonial Records, 1653-1665,* pp. 544-546.

later to £10. Individuals either refused to hold office or took only a conditional oath of office. Bad though union with the liberal Congregationalists of Connecticut might be, it was preferable to inclusion in the province of the Anglican Duke of York. On August 11, 1664, the magistrates and a general court of the colony on the Sound suggested that by virtue of its patent Connecticut assert its claim to the New Haven Colony and in the king's name require it to submit, grant all that had been offered in the long drawn out negotiations, and undertake to defend the recently acquired charter against the royal commissioners, and the New Haven Colony would give in, but on second thought added, "untill the Comissioners of the Colonies doe meete."

In September, 1664, the commissioners of the United Colonies of New England convened at Hartford. Maintaining that the union of Connecticut and the New Haven Colony had been consummated, the council of the River Colony protested against the presence of William Leete and William Jones as commissioners of the New Haven Colony and suggested that a revision of the articles of confederation was in order. Representatives of Massachusetts Bay and New Plymouth advised "theire bretheren and loueing Confeaderates" to come to an agreement in order that "the sadd consequences that will Inevitably follow vpon theire further Contensions one with another might be preuented," and agreed to recommend to their respective governments that if the union of Connecticut and the New Haven Colony were consummated, four out of six commissioners might conclude all matters at meetings of the New England Confederation, and that annual meetings might give way to triennial, but they refused to take cognizance of the dispute.[86]

[86] Connecticut Archives, Miscellaneous Papers, I, 86; *New Haven Colonial Records, 1653-1665,* pp. 546-547; *Plymouth Colony Records,* X, 318-319.

Since the action of the commissioners of the United Colonies of New England was not conclusive, on September 14, 1664, the freemen of the New Haven Colony assembled "to Advise and Consider together, in what state is best for us to appeare, when the Comissioners from England come to visitt us, whether in the state we now are, or under a Regall stampe (as they call it) in joyneing with Connecticutt," but broke up without coming to a decision.[87]

Connecticut considered that the New Haven Colony had come to an end. On October 4 the council authorized Governor Winthrop to appoint officers in the several plantations of New Haven, Milford, Branford, Guilford, and Stamford. On October 13 the general assembly at Hartford sent Samuel Sherman and John Allyn to require the inhabitants of New Haven, Milford, Branford, and Guilford to submit to the government of Connecticut, and Mathew Allyn and James Richards to Stamford for the same purpose, and invested William Leete, William Jones, Mathew Gilbert, Benjamin Fenn, Jasper Crane, Robert Treat, and Richard Law with magisterial power under the government of Connecticut. Unwilling to push its advantage too far, however, on November 3 the council of Connecticut discreetly respited the oath required of freemen within the limits of the former New Haven Colony.[88]

On November 17 the town of Milford submitted to Sherman and Allyn. Two days later the action of the town of New Haven was indecisive. On November 30, 1664, three of the four royal commissioners fixed the southern boundary of Connecticut at the sea and the western boundary at a line running north northwest from the eastern side of the mouth of Mamaroneck Creek or

[87] *New Haven Colonial Records, 1653-1665*, pp. 547-548.
[88] *Ibid.*, p. 548; *Connecticut Colonial Records*, I, 437.

River, and handed Long Island over to the Duke of York, thus recognizing the right of Connecticut and New York to the territory of the New Haven Colony. It was useless for the colony on the Sound to hold out longer. On December 13 a general court attended by freemen of New Haven, Guilford, Branford, and part of Milford, and as many of the inhabitants as cared to come, assembled at New Haven and voted to submit to Connecticut and chose a committee to consummate the union of the two colonies. On January 7, 1665, the town of New Haven surrendered. Disregarding the committee appointed by the freemen of the New Haven Colony, on April 20, 1665, a general court at Hartford placed William Leete, William Jones, Benjamin Fenn, Mathew Gilbert, Jasper Crane, Alexander Bryan, Richard Law, and Robert Treat of the former New Haven Colony in nomination for the office of assistant in the colony of Connecticut, and although freemen from the New Haven Colony considered that they were repulsed at the court of elections at Hartford, May 11, 1665, Leete, Jones, Fenn, and Crane were chosen to office. On May 1, 1665, the town of New Haven refused to pay any part of the charges of procuring the charter which had been the death knell of the kingdom of Christ on the shores of Long Island Sound, but on the following May 22 and August 14 the proceedings of the general assembly of Connecticut and the laws of the River Colony were read to town meetings at New Haven.[89]

In September, 1667, the commissioners of the United Colonies of New England met at Hartford. William Leete, the last governor of the New Haven Colony, attended the meeting as one of the commissioners of Connecticut, and was chosen to the presidency of the New

[89] New York Colonial MSS., XXII, 5; Connecticut Archives, Miscellaneous Papers, I, 87; *New Haven Colonial Records, 1653-1665*, p. 550; *New Haven Town Records, 1662-1684*, pp. 102-104, 125, 142, 144; *Connecticut Colonial Records*, I, 440; II, 13.

England Confederation. Contrary to the articles of confederation, the union of Connecticut and the New Haven Colony had taken place without the consent of the New England Confederation. Massachusetts Bay and New Plymouth asked to know the terms of the union, and when they were not forthcoming, protested, but Connecticut had no intention of releasing its prey. Finally accepting the situation, in 1670 and 1672 the two northerly confederates salved their consciences for the wrong done to a fellow by incorporating in revised articles of confederation the statement that the union of Connecticut and the New Haven Colony "shall alwaies be Interpreted as by theire owne Consession and not otherwise."[90]

When the English conquest of New Netherland seemed assured, the New Haveners preparing to migrate to Achter Col under the jurisdiction of New Netherland turned from Director General Stuyvesant to the Duke of York, and from Achter Col to the Delaware, where the Indian title was already extinguished, and where they had expended much capital. On January 7, 1664, a general court of the New Haven Colony authorized a committee to treat with John Scott, self-appointed agent of the Duke of York, at the moment at the zenith of his power on Long Island, regarding a patent for the Delaware. Scott soon fell before Connecticut, and in the name of the deputies of the several towns of the New Haven Colony, on December 20, 1664, William Jones laid the claim of the colony before Richard Nicolls, deputy of the Duke of York, only to learn that the duke had already granted the Delaware to Berkeley and Carteret. On February 10, 1665, the proprietors commissioned Philip Carteret as governor of their province of New Jersey. Upon the arrival of Philip Carteret in America, Jones and other undertakers of a plantation on Delaware Bay or River received his per-

90 *Plymouth Colony Records,* X, 323-351.

mission to settle in the territory which inhabitants of the New Haven Colony had purchased from the Indians a quarter of a century before this time and the right to govern themselves, subject to a quit-rent of a half-penny per acre to be paid to the proprietors, and the jurisdiction of the governor, council, and assembly of New Jersey. On February 10, 1666, the undertakers of the proposed plantation on the Delaware sent Robert Treat and John Gregory to Philip Carteret to procure changes in the agreement, but the governor had already forwarded it to the proprietors in England.[91]

At this point in the negotiations Philip Carteret seems to have turned the attention of the New Haveners to the region in northern New Jersey for which they had been negotiating with Peter Stuyvesant. On May 21, 1666, inhabitants of Milford, Guilford, and Branford chose a location on the Passaic River. They were driven off by the Hackensack Indians, but Governor Carteret negotiated a purchase of the site, and on May 26, 1666, sent Robert Treat and others with two interpreters to Oratam to complete it. On July 11, 1667, the original agreement with the Indians was embodied in a deed, and on March 13, 1678, the first purchase was extended. In the spring of 1666 the undertakers chose a committee to remain on the site while the others returned to the towns of the extinct New Haven Colony to arrange a removal to New Jersey. In June James Bollen, secretary of the province, was in Milford, doubtless on business relating to the removal. On October 30, 1666, Abraham Pierson and other inhabitants of Branford convened and drafted certain fundamental

[91] *New Haven Colonial Records, 1653-1665*, p. 515; Aaron Leaming and Jacob Spicer, *The Grants, Concessions, and Original Constitutions of the Province of New-Jersey* (1752), pp. 26-27; C. O. 1: 18, no. 155; Yale University Library, Answer to a Bill in Chancery, printed in *New Jersey Archives*, 1st series, I, 51-54; William A. Whitehead, *East Jersey under the Proprietary Governments* (1875), pp. 288-290.

orders reminiscent of those of the New Haven Colony to be enforced in the town on the Passaic. To these orders inhabitants of New Haven, Guilford, and Milford later subscribed.[92]

John Davenport was interested in the migration to New Jersey but he was too old to take part in the founding of a second kingdom of Christ. Placing John Bowers in charge of his congregation at Branford and James Fitch in charge of his work among the Indians, Abraham Pierson became the spiritual leader of the settlement on the Passaic, at first called Milford and later Newark. For William Leete lands were laid out in the new town, and William Jones carried on the negotiations with Philip Carteret, but both remained in Connecticut, the former to become governor of the colony, the latter an assistant. Robert Treat of Milford and Samuel Swayne and Jasper Crane of Branford, all at one time magistrates of the New Haven Colony, removed to the new settlement and served as deputies to the early assemblies of New Jersey, but at a later time Treat returned to Connecticut and served as assistant, deputy governor, and governor of the colony from which in the years immediately following the Restoration he had tried so hard to escape.[93]

The town on the Passaic started off as a self-governing community differing little from the original plantation of Quinnipiac. Homelots of six acres were laid out. A church and mill were built. Magistrates to preside at town courts, deputies to assist the magistrates, and a second lot of deputies to attend the general assembly of the province,

[92] "Answer of the Rioters to the Publications of the Proprietors and Speech of Samuel Nevill," *New Jersey Archives*, 1st series, VII, 31-32; "Newark Town Records," New Jersey Historical Society *Collections*, VI; William A. Whitehead, *East Jersey under the Proprietary Governments* (1875), pp. 49-53, 290-293.

[93] "Newark Town Records," New Jersey Historical Society *Collections*, VI.

a town constable, treasurer, and clerk were annually elected. Newark never expanded into a second New Haven Colony, however. The town was always subject to the superior jurisdiction of governor, council, and assembly of the province of New Jersey, and for its lands it owed a quit-rent to the proprietors in England. A population of eighty-six families in 1673 had increased to only a hundred families seven years later.[94]

For a time John Davenport tarried at New Haven, busying himself with preaching and writing.[95] In 1651 he had refused a call to the pastorate of the Second Church at Boston in Massachusetts Bay, but with the suppression of the colony he had founded and the ecclesiastical and civil systems he had fought to maintain, the cause of Christ on the shores of Long Island Sound seemed miserably lost, and he no longer considered himself bound to the church at New Haven.[96] In September, 1667, an invitation to fill the pulpit of the First Church in Boston, made vacant by the death of John Wilson, came to him, and he desired to accept it. The call was not unanimous, however, for a minority of twenty-eight in the Boston church opposed Davenport, both because he was an old man of seventy and because he had never accepted the conclusions of the synod of 1662, and refused to baptize the children of those who had not been admitted to full communion with

[94] New York Colonial MSS., XXIII, 69; George Scot, *The Model of the Government of the Province of East-New-Jersey in America* (1685), p. 136, reprinted in William A. Whitehead, *East Jersey under the Proprietary Governments* (1875), p. 406.

[95] An epistle to the reader prefixed to Increase Mather's *The Mystery of Israel's Salvation* (London, 1669) is signed "From my study in N. Haven in N. E. the 18th. day of Sept. 1667. Thine in the Truth truly, John Davenporte."

[96] *New Haven Town Records, 1649-1662*, p. 86; John Davenport to John Leverett, June 24, 1665, printed in Thomas Hutchinson, *A Collection of Original Papers* (1769), pp. 392-396.

the church. Desiring to spare the tender spirit of their aged pastor from the strife and contention which his removal to the church in Boston would render inevitable, the church at New Haven refused to admit that the dissolution of the New Haven Colony had severed the bond between pastor and church, and opposed his departure. On the occasion of a visit of Davenport to Boston in May, 1668, the majority of the church at Boston repeated their invitation, and for the second time Davenport asked the church at New Haven to dismiss him. An unsatisfactory reply of July 15, 1668, was made known to only a few warm supporters in the church at Boston and a third request for a dismissal was dispatched to the church at New Haven. A letter of October 12, 1668, was again unsatisfactory, but with the knowledge of Davenport, James Allen, candidate for the office of teacher in the church, and James Peck, ruling elder, abstracted such passages as would pass for a dismissal, and these John Davenport, Jr., copied in the form of a letter and to them appended the signature of Nicholas Street. On October 25, 1668, the revised document was read to the First Church in Boston, and John Davenport, his son, and their wives were propounded for membership. On November 1 the candidates were admitted. On November 9 Davenport was called to the pastorate of the First Church in Boston. One month later he received his final ordination at a service solemn enough to have converted Charles II to Congregationalism.[97]

Meanwhile, on August 6, 1668, messengers of the

[97] C. O. 1: 21, no. 135; Massachusetts Historical Society, Letters and Papers, Boston, 1631-1783, II, 1; III, 1; IV, 1-2; V, 1-5; Massachusetts Archives, X, 56; John Davenport, James Allen, and James Penn to the Church at Roxbury, undated, American Antiquarian Society; Massachusetts Historical Society, John Hull's Narrative; Yale University Library, The Third Church Narrative, printed in Hamilton Andrews Hill, *History of the Old South Church*, I.

churches at Dorchester, Dedham, Roxbury, and Cambridge convened at Boston and authorized the dissatisfied minority of the First Church to demand letters of dismissal and to gather a third church. When the demand was refused, a second gathering of representatives of fifteen churches met at Boston, April 13, 1669, and sanctioned the secession of the minority. With the approval of a majority of the magistrates of the colony, on May 12, 1669, the secessionists met at Charlestown and gathered the Third or Old South Church of Boston. A week later Davenport preached a sermon which was a plea for the old order, lest "the golden Candlesticks, and the burning and shining Lights in them" be lost, before the court of elections of Massachusetts Bay. The deputies to the general court approved of his efforts but the assistants condemned the sermon as a partisan argument.[98] In the following month Nicholas Street of New Haven visited Boston, and the fact that Davenport himself had not had a *bona fide* dismissal from the church at New Haven became known. Seventeen ministers of the Bay Colony, among them John Higginson and John Sherman, at one time ministers of the New Haven Colony, and Increase Mather, the friend who had supported Davenport in his stand on baptism in 1662, condemned the obvious deception that had been practiced on the First Church at Boston. Davenport charged Street with misguiding the church at New Haven, and vowed never again to set foot in the territory of the colony he had founded. In the midst of strife and contention in churches and colony, on the evening of Sunday, March 13, 1670, he was stricken with the dead palsy, and after a twenty-four hours' illness, on

[98] *A Sermon Preach'd at The Election of the Governour, At Boston in New-England, May 19th 1669* (1670), reprinted in Colonial Society of Massachusetts *Publications,* X, 6; Massachusetts Archives, X, 7.

"the 15th day about 9. at night the Lord tooke him out of a troublesome unthanckfull evill world."[99]

[99] John Davenport, Jr., to John Winthrop, Jr., March 28, 1670, in Massachusetts Historical Society, Winthrop MSS., XII, 105; The Third Church Narrative, printed in Hamilton Andrews Hill, *History of the Old South Church,* I, 165; "John Hull's Diary," American Antiquarian Society *Transactions and Collections,* III, 230. In the last two sources the date of Davenport's death is given as March 16, 1670, but the letter of John Davenport, Jr., would seem to be conclusive proof that March 15, 1670, is the correct date.

CHAPTER XII

EPILOGUE

AT a time when the monarchy of the early Stuarts was at its lowest ebb, after vain struggles to better their ecclesiastical, civil, and economic conditions in England, John Davenport and Theophilus Eaton led a company of ultra-conservative Puritans from London to Boston in Massachusetts Bay. The immigrants found the Bay Colony torn with religious dissension, its harbors occupied, and conditions little more to their liking than conditions in England. Catching the vision of a kingdom of Christ on the shores of Long Island Sound, they added to their number and pushed on to a more distant frontier.

Without royal patent to the soil, or authorization to establish a colonial government, the group had in its favor only distance and the preoccupation of the crown with affairs in England and Scotland. Purchasing the rights of the Indians to large stretches of territory on the northern shore of Long Island Sound, on Long Island, and on Delaware Bay and River, the first arrivals staked out a colony. They received recognition from James Forrett, agent of William Alexander, Earl of Stirling, one Miles, agent of Sir Edmund Plowden, and George Fenwick, representative of the grantees of Robert Rich, Earl of Warwick. To people their territory they drew colonists from New England and Old. The first plantation at Quinnipiac soon expanded into the New Haven Colony, with jurisdiction over the towns of New Haven, Guilford, Milford, Stamford, and Branford on the mainland, and the town of Southold on Long Island, and a foothold on the Delaware River.

Copying the non-separating Congregationalism of Massachusetts Bay, in each town of the colony little groups of saints entered into covenant with God and with one another to walk in all the ways of truth. Each church thus gathered became a unit independent of outside control. To their fellowship the elect admitted others who had proved their worthiness, and from it they excluded those who fell from grace. All attempts to liberalize the system met with failure.

In establishing a government the settlers of the colony on the Sound adopted a frame of government and code of laws which John Cotton had prepared for Massachusetts Bay. In harmony with this code they restricted all ecclesiastical and civil privileges to church-members. Only saints who had entered into covenant with God and with one another partook of the Lord's Supper, offered their children for baptism, and participated in civil affairs.

At early dates schools offering instruction in elementary and grammar-school subjects appeared in the towns of the colony but the college which John Davenport endeavored to found at New Haven to train leaders "for the service of god in Church and comonwealth" failed to materialize until long after the New Haven Colony had come to an end. To establish the commercial commonwealth of which the immigrants from London dreamed, two decades also proved too brief a time.

One of the United Colonies of New England, the New Haven Colony conducted its relations with its Puritan neighbors, with the Indians, and with New Netherland and New Sweden through the channels of the confederation. Although the colony copied the ecclesiastical and civil practices of Massachusetts Bay, and enforced them even more stringently than did that colony, its economic and intercolonial interests parallelled those of the more liberal Connecticut, and for a period of twenty-two years the two southerly confederates saw eye to eye. With the straightforward and honest Dutchmen on the Hudson and with the Swedes on the Delaware, the merchants of the New Haven Colony traded and intermarried, at the same time casting envious glances at the territories of their continental friends and planning the eventual subjugation of both New Netherland and New Sweden. This duplicity can best be explained by believing that they sincerely thought that Dutch and Swedes were encroaching upon English soil.

Meanwhile, in England the wheel of fortune had turned. War in Scotland was followed by the convening of the Long Parliament and the rise of the Puritan party to a position of influence. For twenty-two years the right of the colony on the Sound to exist went unchallenged. An attempt to secure a charter to cover the territory of both the New Haven Colony and Connecticut in 1646 was frustrated by the loss of the vessel carrying the agent of the colonies to England. An attempt to secure a patent for the Delaware region in 1651 was also without result. With friends in high office in the mother country authorization became less vital, however, and the matter was not pressed.

Although speculation lies beyond the province of the historian, one may pause to consider the possibilities in the case. Had the Puritans retained control of the government in England, the New Haven Colony would probably have continued to exist; and had England subdued New Netherland in 1654, the territory between Greenwich and the Delaware might have passed to the New Haven Colony, and in place of the states of Connecticut, New York, and New Jersey, the map of the United States might show today a state of New Haven stretching from the western boundary of Rhode Island to the Delaware River.

But this was not to be. In 1660 the wheel of fortune completed its revolution, and the Stuarts again ruled England. With its whole history standing as a barrier between it and the crown, and without competent leaders, the New Haven Colony could do nothing. On the other hand, Connecticut, with less to make it fearful and with more competent statesmen, secured a charter in 1662 covering the territory which the New Haven Colony had at one time hoped to possess. For a long two years the latter jurisdiction refused to merge its identity with that of its former ally. Finally, to escape arbitary inclusion in the province of the Anglican Duke of York, it submitted. John Davenport betook himself to Boston in Massachusetts Bay; other malcontents migrated to Newark in New Jersey.

To the privileged inner circle of the New Haven Colony the disappearance of Christ's kingdom on the shores of Long Island Sound represented the depth of human tragedy—the plans and efforts of a lifetime come to naught. Yet even before 1665 the ecclesiastical and civil systems of the New Haven Colony were crumbling, and as seventeenth-century intolerance fell before eighteenth-century tolerance, they were bound to disappear. Saints seemed fewer, and a less articulate if not less godly generation clamoured to participate in the affairs of the church and of the state. Somewhat sooner than might otherwise have been the case, the New Haven Colony was absorbed by a government "amazingly advanced for the day," and destined to survive until 1818.[1] After the lapse of nearly three hundred years it is possible to see that the disappearance of the colony on the Sound represented not tragedy but progress.

[1] Charles M. Andrews, *Our Earliest Colonial Settlements* (1933), pp. 139-140.

BIBLIOGRAPHICAL NOTE

MANUSCRIPTS.

Much light on the English background of the settlers of the New Haven Colony can be gleaned from the records and account books of the parishes in England from which they came. The vestry book of St. Lawrence's, Old Jewry, London, now deposited in the Guildhall Library, the minutes of general vestries and of vestries of committees of St. Stephen's, Coleman Street, London, the churchwardens' accounts, and the register of the parish, in charge of Mr. H. Graham Bennet, clerk of the parish council, transcripts of the register of St. Peter's at Rowley in Yorkshire for the years 1620 to 1625 and 1630 to 1640, and the institution books of the diocese of York, in the office of the registrar of the diocese at York, add to the knowledge of the settlers of the plantation of Quinnipiac or New Haven. A transcript of the register of St. Margaret's at Ockley in Surrey, in charge of Mr. H. C. Martin, rector, and the register of St. Dunstan's at Cranbrook in Kent, in charge of Mr. H. T. Swingler, vicar, throw light on the settlers of Menunkatuck or Guilford. A copy of the register of St. Edmund's at Southwold, Suffolk County, England, deposited in the office of the town clerk at Southold, Long Island, New York, gives information regarding John Youngs, the first pastor at Southold, and his family. Further knowledge of the settlers and the colony is to be found in the State Papers, Domestic Series, for the reigns of James I and Charles I; Bills, Answers, etc., Charles I, London and Middlesex, no. 533; Exchequer Decrees, IV, 88–91; State Papers, Holland; State Papers, Poland; State Papers, Colonial Series; the Order Books of the Council of State; and the Privy Council Registers for the early years of Charles II; all deposited in the Public Record Office, London; and in The Trial of the Company of Feoffees for the Purchase of Impropriations, Harleian MSS., 832; Papers of Thomas Povey, Egerton MSS., 2395; Papers of General Desborough 1651–1660, Egerton MSS., 2519; the Barrington Papers, Egerton MSS., 2643–2650; sections of John Scott's Proposed History of America, Sloane MSS., 3662; letters of John Davenport and Ezekiel Rogers in Additional MSS., 4275 and 4276; the Boswell Papers, Additional MSS., 6394; and manuscript tracts relating to the English church in Amsterdam, Additional MSS., 24666; all deposited in the British Museum.

Information regarding the career of John Davenport in Amsterdam can be found in the Records of the Consistory of the English Reformed Church at Amsterdam, in charge of Dr. William Thomson, pastor of the church; in the Resolutie-boek of the burgomasters of Amsterdam, 1603–1649, in the archives of the city; and in Acta Classis Amstelodamensis, deposited in Nieuwezijds Kapel, Amsterdam.

The chief sources of information for a history of the New Haven Colony in America are the colonial and town records for the period from 1638 to 1649 and the colonial records for the period from 1653 to 1665. The first-mentioned volume was originally in the custody of the town clerk at New Haven, and the second, in the custody of the clerk of the county court at New Haven. By a resolution of the general assembly of the colony of Connecticut in 1772, the secretary of the colony was ordered to receive into his hands and deposit in his office the records of the New Haven Colony from 1653 to 1665. By an act of the general assembly of the state of Connecticut in 1921, both volumes were removed to the Connecticut State Library. Although apparently used in the nineteenth century by Benjamin Thompson, the historian of Long Island, a volume of records of the colony for the period from 1644 to 1653 has been lost. In accordance with a resolution of the general assembly of Connecticut, the two existing volumes were edited and published by Charles J. Hoadly as *Records of the Colony and Plantation of New Haven, from 1638 to 1649,* and *Records of the Colony or Jurisdiction of New Haven, from May, 1653, to the Union,* Hartford, 1857 and 1858. In this study, citations are to these printed volumes. All quotations, however, have been checked against the original manuscripts, and this accounts for variations in spelling, capitalization, and punctuation from the printed version. A Booke Conteyning The Accounts of Newhaven Jurisdiction began the 3^{d} mo. 1652, and extending to June, 1653, is the only account book of the colony that has survived. It is still in the office of the town clerk at New Haven.

Information regarding the relations of the New Haven Colony with its neighbors can be derived from Connecticut Archives: Town and Lands, I; Foreign Correspondence, I and II; Colonial Boundaries, I; and Miscellaneous Papers, I. These are deposited in the Connecticut State Library at Hartford. Massachusetts Archives in the State House at Boston yield some information. New York Colonial MSS. and General Entries, I, 1664–1665, in the New York State Library at Albany, and Deeds, I and II, in the office of the secretary of state at Albany, throw light on the relations between the New Haven Colony and New Netherland. Although badly damaged in the fire of 1911, the material in the New York State Library has been repaired, mounted between silk gauze, and is in process of being rebound. Fortunately for the student of colonial history, New York Colonial MSS. were calendared by E. B. O'Callaghan, 2 vols., Albany, 1865, 1866, and General Entries, I, 1664–1665, were published by the University of the State of New York, *State Library Bulletin, History No. 2,* May 1899.

The earliest records of the town of New Haven are included in the volume of colonial and town records deposited in the Connecticut State Library. Later records of the town of New Haven and those of the other towns within the limits of the New Haven Colony are to be found in the offices of the various town clerks. The records of the town of New Haven are unusually detailed. They were edited and published by Franklin Bowditch Dexter as *New Haven Town Records, 1649–1684,* 2 vols., New Haven, 1917, 1919. New Haven Probate Records, I, Wills, Inventories, Etc., 1647–1687, in the custody of the clerk of the probate court at New Haven, and A Booke of all the landes w^{c}h Planters at first or by allienations since possesse w^{t}hin New Haven Towne, compiled by Richard Pery, secretary, in 1645 and 1646, now deposited in Yale University Library, must be considered with the town records. The records of Guilford are almost as detailed as are those of New Haven. They are the only records which throw light on the number of votes cast in town elections. For the years when the New Haven Colony existed, they consist of: Guilford Records, A, 1645–1662; Guilford Records, B, also called Guilford Book of More Fixed Orders for This Plantation, a recapitulation made in 1650 of orders passed at earlier dates; and a Terrier of all the divided lands in Guilford, 1648. The earliest records of the town of Milford are no longer extant. Milford Land Records, I, also called Milford Third Book of Records, is a transcript made in 1677 of items at that time considered most important in two earlier volumes. Stamford Records, 1641–1726, are meager, as are those of Branford, 1645–1679. Greenwich Land Records, 1640–1711, contain a few items relating to the New Haven Colony. The records of all towns on Long Island in which the colony on the Sound was interested have been published.

New Haven First Church Records and Milford First Congregational Church Records are now deposited in the Connecticut State Library.

A volume of sermons preached by John Davenport at Hilton Castle in the parish of Monk Wearmouth, palatinate of Durham, between November, 1615, and March, 1616; a Note-Book kept by John Davenport; The Trial of Ezekiel Cheever before the Church at New Haven, printed in Connecticut Historical Society *Collections,* I, 22–51; Boston, Third Church, The Third Church Narrative, 1667–1674, attested by Josh. Scottow, 2 Feb. 1695, in Ezra Stiles, Folio Letters, I, printed in Hamilton Andrews Hill, *History of the Old South Church,* 2 vols., Boston and New York, 1890; and An Answer to a Bill in Chancery, in New Jersey Deeds, etc., printed in *New Jersey Archives,* 1st series, I, 51–54, are all in the Yale University Library.

A few Davenport manuscripts in the library of the American Antiquarian Society; the Winthrop MSS. in the library of the Massachusetts Historical Society; the Robert C. Winthrop Collection of Connecticut Manuscripts, 1631–1794, in three bound volumes in the Connecticut State Library; the Winthrop-Davenport correspondence in the New York Public Library, partly published as "Winthrop-Davenport Papers," in New York, Public Library, *Bulletin,* III, 393–408; the Mather Papers in the Boston Public Library, in part published in Massachusetts Historical Society *Collections,* 4th series, VIII; and the Leete MSS. in the library of the Massachusetts Historical Society all yield information regarding seventeenth-century New England and the New Haven Colony.

PRINTED SOURCES.

The *Calendar of State Papers, Domestic Series;* the *Calendar of State Papers, Colonial Series;* and the *Acts of the Privy Council, Colonial Series,* calendar some of the material in the Public Record Office already referred to. *A Collection of the State Papers of John Thurloe,* edited by Thomas Birch, 7 vols., London, 1742; and *The New England Company of 1649 and John Eliot,* Prince Society, Boston, 1920, throw further light on the relations of the New Haven Colony with England.

The *Records of the Colony and Plantation of New Haven, from 1638 to 1649,* and the *Records of the Colony or Jurisdiction of New Haven, from May, 1653, to the Union,* edited by Charles J. Hoadly, Hartford, 1857 and 1858, have been commented upon above. Among the records of neighboring colonies, mention should be made of *The Public Records of the Colony of Connecticut,* especially I and II, edited by J. Hammond Trumbull, Hartford, 1850 and 1852; *Records of the Governor and Company of the Massachusetts Bay in New England,* edited by Nathaniel B. Shurtleff, 5 vols. in 6, Boston, 1853–1854; *Records of the Colony of New Plymouth in New England,* especially I to IV, edited by Nathaniel B. Shurtleff, and "Acts of the Commissioners of the United Colonies of New England, 1643–1679," IX and X, edited by David Pulsifer, Boston, 1855–1859; and *Documents Relative to the Colonial History of the State of New York,* containing material culled from the archives of England, France, the United Netherlands, Sweden, and New York Colonial MSS., especially I, II, and III, edited by E. B. O'Callaghan and indexed in XI, and XII, XIII, and XIV, edited by B. Fernow, Albany, 1853–1883. With this group of works, Amandus Johnson, *The Instruction for Johan Printz, Governor of New Sweden,* Philadelphia, 1930, should be included.

New Haven Town Records, 1649–1684, edited by Franklin

Bowditch Dexter, 2 vols., New Haven, 1917 and 1919, have already been mentioned. *Southold Town Records,* 2 vols., Southold and Riverhead, 1882 and 1884, are the only other published records of a town within the limits of the New Haven Colony. *The First Book of Records of the Town of Southampton,* Sag-Harbor, 1874; *Oyster Bay Town Records, 1653–1704,* 2 vols., New York, 1916 and 1924; and *Huntington Town Records, 1653–1873,* 3 vols., Huntington, 1887–1889, are records of towns settled under the influence of the colony on the Sound although they never actually coalesced with it. With this group of works might be mentioned "Boston Records, 1634–1660," Record Commissioners of the City of Boston, *Second Report,* Boston, 1877, 2d edition, 1881; "Town Records of Salem 1634–1659," Essex Institute *Historical Collections,* IX, Part I; *The Records of New Amsterdam from 1653 to 1674,* edited by B. Fernow, 7 vols., New York, 1897; "Records of the Town of Newark, New Jersey," New Jersey Historical Society *Collections,* VI; and the *Historical Catalogue of the Members of the First Church of Christ in New Haven, Connecticut* (*Center Church*) *A. D. 1639–1914,* compiled by Franklin Bowditch Dexter, New Haven, 1914.

In the field of legislation, mention should be made of the Cotton Code, published as *An Abstract or* [sic] *the Lawes of New England, As they are now established,* London, 1641, and again as *An Abstract of Laws and Government. Wherein as in a Mirrour may be seen the wisdome and perfection of the Government of Christs Kingdome. Accomodable to any State or form of Government in the world, that is not Antichristian or Tyrannicall,* London, 1655. The code was included in Thomas Hutchinson, *A Collection of Original Papers,* Boston, 1769, pp. 161–179, and Albany, 1865, I, 181–205; Massachusetts Historical Society *Collections,* 1st series, V, 171–192; and Peter Force, *Tracts and Other Papers,* III, 1844, no. 9. The Massachusetts Body of Liberties, akin to the Cotton Code, is to be found in Massachusetts Historical Society *Collections,* 3d series, VIII, 216–237, and in William H. Whitmore, *A Bibliographical Sketch of the Laws of Massachusetts Colony,* Boston, 1890. The code compiled for the New Haven Colony by Theophilus Eaton was published as *New-Haven's Settling in New-England. And Some Lawes for Govern-*

ment: Published for the Use of that Colony. Though some of the Orders intended for present convenience, may probably be hereafter altered, and as need requireth other Lawes added, London, 1656. Copies of the original edition are to be found in the library of the American Antiquarian Society and the Connecticut State Library. It has been reprinted in *Records of the Colony or Jurisdiction of New Haven, from May, 1653, to the Union,* Hartford, 1858, pp. 559–616.

In the field of contemporary correspondence, the Winthrop Papers, partly published in the Massachusetts Historical Society *Collections,* 3d series, IX, 226–301; X, 1–126; 4th series, VI and VII; 5th series, I; IV, 287–313; VIII; and 6th series, III and V, especially the correspondence addressed to John Winthrop, Jr.; and the Mather Papers, also partly published in the Massachusetts Historical Society *Collections,* 4th series, VIII, are invaluable sources of information for seventeenth-century New England.

Among contemporary writings, those of John Cotton and John Davenport are most important. Of Cotton's writings, see *Gods Promise to His Plantation,* London, 1630; *A Discourse About Civil Government in a New Plantation Whose Design is Religion,* Cambridge, 1663; and *A Copy of a Letter of Mr Cotton of Boston, in New England, sent in answer of certaine Objections made against their Discipline and Orders there, directed to a Friend,* London, 1641. Of Davenport's writings, see *An Apologeticall Reply To a booke Called An Answer to the unjust complaint of W. B[est],* Rotterdam, 1636; *The Profession of the Faith of that Reverend and worthy Divine Mr J. D. sometimes Preacher of Stevens Coleman-street. London.,* London, 1642; *Another Essay for Investigation of the Truth in Answer to Two Questions Concerning, I. The Subject of Baptism. II. The Consociation of Churches,* Cambridge, 1663; *The Power of Congregational Churches Asserted and Vindicated, In Answer to a Treatise of Mr. J. Paget, Intituled The Defence of Church-Government exercised in Classes and Synods,* London, 1672; *A Sermon Preach'd at The Election of the Governour, At Boston in New-England, May 19th 1669,* 1670, reprinted in Colonial Society of Massachusetts *Publications,* X, 6; and with William Hooke, *A Catechisme containing the Chief Heads of Christian Religion,* London, 1659. For a more complete list of the writings of the founder of the colony on the Sound, see Franklin Bowditch Dexter, "Sketch of the Life and Writings of John Davenport," New Haven Colony Historical Society *Papers,* II, 205–238. With this group of works, John Norton, *Abel being dead yet speaketh; or, The Life and Death of that Deservedly famous man of God, Mr. John Cotton,* Cambridge, 1657, and London, 1658, is of importance because Norton used a biography of John Cotton by John Davenport which has since disappeared.

For contemporary accounts of the relations between Archbishop Laud and John Davenport, see Thomas Fuller, *The Church-History of Britain; from the birth of Jesus Christ, untill the year 1648,* London, 1655, republished in 6 vols., Oxford, 1845; Peter Heylyn, *Cyprianus Anglicus: or the history of the life and death of . . . William [Laud] . . . Archbishop of Canterbury,* London, 1668; William Laud, *Works,* 7 vols. in 9, Oxford, 1847–1860; William Prynne, *A Breviate of the Life of William Laud, Arch-bishop of Canterbury,* London, 1644; and the same author's *Canterburies Doome; or the first part of a compleat history of the commitment, charge, tryall, condemnation, execution of William Laud, late Arch-bishop of Canterbury,* London, 1646.

For contemporary accounts of the Antinomian controversy, see Charles Francis Adams, *Antinomianism in the Colony of Massachusetts Bay, 1636–1638,* Prince Society, Boston, 1894.

For contemporary histories of New England, see John Winthrop, *The History of New England from 1630 to 1649. . . . With notes . . . by James Savage,* 2 vols., Boston, 1825 and 1826, 2d edition, Boston, 1853, and reedited as *Winthrop's Journal "History of New England" 1630–1649,* by James Kendall Hosmer, 2 vols., New York, 1908; and William Hubbard, "A General History of New England, from the discovery to MDCLXXX," Massachusetts Historical Society *Collections,* 2d series, V and VI.

SECONDARY WORKS.

The brief treatment of the New Haven Colony in Cotton Mather, *Magnalia Christi Americana,* London, 1702, has been somewhat expanded in Edward R. Lambert, *History of the*

Colony of New Haven, before and after the Union with Connecticut, New Haven, 1838, and Leonard Bacon, *Thirteen Historical Discourses,* New York, 1839. Edward E. Atwater, *History of the Colony of New Haven to Its Absorption into Connecticut,* New Haven, 1881, 2d edition, Meriden, 1902, and Charles H. Levermore, *The Republic of New Haven,* Baltimore, 1886, are longer works but far from adequate studies of the smallest of the Puritan commonwealths in New England.

The neighboring colonies have received more attention from historians. Thomas Hutchinson, *The History of the Colony of Massachusets-Bay, from the first Settlement thereof in 1628. Until its Incorporation with the Colony of Plimouth, Province of Main, etc. by the Charter of King William and Queen Mary, in 1691,* the first volume of a three-volume history of Massachusetts Bay issued at Boston, 1764–1828, and 1795–1828, and in London, 1760 [*sic*] and 1765–1828; and Benjamin Trumbull, *A Complete History of Connecticut,* I, Hartford, 1797, 2 vols., New Haven, 1818, and 2 vols., New London, 1898, are excellent accounts of Massachusetts Bay and Connecticut. E. B. O'Callaghan, *History of New Netherland,* 2 vols., New York and Philadelphia, 1846 and 1848; and Amandus Johnson, *The Swedish Settlements on the Delaware; their history and relation to the Indians, Dutch and English, 1638–1664,* 2 vols., Philadelphia and New York, 1911, are adequate accounts of the Dutch and Swedish colonies to the west and south.

Among town histories, only Bernard C. Steiner, *A History of the Plantation of Menunkatuck and of the Original Town of Guilford, Connecticut,* Baltimore, 1897; and E. B. Huntington, *History of Stamford, Connecticut, from Its Settlement in 1641, to the Present Time,* Stamford, 1868, are worthy of mention.

Among biographies, reference should be made to A. Benedict Davenport, *A History and Genealogy of the Davenport Family,* New York, 1851, with *A Supplement to the History and Genealogy of the Davenport Family,* Stamford, 1876; Franklin Bowditch Dexter, "Sketch of the Life and Writings of John Davenport," New Haven Colony Historical Society *Papers,* II, 205–238; Jacob Bailey Moore, "Memoir of Theophilus Eaton," New York Historical Society *Collections,* 2d series, II, 467–493; and

Charles Ray Palmer, "Rev. William Hooke, 1601–1678," New Haven Colony Historical Society *Papers,* VIII, 56–81.

Noteworthy studies of special subjects are: Champlin Burrage, *The Early English Dissenters in the Light of Recent Research,* 2 vols., Cambridge, 1912; Henry Martyn Dexter, *The Congregationalism of the Last Three Hundred Years, as Seen in Its Literature,* New York, 1880; Williston Walker, *The Creeds and Platforms of Congregationalism,* New York, 1893; Perry Miller, *Orthodoxy in Massachusetts, 1630–1650,* Cambridge, 1933; F. C. Gray's identification of the Body of Liberties in Massachusetts Historical Society *Collections,* 3d series, VIII, 191–215; Leonard W. Labaree, *Milford, Connecticut: The Early Development of a Town as Shown in Its Land Records,* Tercentenary Commission of the State of Connecticut, New Haven, 1933; and Lemuel A. Welles, *The History of the Regicides in New England,* New York, 1927.

INDEX